Rockville Campus

THE WRITING
OF INFORMAL ESSAYS

THE WRITING
OF INFORMAL ESSAYS

BY

MARY ELLEN CHASE

AND

MARGARET ELIOT MACGREGOR

Essay Index Reprint Series

BOOKS FOR LIBRARIES PRESS
FREEPORT, NEW YORK

STANDARD BOOK NUMBER:
8369-1556-9

LIBRARY OF CONGRESS CATALOG CARD NUMBER:
79-93326

PRINTED IN THE UNITED STATES OF AMERICA

PREFACE

This book is not merely a collection of excellent essays. Those are issued each year, attractively bound, often well edited, and designed by able and conscientious college professors for the use and inspiration of college students. The editors of this book hope that it may facilitate at once that use and that inspiration by the clearness of its plan and by the constructiveness of its suggestions. That plan and those suggestions are based upon and arise from a dozen years of teaching Informal Exposition to both university and college students. No system or method of teaching any form of composition can safely be adjudged fool-proof; and yet from our own experience and that of colleagues we believe that the one outlined in the following pages is at least relatively successful.

We have had two chief aims in writing and compiling this book:

1. To divorce the student mind from the idea that the writing of creditable essays is barred from all except the most gifted.

2. To outline a coherent and constructive plan of procedure, suggestive rather than didactic, by which the student, beginning with the more simple, more objective essay of fact and experience, may advance toward the difficult subjective type based on opinions and ideas, on perception and imagination.

Now that higher education has become a fad among all sorts and conditions of men, the fact remains, whether we will or no, that college classes are largely made up of average rather than of exceptional students. Again, whether we will or no, the popularity of the study and practice of composition is not yet on the wane. The situation presented by these facts makes two demands on the instructor who chooses or is compelled to teach the writing of Informal Exposition. He must, first of all, for the sake of the majority of his students, banish to Coventry the idea that in the words of Alexander Smith the essayist is a "poet in prose," that the writing of essays, in itself a subtle and elusive process, demands a mind teeming with ideas, one at least occasionally possessed by an inspired imagination. And, secondly, having done this, he must present his students with some practical and simple method of procedure by means of which they may be encouraged to appreciate and to utilize their own experience and through which, it may not be entirely vain to hope, opinions and ideas, yea even perceptions, may eventually find ample room in their somewhat expanded minds.

We hope that this volume may prove helpful both to teachers and students. Quite aside from the selections themselves, it is by no means our own. Suggestions given willingly by former colleagues, especially at the University of Minnesota, have been freely used; and hundreds of students over a period of twelve years have vastly aided us by their own needs, demands, and suggestions. To those among their number who have graciously allowed us to include their essays in the appendix of this book we are especially indebted; for it is essays such as these which help to establish the effectiveness of the method here outlined and of the selections quoted. Acknowledgment of permissions to use material is made in the text itself; and to those acknowledgments we here add our sincere thanks to both publishers and authors. We must especially express our appreciation to Mr. Stark Young of the *New Republic*, himself an essayist of note and charm, for his kind interest in this book and for his unfailing generosity.

M. E. C.
M. E. M.

Smith College,
January, 1928.

CONTENTS

CONTENTS

CONTENTS vii

THE WRITING OF INFORMAL ESSAYS

CHAPTER I

THE OBJECTIVE ESSAY

THIS title, properly speaking, is an inaccuracy since no informal essay can be truly termed objective. Its very informality suggests the presence of the author, the expression of his likes and dislikes, his frank assumption that the reader will not only bear good-naturedly with his prejudices and memories, foibles and notions, but will be interested in them as well. The writer of informal essays promises always to talk about himself. He is above all else subjective.

And yet a study of the selections that are included under this heading shows that the term is not wholly a misnomer. Personal and subjective as are all the essays in that they reflect the opinions, predilections, and feelings of their writers, they are yet objective in that each and every one of them is actuated by some *object* upon which the individual essayist has centered his attention. This object is in one essay a person, in another, a pet animal, in a third, a much-loved place, in a fourth, an author; and in every case the person, the animal, the place or the author dominates the essay by virtue of certain features which have engaged the admiration, the memory, or the affection of the essayist.

From our experience we have come to believe that to attempt to write this objective kind of essay is the most reasonable beginning for the would-be informal essayist. There are many arguments for such a point of view. In the first place, such essays are based upon one's own experience. No occurrence or association in one's life is too paltry to be regarded as possible subject matter. Again, the motivating power in the writing of such essays is feeling, which, no modern psychologist need tell us, is more basic, fundamental, and natural than thought. Like Charles Lamb, we are "made up of likings and dislikings," and that condition is true of us long before we bring to bear any thought upon the matter of our prejudices. In the third place, an essay which has for its aim the portrayal of some interesting person, real or imaginary, or of some animal, dear or detestable to the writer, is far easier for the average student to tackle than is an essay based primarily on ideas, for the simple reason that in the first kind of essay there is from the very outset an object as well as an objective to tie to. The object is the subject chosen, be it one's favorite teacher or one's lamented dog; the objective, the delineation of that subject by the employment of every means at hand. What those means may be, the essays that follow exemplify. Precept must always give place to example.

A. Essays on Persons and Animals

One of the richest, most interesting, and most whimsical of objective essays is the essay which attempts to present some person or some animal, chosen by the writer because of the admiration, devotion, gratitude or amusement inspired in him by the subject under consideration. If then there has entered intimately into your life some teacher,

minister, priest, doctor, as Francis Barton Gummere
entered into the life of Christopher Morley, or if
such person has compelled your admiration even
though you have not known him closely, you have
a subject ready to your hand. Nor is it necessary
that like Dr. Gummere he has elicited your respect
and devotion. He may be simply a quaint and
charming person who has interested and amused
you because of his traits and viewpoints, his prejudices and habits. Few children or young people
have lived through their early years without being
touched by their love for a pet animal. See what
good use Miss Repplier as a grown-up has made of
her devoted slavery to Agrippina. You will hardly
be able to command such a wealth of literary references as hers; your own essay may be one-fourth as
long; but, helped by her enthusiasm and your own
cat, you may do a creditable piece of work. Or, if
you are possessed of a reflective turn of mind, you
will like to see what you can do after the manner
of Edward Verrall Lucas, who writes his appreciation of an old English scholar by employing the
means of setting and of contrast to help him in his
pleasant task.

The field of this essay on persons or animals is a
wide one. It is by no means relegated to the actual
or circumscribed by the narrow horizons of one's
physical existence. It may well be that you are
more interested in the people of books or of history
and legend, that they are far more real and valuable
to you than any companion near at hand. See what
a delightful appreciation Robert M. Gay has written
of Noah's wife, that much-maligned lady of legend.
Famous or infamous animals might well supply the

material for a dozen whimsical essays. Why not an essay on Dick Whittington's Cat or Bucephalus, Balaam's ass or the shrewd Reynard, the Fox? Then there are the people of your own imagination. An imaginary playmate might well be the subject of a delightful essay.

It is our aim in these suggestions only to point the way to the discovery of more. The centuries are strewn with better guide posts than we have given. From an appreciation, such as Marjorie Lawson has contributed in the collection of student essays, of some quaint servant, who once frightened you with tales of banshee, you may journey back if you like thousands of years to Argus, the dog of Ulysses, and find along the way material ready for your pen and your imagination.

IN MEMORIAM

FRANCIS BARTON GUMMERE [1]

BY

Christopher Morley

I OFTEN wonder what inward pangs of laughter or despair he may have felt as he sat behind the old desk in Chase Hall and watched us file in, year after year! Callow, juvenile, ignorant, and cocksure—grotesquely confident of our own manly fullness of worldly *savoir*—an absurd rabble of youths, miserable flintheads indeed for such a steel! We were the most unpromising of all material for the scholar's eye; comfortable, untroubled middle-class lads most of us, to whom study was neither a privilege nor a passion, but only a sober and decent way of growing old enough to enter business.

We did not realize how accurately—and perhaps a trifle grimly—the strong, friendly face behind the desk was searching us and sizing us up. He knew us for what we were—a group of nice boys, too sleek, too cheerfully secure to show the ambition of the true student. There was among us no specimen of the lean and dogged crusader of learning that kindles the eye of the master: no fanatical Scot, such as rejoices the Oxford or Cambridge don; no liquid-orbed and hawk-faced Hebrew with flushed cheek bones,

[1] From *Plum Pudding* by Christopher Morley, published by Doubleday, Page and Company.

7

such as sets the pace in the classrooms of our large universities. No: we were a hopelessly mediocre, well-fed, satisfied, and characteristically Quakerish lot. As far as the battle for learning goes, we were pacifists—conscientious objectors.

It is doubtful whether any really great scholar ever gave the best years of his life to so meagerly equipped a succession of youngsters! I say this candidly, and it is well it should be said, for it makes apparent the true genius of Doctor Gummere's great gift. He turned this following of humble plodders into lovers and zealots of the great regions of English letters. There was something knightly about him— he, the great scholar, who would never stoop to scoff at the humblest of us. It might have been thought that his shining gifts were wasted in a small country college, where not one in fifty of his pupils could follow him into the enchanted lands of the imagination where he was fancy free. But it was not so. One may meet man after man, old pupils of his, who have gone on into the homely drudging rounds of business, the law, journalism—men whose faces will light up with affection and remembrance when Doctor Gummere's name is mentioned. We may have forgotten much of our Chaucer, our Milton, our Ballads—though I am sure we have none of us forgotten the deep and thrilling vivacity of his voice reciting:

O where hae ye been, Lord Randal, my son?
O where hae ye been, my handsome young man?
I hae been to the wild wood; mither, make my bed soon,
For I'm weary wi' hunting and fain wad lie doun.

But what we learned from him lay in the very charm of his personality. It was a spell that no one in his classroom could escape. It shone from his sparkling eye; it spoke in his irresistible humor; it moved in every line of that well-loved face, in his characteristic gesture of leaning forward and tilting his head a little to one side as he listened, patiently, to whatever juvenile surmises we stammered to express. It was the true learning of which his favorite Sir Philip Sidney said:

This purifying of wit, this enriching of memory, enabling of judgment, and enlarging of conceit, which commonly we call learning, under what name soever it come forth or to what immediate end soever it be directed, the final end is to lead and draw us to as high a perfection as our degenerate souls, made worse by their clay lodgings, can be capable of.

Indeed, just to listen to him was a purifying of wit, an enriching of memory, an enabling of judgment, an enlarging of imagination. He gave us "so sweet a prospect into the way as will entice any man to enter into it."

He moved among all human contacts with unerring grace. He was never the teacher, always the comrade. It was his way to pretend that we knew far more than we did; so with perfect courtesy and gravity, he would ask our opinion on some matter of which we knew next to nothing; and we knew it was only his exquisiteness of good manners that impelled the habit; and we knew he knew the laughableness of it; yet we adored him for it. He always suited his strength to our weakness; would tell us things almost with an air of apology for seeming to know more than we; pretending that we doubtless had known it all along, but it had just slipped our memory. Marvelously he set us on our secret honor to do justice to this rare courtesy. To fail him in some task he had set became, in our boyish minds, the one thing most abhorrent in dealing with such a man—a discourtesy. He was a man of the rarest and most delicate breeding, the finest and truest gentleman we had known. Had he been nothing else, how much we would have learned from that alone.

What a range, what a grasp, there was in his glowing, various mind! How open it was on all sides, how it teemed with interests, how different from the scholar of silly traditional belief! We used to believe that he could have taught us history, science, economics, philosophy—almost anything; and so indeed he did. He taught us to go adventuring among masterpieces on our own account, which is the most any teacher can do. Luckiest of all were those who, on one pretext or another, found their way to his fireside of an evening. To sit entranced, smoking one of his cigars,[1] to hear him talk of Stevenson, Meredith, or Hardy—(his favorites among the moderns) to marvel anew at the infinite scope and vivacity of his learning—this was to live on the very doorsill of enchantment. Homeward we would go, crunching across the snow to where Barclay crowns the slope with her evening blaze of lights, one glimpse nearer some realization of the magical colors and tissues of the human mind, the rich perplexity and many-sided glamour of life.

It is strange (as one reviews all the memories of

---

[1] It was characteristic of him that he usually smoked *Robin Hood*, that admirable five-cent cigar, because the name, and the picture of an outlaw on the band, reminded him of the fourteenth century ballads he knew by heart.

that good friend and master) to think that there is
now a new generation beginning at Haverford that
will never know his spell.   There is a heavy debt
on his old pupils.   He made life so much richer and
more interesting for us.   Even if we never explored
for ourselves the fields of literature toward which he
pointed, his radiant individuality remains in our
hearts as a true exemplar of what scholarship can
mean.   We can never tell all that he meant to us.

Gropingly we turn to little pictures in memory.
We see him crossing Cope Field in the green and
gold of spring mornings, on his way to class.   We
see him sitting on the veranda steps of his home
on sunny afternoons, full of gay and eager talk on a
thousand diverse topics.   He little knew, I think,
how we hung upon his words.   I can think of no
more genuine tribute than this: that in my own class
—which was a notoriously cynical and scoffish band
of young sophisters—when any question of religious
doubt or dogma arose for discussion among some
midnight group, some one was sure to say, "I wish
I knew what Doctor Gummere thought about it!"
We felt instinctively that what he thought would
have been convincing enough for us.

He was a truly great man.   A greater man than
we deserved, and there is a heavy burden upon us
to justify the life that he gave to our little college.
He has passed into the quiet and lovely tradition
that surrounds and nourishes that place we all love
so well.   Little by little she grows, drawing strength
and beauty from human lives around her, confirming
herself in honor and remembrance.   The teacher is
justified by his scholars. Doctor Gummere might have
gone elsewhere, surrounded by a greater and more

ambitiously documented band of pupils. He whom we knew as the greatest man we had ever seen, moved little outside the world of learning. He gave himself to us, and we are the custodians of his memory.

Every man who loved our vanished friend must know with what realization of shamed incapacity one lays down the tributary pen. He was so strong, so full of laughter and grace, so truly a man, his long vacation still seems a dream, and we feel that somewhere on the well-beloved campus we shall meet him and feel that friendly hand. In thinking of him I am always reminded of that fine old poem of Sir Henry Wotton, a teacher himself, the provost of Eton, whose life has been so charmingly written by another Haverfordian—Logan Pearsall Smith.

The Character of a Happy Life

How happy is he born and taught
That serveth not another's will;
Whose armor is his honest thought,
And simple truth his utmost skill!

Whose passions not his masters are;
Whose soul is still prepared for death
Not tied unto the world by care
Of public fame or private breath;

Who envies none that chance doth raise,
Nor vice; who never understood
How deepest wounds are given by praise;
Nor rules of state, but rules of good;

Who hath his life from rumors freed;
Whose conscience is his strong retreat;
Whose state can neither flatterers feed,
Nor ruin make oppressors great;

Who God doth late and early pray
   More of His grace than gifts to lend;
And entertains the harmless day
   With a well-chosen book or friend;

This man is freed from servile bands
   Of hope to rise or fear to fall:
Lord of himself, though not of lands,
   And having nothing, yet hath all.

Such was the Happy Man as Sir Henry Wotton described him. Such, I think, was the life of our friend. I think it must have been a happy life, for he gave so much happiness to others.

NOAH'S WIFE: OR, WHAT'S IN A NAME?[1]

Robert M. Gay

> Noah of old, and Noah's dame,
> I think I never heard her name,
> But she went in tho' all the same.
> —MOTHER GOOSE

I WISH to say a word for Noah s wife. For all I know to the contrary, she has waited 4269 years (according to Archbishop Ussher's computation) for a sympathetic voice to be raised in her behalf. For this very considerable period there has been a shadow upon her reputation, due to no fault of hers; and it is high time that the grounds of this injustice be looked into.

I became interested in Noah's wife, more years ago than I can say, by way of her husband. Noah was my earliest hero. Almost every Christmas I received a Noah's Ark, with a red roof, half of which was hinged along the ridgepole like a lid, and with a row of windows painted on each side, out of which peered a variety of goggle-eyed animals. Lifting the roof I drew forth, first, Noah and his wife, and Shem, Ham, and Japhet. For some mysterious reason, Noah's daughters-in-law were never present. Father, mother, and the three sons comprised the human passengers—all dressed in bodices and long

[1] Reprinted by the kind permission of the author and of *The Atlantic Monthly*.

14

skirts, and wearing hats like those worn by Chinese coolies, and all standing stiff as grenadiers.

After them, I lifted out the animals, twenty or thirty of them, violently striped or spotted, and smelling of paint. One could tell the horse, cow, and deer apart by the horns. I think that Christmas held no joy quite comparable to this of pulling the slightly sticky beasts out, one after another, guessing at their species, matching them up, and arranging them two by two on the hearthrug, while Noah and his wife supervised the shipment from the quarter-deck, and Shem, Ham, and Japhet shooed the animals in from behind.

I thought then, and I think still, that Noah's doings were the most remarkable in history. The Ark, we are told, was made of gopher wood, every plank and joist of which he had to fell, cut, and finish, himself. He had then to assemble his lumber, according to specifications that had been given him, into a seaworthy structure, 300 x 50 x 30 cubits or, as I estimate it, about 525 x 87 x 52 feet, built in three stories, with one door and one window. Meanwhile, he had to collect the animals, sort them out, arrange them in couples and sevens, drive them into the Ark, and—most appalling of all—live with them for one hundred and fifty days, before he even made Mount Ararat. And at this time he was six hundred years old! Even for a man much younger, this would have been the most difficult undertaking in all history.

About the Old Testament characters, however, there is an air which I find hard to describe. I can perhaps suggest what I feel about them by saying that they are always doing the most surprising things

in the most matter-of-fact way.   There is nothing
just like this in any other book, I think.   The labors
of Hercules or Jason or Jack-the-Giant-Killer, though
remarkable, were still represented as laborious; but
these Old Testament worthies thought nothing of
undertaking to do, and of doing, things that would
have made even Hercules or Jack resign his commission in despair.   And they did these things
calmly and competently, and without wasting any
breath in talking about them.

Noah seems to have gone about catching the
animals, for example, quietly, methodically, and
modestly.   Not a word is said about any difficulties
he may have had.   And yet anyone who has ever
tried to catch an unwilling hen, or drive a pig through
a gate, or keep a grasshopper or a frog in a box, or
put salt on a bird's tail, must have wondered what
his method was; how this astonishing man went
about collecting his beasts, birds, and creeping things,
arranging them in rank and file, and persuading
them to march decorously up the gangplank; and
one can only echo the words of an old French writer,
who concludes an examination of this incident with
the following reflection: "There are many persons
who have spoiled a good deal of paper trying to
discover the truth of this affair; but there is no one
who has been able to arrive at a perfect assurance
or certitude."

When I was a little boy, although my playmates
and I were lost in admiration of Noah, we paid
little attention to the ladies of the party.   We early
noticed, nevertheless, that his wife had no name, and
she quickly became associated in our minds with
Lot's wife, who suffers from the same anonymity.

Now, this linking of Noah's wife with Lot's wife seems to have been constant throughout history, and furnishes a bit of evidence of the importance of a name that escaped even the researches of Mr. Shandy. For Lot's wife's reputation has never been any better than might be; and the shadow that rests upon her namelessness has been extended by the unthinking to cover the only other matriarch who seems to have had no given name. Poor Noah's wife! And this in spite of the fact that, though she had a much better reason than Lot's wife for casting a longing, lingering look behind, there is no evidence whatever that she did so. As a boy I felt sorry even for Lot's wife, and could never see that she was guilty of anything deserving a fate so disagreeable. I heard ministers explain her saline conclusion more than once; but their explanation explained so little that it became grouped in my mind with other "wingy mysteries in divinity, and airy subtleties in religion," such as Balaam's ass and Elisha's bears and Jonah's whale, about which we children had many rationalistic controversies. I lived for years in the hope that a preacher might some Sunday explain the Flood, and drop a hint concerning the anonymity of Noah's wife; but none ever did; and it was only after a long while that I began to suspect that preachers were accustomed to skip rather lightly over these matters.

But the story of Noah was such a good one that, despite some difficulties in the higher criticism, it engaged my imagination for many a day. The world of waters, and the lonely Ark with its unique tonnage floating upon it, the windows of heaven being opened and closed, the flight of the raven and the dove, the lifting-up of the cover of the Ark and, above all, the disposition of the animals and the daily routine that must have been gone through to keep them all healthy and happy—these furnished materials for a good many hours of pleasant day-dreaming. It was my earliest sea story, and no other story in the world can hold a candle to a good sea story. Some details bothered me; particularly how the Ark was lighted, since it had only one window. I had never read the Koran, and therefore did not know that there was a gigantic carbuncle suspended from the rooftree; nor did I know several other facts about which the Koran is explicit—such as that Noah's wife had a name, and that it was Wahela, and that the Ark sailed clear around the earth six times. Anyway, this information is clearly heterodox, and therefore not worthy of much notice.

A good many years later, I was amused to discover that Noah's family had engaged the curiosity of others, and that there had grown up a tradition even round Noah's wife. Among the Mohammedans, I learned, there was a notion abroad that, like Lot's wife, she was a freethinker, and in the Middle Ages it was the general opinion that she was a shrew, as Chaucer records:—

> Hastow nought herd, quod Nicholas, also
> The sorwe of Noë with his felashippe
> That he had or he gat his wyf to schipe?

It was whispered also that she deceived her husband regarding her secret views on many subjects; that she tried to persuade the neighbors that he was crazy; and that, finally, as the old mystery plays relate, she refused flatly to go into the Ark, and had in the end to be carried in bodily, kicking and squalling.

This is a damaging indictment, if there is any evidence to support it; but there is no doubt in my mind that an estimable woman has been done a grave injustice, and for no reason whatever except that the narrator of the Flood incident either forgot to record, or did not know, her name. He was equally careless regarding her three daughters-in-law; but, so far as I know, no one has ever gossiped about them. They are simply Shem's, Ham's, and Japhet's wives, and posterity has been willing to let them go at that; but their poor mother-in-law has been singled out for obloquy merely, so far as the testimony indicates, because she enjoyed a certain social prominence as the wife of the first and most remarkable of skippers.

The medieval legend is, it is true, an excellent bit of irony, quite in the vein of Anatole France, intimating as it does that the man who could manage all the rest of animate creation with such efficiency could not manage his wife—that he was, in fact, henpecked. But we need not give too much credence to it on the score of its plausibility; for in the Middle Ages, when humor was a robuster growth than it is nowadays, men never hesitated to rationalize the Scriptural stories and to embroider them with amusing suggestions. They handled the story of Balaam and his ass so freely that they, or the ass at least, became the most ribald fun maker of the age, and they seem never to have tired of spinning new yarns about Jonah and his whale. Even the Devil, afraid as they were of him, struck them as funny; and they knew no joke quite so good as

Beelzebub pitchforking sinners out of this world into a warmer. Finally, they had a theory that Satan somehow got into the Ark, possibly disguised as an animal, and that he made trouble throughout the voyage. Such a story is quite in character, if we are to believe Milton, who says that Satan first got into Eden by using the same ruse.

In the light of such inventions, what they said about Noah's wife need not cause us much perturbation. Since I have grown up and have observed the attitude of her descendants of her own sex toward such experiences as were hers, I have come to sympathize with her whole-heartedly. Think of having to watch a taciturn husband neglecting his business for years, to build a boat on dry land, miles from any water; think what impressions must have been hers, as he went to and fro collecting animals that smelled unpleasantly, most of which she of course detested; think of her premonitions when she was invited to enter the Ark, still on dry land, and to permit herself to be shut in with all the creeping things in their kinds there were in the world! And after she was in the Ark—to live almost a year in a box, in which there was only one window to look out at, and nothing to see even from that except water; to have nobody to talk to except her sons, who seem to have taken after their father, and her daughters-in-law, who seem to have been women of no importance; to walk for exercise between interminable rows of snorting, snuffling, growling creatures; and to wake in the small hours of the morning, wondering how many of the creeping things might have got into the bedroom! Where is there an instance of feminine heroism comparable to this?

Noah can hardly have been much in the way of company for her, because he had to feed the animals. I cannot see how he ever had a moment to sit down, or how, if he ever did sit down, there was anything to talk about except the animals—the last subject a woman wants to talk about. Was ever woman subjected to such an ordeal? And yet, is there a single indication that she added to Noah's worries, that she complained, scolded, moped, or wept? Not one. On the contrary, all the evidence available suggests that she went through her trying experience as calmly as her husband. She could not have been a high-strung, nervous woman, or a woman with a temper, or a woman full of the irrational fears usually ascribed to her sex; for, if she had been any of these, she would have jumped overboard after the first week. No. I am convinced that she was rather a quiet, self-possessed body, with a sense of humor, fond of flowers, which she cultivated on the sill of her only window, and gifted with unusual intellectual resources. Probably she played on the harp, mended the bodices and skirts of her family, scratched the noses of the less ferocious animals, fed the birds, and kept a diary; a silent, self-effacing woman, who knew how to milk the cows and goats, and make butter and cheese, and keep things tidied up in the cabin. She was, I have no doubt, loved by her husband and her sons, and even by her daughters-in-law.

I am led to these conclusions, not only by the Anglo-Saxon principle of justice, that a person is innocent until proved guilty, but also on grounds of general probability. For, if Noah's wife had been what is known as a strong-minded woman, is there any doubt that her name would have come down to us? Is it not at least likely that she would have been careful to see that it did? Or, if she had been noted for a bad temper or a shrewish tongue, is it not almost certain that some of her sayings or doings would have been recorded? The evil that men (and women) do lives after them, the good is oft interred with their bones.

An Additional Note.—After I had written my purely impulsive defense of Noah's wife, I discovered that, according to certain rabbinical legends, she had a name. She was Naamah, and she was the daughter of the saintly Enoch. But, more noteworthy than this, I also discovered that she was called the "pious Naamah!" Noah, the legends intimate, really did not deserve to be saved, but was somewhat less wicked than the rest of mankind. It is very gratifying to have one's intuitions ratified by the facts. The pious Naamah, on whose account, in all probability, the entire family was saved, and therefore the animals, has come down in history merely as "Noah's wife," and Noah has received all the credit. Many of my feminine readers will exclaim, "Now isn't that just like a man!"

A FUNERAL [1]

BY

E. V. Lucas

IT was in a Surrey churchyard on a gray, damp afternoon—all very solitary and quiet, with no alien spectators and only a very few mourners; and no desolating sense of loss, although a very true and kindly friend was passing from us. A football match was in progress in a field adjoining the churchyard, and I wondered, as I stood by the grave, if, were I the schoolmaster, I would stop the game just for the few minutes during which a body was committed to the earth; and I decided that I would not. In the midst of death we are in life, just as in the midst of life we are in death; it is all as it should be in this bizarre, jostling world. And he whom we had come to bury would have been the first to wish the boys to go on with their sport.

He was an old scholar—not so very old, either— whom I had known for some five years, and had many a long walk with: a short and sturdy Irish gentle- man, with a large, genial gray head stored with odd lore and the best literature; and the heart of a child. I never knew a man of so transparent a character. He showed you all his thoughts: as some one once said, his brain was like a beehive under glass—you could watch all its workings. And the honey in it! To walk with him at any season of the year was to

[1] From *Character and Comedy* by E. V. Lucas. Reprinted by permission of The Macmillan Company.

23

be reminded or newly told of the best that the English poets have said on all the phenomena of wood and hedgerow, meadow and sky. He had the more lyrical passages of Shakespeare at his tongue's end, and all Wordsworth and Keats. These were his favorites; but he had read everything that has the true rapturous note, and had forgotten none of its spirit.

His life was divided between his books, his friends, and long walks. A solitary man, he worked at all hours without much method, and probably courted his fatal illness in this way. To his own name there is not much to show; but such was his liberality that he was continually helping others, and the fruits of his erudition are widely scattered, and have gone to increase many a comparative stranger's reputation. His own *magnum opus* he left unfinished; he had worked at it for years, until to his friends it had come to be something of a joke. But though still shapeless, it was a great feast, as the world, I hope, will one day know. If, however, this treasure does not reach the world, it will not be because its worth was insufficient, but because no one can be found to decipher the manuscript; for I may say incidentally that our old friend wrote the worst hand in London, and it was not an uncommon experience of his correspondents to carry his missives from one pair of eyes to another, seeking a clue; and I remember on one occasion two such inquirers meeting unexpectedly, and each simultaneously drawing a letter from his pocket and uttering the request that the other should put everything else on one side in order to solve the enigma.

Lack of method and a haphazard and unlimited generosity were not his only Irish qualities. He had a quick, chivalrous temper, too, and I remember the difficulty I once had in restraining him from leaping the counter of a small tobacconist's in Great Portland Street, to give the man a good dressing for an imagined rudeness—not to himself, but to me. And there is more than one bus conductor in London who has cause to remember this sturdy Quixotic passenger's championship of a poor woman to whom insufficient courtesy seemed to him to have been shown. Normally kind and tolerant, his indignation on hearing of injustice was red hot. He burned at a story of meanness. It would haunt him all the evening. "Can it really be true?" he would ask, and burst forth again to flame.

Abstemious himself in all things, save reading and writing and helping his friends and correspondents, he mixed excellent whisky punch, as he called it. He brought to this office all the concentration which he lacked in his literary labors. It was a ritual with him; nothing might be hurried or left undone, and the result, I might say, justified the means. His death reduces the number of such convivial alchemists to one only, and he is in Tasmania, and, so far as I am concerned, useless.

His avidity as a reader—his desire to master his subject—led to some charming eccentricities, as when, for a daily journey between Earl's Court Road and Addison Road stations, he would carry a heavy hand bag filled with books, "to read in the train." This was no satire on the railway system, but pure zeal. He had indeed no satire in him; he spoke his mind and it was over.

It was a curious little company that assembled to do honor to this old kindly bachelor—the two or

three relatives that he possessed, and eight of his
literary friends, most of them of a good age, and for
the most part men of intellect, and in one or two
cases of world-wide reputation, and all a little
uncomfortable in unwonted formal black. We were
very grave and thoughtful, but it was not exactly a
sad funeral, for we knew that had he lived longer—
he was sixty-three—he would certainly have been an
invalid, which would have irked his active, restless
mind and body almost unbearably; and we knew,
also, that he had died in his first real illness after
a very happy life. Since we knew this, and also
that he was a bachelor and almost alone, those of
us who were not his kin were not melted and unstrung
by that poignant sense of untimely loss and irrepa-
rable removal that makes some funerals so tragic;
but death, however it come, is a mystery before
which one cannot stand unmoved and unregretful;
and I, for one, as I stood there, remembered how easy
it would have been oftener to have ascended to his
aerie and lured him out into Hertfordshire or his
beloved Epping, or even have dragged him away to
dinner and whisky punch; and I found myself
meditating, too, as the profoundly impressive service
rolled on, how melancholy it was that all that storied
brain, with its thousands of exquisite phrases and its
perhaps unrivaled knowledge of Shakespearean
philology, should have ceased to be. For such a
cessation, at any rate, say what one will of immortality, is part of the sting of death, part of the victory
of the grave, which St. Paul denied with such
magnificent irony.

And then we filed out into the churchyard, which
is a new and very large one, although the church is

old, and at a snail's pace, led by the clergyman, we crept along, a little black company, for, I suppose, nearly a quarter of a mile, under the cold gray sky. As I said, many of us were old, and most of us were indoor men, and I was amused to see how close to the head some of us held our hats—the merest barleycorn of interval being maintained for reverence's sake; whereas the sexton and the clergyman had slipped on those black velvet skull-caps which God, in His infinite mercy, either completely overlooks, or seeing, smiles at. And there our old friend was committed to the earth, amid the contending shouts of the football players, and then we all clapped our hats on our heads with firmness (as he would have wished us to do long before), and returned to the town to drink tea in an ancient hostelry, and exchange memories, quaint, and humorous, and touching, and beautiful, of the dead.

AGRIPPINA [1]

BY

Agnes Repplier

SHE is sitting now on my desk, and I glance at her with deference, mutely begging permission to begin. But her back is turned to me, and expresses in every curve such fine and delicate disdain that I falter and lose courage at the very ttheshold of my task. I have long known that cats are the most contemptuous of creatures, and that Agrippina is the most contemptuous of cats. The spirit of Bouhaki, the proud Theban beast that sat erect, with gold earings in his ears, at the feet of his master, King Hana; the spirit of Muezza, whose slumbers Mahomet himself was not bold enough to disturb; the spirit of Micetto, Chateaubriand's ecclesiastical pet, dignified as a cardinal, and conscious ever that he was the gift of a sovereign pontiff,—the spirits of all arrogant cats that have played scornful parts in the world's great comedy look out from Agrippina's yellow eyes, and hold me in subjection. I should like to explain to her, if I dared, that my desk is small, littered with many papers, and sadly over-crowded with the useful inutilities which affectionate friends delight in giving me at Christmas time. Sainte-Beuve's cat, I am sure, sat on his desk, and

[1] From "*Essays in Idleness* by Agnes Repplier. By permission of and by arrangement with Houghton, Mifflin Company, authorized publisher.

28

roamed at will among those precious manuscripts which no intrusive hand was ever permitted to touch; but Sainte-Beuve probably had sufficient space reserved for his own comfort and convenience. I have not; and Agrippina's beautifully ringed tail flapping across my copy distracts my attention, and imperils the neatness of my penmanship. Even when she is disposed to be affable, turns the light of her countenance upon me, watches with attentive curiosity every stroke I make, and softly, with curved paw, pats my pen as it travels over the paper,— even in these halcyon moments, though my self-love is flattered by her condescension, I am aware that I should work better and more rapidly if I denied myself this charming companionship.

But in truth it is impossible for a lover of cats to banish these alert, gentle, and discriminating little friends, who give us just enough of their regard and complaisance to make us hunger for more. M. Fée, the naturalist, who has written so admirably about animals, and who understands, as only a Frenchman can understand, the delicate and subtle organization of a cat, frankly admits that the keynote of its character is independence. It dwells under our roof, sleeps by our fire, endures our blandishments, and apparently enjoys our society, without for one moment forfeiting its sense of absolute freedom, without acknowledging any servile relation to the human creature who shelters it. "The cat," says M. Fée, "will never part with its liberty; it will neither be our servant, like the horse, nor our friend, like the dog. It consents to live as our guest; it accepts the home we offer and the food we give; it even goes so far as to solicit our caresses, but capri-

ciously, and when it suits its humor to receive
them."

Rude and masterful souls resent this fine self-
sufficiency in a domestic animal, and require that
it should have no will but theirs, no pleasure that
does not emanate from them. They are forever
prating of the love and fidelity of the dog, of the
beast that obeys their slightest word, crouches
contentedly for hours at their feet, is exuberantly
grateful for the smallest attention, and so affectionate that its demonstrations require to be curbed
rather than encouraged. All this homage is pleasing
to their vanity; yet there are people, less magisterial
perhaps, or less exacting, who believe that true
friendship, even with an animal, may be built upon
mutual esteem and independence; that to demand
gratitude is to be unworthy of it; and that obedience
is not essential to agreeable and healthy intercourse.
A man who owns a dog is, in every sense of the
word, its master; the term expresses accurately their
mutual relations. But it is ridiculous when applied
to the limited possession of a cat. I am certainly
not Agrippina's mistress, and the assumption of
authority on my part would be a mere empty dignity,
like those swelling titles which afford such innocent
delight to the Freemasons of our severe republic.
If I call Agrippina, she does not come; if I tell her to
go away, she remains where she is; if I try to persuade
her to show off her one or two little accomplishments,
she refuses, with courteous but unswerving decision.
She has frolicsome moods, in which a thimble, a
shoe-buttoner, a scrap of paper, or a piece of string
will drive her wild with delight; she has moods of
inflexible gravity, in which she stares solemnly at

her favorite ball rolling over the carpet, without stirring one lazy limb to reach it. "Have I seen this foolish toy before?" she seems to be asking herself with musing austerity; "and can it be possible that there are cats who run after such frivolous trifles? Vanity of vanities, and all is vanity, save only to lie upon the hearth-rug, and be warm, and 'think grave thoughts to feed a serious soul.'" In such moments of rejection and humiliation, I comfort myself by recalling the words of one too wise for arrogance. "When I play with my cat," says Montaigne, "how do I know whether she does not make a jest of me? We entertain each other with mutual antics; and if I have my own time for beginning or refusing, she too has hers."

This is the spirit in which we should approach a creature so reserved and so utterly self-sufficing; this is the only key we have to that natural distinction of character which repels careless and unobservant natures. When I am told that Agrippina is disobedient, ungrateful, cold-hearted, perverse, stupid, treacherous, and cruel, I no longer strive to check the torrent of abuse. I know that Buffon said all this, and much more, about cats, and that people have gone on repeating it ever since, principally because these spirited little beasts have remained just what it pleased Providence to make them, have preserved their primitive freedom through centuries of effete and demoralizing civilization. Why, I wonder, should a great many good men and women cherish an unreasonable grudge against one animal because it does not chance to possess the precise qualities of another? "My dog fetches my slippers for me every night," said a friend triumphantly, not

long ago. "He puts them first to warm by the fire,
and then brings them over to my chair, wagging his
tail, and as proud as Punch. Would your cat do as
much for you, I'd like to know?" Assuredly not!
If I waited for Agrippina to fetch me shoes or slippers,
I should have no other resource save to join as
speedily as possible one of the barefooted religious
orders of Italy. But, after all, fetching slippers is
not the whole duty of domestic pets. As La Fontaine
gently reminds us:—

Tout animal n'a pas toutes propriétés.

We pick no quarrel with a canary because it does
not talk like a parrot, nor with a parrot because it
does not sing like a canary. We find no fault with
a King Charles spaniel for not flying at the throat
of a burglar, nor with a St. Bernard because we
cannot put it in our pocket. Agrippina will never
make herself serviceable, yet nevertheless is she of
inestimable service. How many times have I rested
tired eyes on her graceful little body, curled up in
a ball and wrapped round with her tail like a parcel;
or stretched out luxuriously on my bed, one paw
coyly covering her face, the other curved gently
inwards, as though clasping an invisible treasure!
Asleep or awake, in rest or in motion, grave or gay,
Agrippina is always beautiful; and it is better to be
beautiful than to fetch and carry from the rising to
the setting of the sun. She is droll, too, with an
unconscious humor, even in her most serious and
sentimental moods. She has quite the longest ears
that ever were seen on so small a cat, eyes more
solemn than Athene's owl blinking in the sunlight,
and an air of supercilious disdain that would have

made Diogenes seem young and ardent by her side.
Sitting on the library table, under the evening lamp,
with her head held high in air, her tall ears as erect
as chimneys, and her inscrutable gaze fixed on the
darkest corner of the room, Agrippina inspires in the
family sentiments of mingled mirthfulness and awe.
To laugh at her in such moments, however, is to
incur her supreme displeasure. I have known her to
jump down from the table, and walk haughtily out
of the room, because of a single half-suppressed but
wholly indecorous giggle.

Schopenhauer has said that the reason domestic
pets are so lovable and so helpful to us is because
they enjoy, quietly and placidly, the present moment.
Life holds no future for them, and consequently no
care; if they are content, their contentment is absolute; and our jaded and wearied spirits find a natural
relief in the sight of creatures whose little cups of
happiness can so easily be filled to the brim. Walt
Whitman expresses the same thought more coarsely
when he acknowledges that he loves the society of
animals because they do not sweat and whine over
their condition, nor lie awake in the dark and weep
for their sins, nor sicken him with discussions of their
duty. In truth, that admirable counsel of Sydney
Smith's, "Take short views of life," can be obeyed
only by the brutes; for the thought that travels
even to the morrow is long enough to destroy our
peace of mind, inasmuch as we know not what the
morrow may bring forth. But when Agrippina has
breakfasted, and washed, and sits in the sunlight
blinking at me with affectionate contempt, I feel
soothed by her absolute and unqualified enjoyment.
I know how full my day will be of things that I

don't want particularly to do, and that are not
particularly worth doing; but for her, time and the
world hold only this brief moment of contentment.
Slowly the eyes close, gently the little body is
relaxed. Oh, you who strive to relieve your over-
wrought nerves, and cultivate power through repose,
watch the exquisite languor of a drowsy cat, and
despair of imitating such perfect and restful grace!
There is a gradual yielding of every muscle to the
soft persuasiveness of slumber; the flexible frame is
curved into tender lines, the head nestles lower, the
paws are tucked out of sight; no convulsive throb
or start betrays a rebellious alertness; only a faint
quiver of unconscious satisfaction, a faint heaving of
the tawny sides, a faint gleam of the half-shut
yellow eyes, and Agrippina is asleep. I look at her
for one wistful moment, and then turn resolutely to
my work. It were ignoble to wish myself in her
place, and yet how charming to be able to settle
down to a nap, *sans peur et sans reproche*, at ten
o'clock in the morning!

These, then, are a few of the pleasures to be
derived from the society of an amiable cat; and by
an amiable cat I mean one that, while maintaining
its own dignity and delicate reserve, is nevertheless
affable and condescending in the company of human
beings. There is nothing I dislike more than newspaper and magazine stories about priggish pussies—
like the children in Sunday-school books—that share
their food with hungry beasts from the back alleys,
and show touching fidelity to old blind masters, and
hunt partridges, in a spirit of noble self-sacrifice, for
consumptive mistresses, and scorn to help themselves
to delicacies from the kitchen tables, and arouse

their households so often in cases of fire that I should suspect them of starting the conflagrations in order to win applause by giving the alarm. Whatever a real cat may or may not be, it is never a prig, and all true lovers of the race have been quick to recognize and appreciate this fact.

"I value in the cat," says Chateaubriand, "that independent and almost ungrateful temper which prevents it from attaching itself to anyone; the indifference with which it passes from the salon to the housetop. When you caress it, it stretches itself out and arches its back responsively; but that is caused by physical pleasure, and not, as in the case of the dog, by a silly satisfaction in loving and being faithful to a master who returns thanks in kicks. The cat lives alone, has no need of society, does not obey except when it likes, pretends to sleep that it may see the more clearly, and scratches everything that it can scratch."

Here is a sketch spirited enough, and of good outline, but hardly correct in detail. A cat seldom manifests affection, yet is often distinctly social, and likes to see itself the petted minion of a family group. Agrippina, in fact, so far from living alone, will not, if she can help it, remain for a moment in a room by herself. She is content to have me as a companion, perhaps in default of better; but if I go upstairs or downstairs in search of a book, or my eye-glasses, or any one of the countless things that are never where they ought to be, Agrippina follows closely at my heels. Sometimes, when she is fast asleep, I steal softly out of the door, thinking to escape her vigilance; but before I have taken a dozen steps she is under my feet, mewing a gentle reproach, and

putting on all the injured airs of a deserted Ariadne.
I should like to think such behavior prompted by
affection rather than by curiosity; but in my candid
moments I find this "pathetic fallacy" a difficult
sentiment to cherish. There are people, I am aware,
who trustfully assert that their pets love them; and
one such sanguine creature has recently assured the
world that "no man who boasts the real intimacy
and confidence of a cat would dream of calling his
four-footed friend 'puss.' " But is not such a boast
rather ill-timed at best? How dare any man venture
to assert that he possesses the intimacy and confidence of an animal so exclusive and so reserved?
I doubt if Cardinal Wolsey, in the zenith of his
pride and power, claimed the intimacy and confidence
of the superb cat who sat in a cushioned armchair
by his side, and reflected with mimic dignity the
full-blown honors of the Lord High Chancellor of
England. Agrippina, I am humbly aware, grants
me neither her intimacy nor her confidence, but
only her companionship, which I endeavor to receive
modestly, and without flaunting my favors to the
world. She is displeased and even downcast when
I go out, and she greets my return with delight,
thrusting her little gray head between the banisters
the instant I open the house door, and waving a
welcome in mid-air with one ridiculously small paw.
Being but mortal, I am naturally pleased with these
tokens of esteem, but I do not, on that account, go
about with arrogant brow, and boast of my intimacy
with Agrippina. I should be laughed at, if I did,
by everybody who is privileged to possess and
appreciate a cat.

As for curiosity, that vice which the Abbé Galiani

held to be unknown to animals, but which the more astute Voltaire detected in every little dog that he saw peering out of the window of its master's coach, it is the ruling passion of the feline breast. A closet door left ajar, a box with half-closed lid, an open bureau drawer,—these are the objects that fill a cat with the liveliest interest and delight. Agrippina watches breathlessly the unfastening of a parcel, and tries to hasten matters by clutching actively at the string. When its contents are shown her, she examines them gravely, and then, with a sigh of relief, settles down to repose. The slightest noise disturbs and irritates her until she discovers its cause. If she hears a footstep in the hall, she runs out to see whose it is, and, like certain troublesome little people I have known, she dearly loves to go to the front door every time the bell is rung. From my window she surveys the street with tranquil scrutiny, and, if boys are playing below, she follows their games with a steady, scornful stare, very different from the wistful eagerness of a friendly dog, quivering to join in the sport. Sometimes the boys catch sight of her, and shout up rudely at her window; and I can never sufficiently admire Agrippina's conduct upon these trying occasions, the well-bred composure with which she affects neither to see nor to hear them, nor to be aware that there are such objectionable creatures as children in the world. Sometimes, too, the terrier that lives next door comes out to sun himself in the street, and, beholding my cat sitting well out of reach, he dances madly up and down the pavement, barking with all his might, and rearing himself on his short hind legs, in a futile attempt to dislodge her. Then the spirit of evil enters Agrippina's little heart. The window is open, and she creeps to the extreme edge of the stone sill, stretches herself at full length, peers down smilingly at the frenzied dog, dangles one paw enticingly in the air, and exerts herself with quiet malice to drive him to desperation. Her sense of humor is awakened by his frantic efforts, and by her own absolute security; and not until he is spent with exertion, and lies panting and exhausted on the bricks, does she arch her graceful back, stretch her limbs lazily in the sun, and with one light bound spring from the window to my desk. Wisely has Moncrif observed that a cat is not merely diverted by everything that moves, but is convinced that all nature is occupied exclusively with catering to her diversion.

There is a charming story told by M. Champfleury, who has written so much and so admirably about cats, of a poor hermit whose piety and asceticism were so great that in a vision he was permitted to behold his place in heaven, next to that of St. Gregory, the sovereign pontiff of Christendom. The hermit, who possessed nothing upon earth but a female cat, was abashed by the thought that in the next world he was destined to rank with so powerful a prince of the Church; and perhaps—for who knows the secret springs of spiritual pride?—he fancied that his self-inflicted poverty would win for him an even higher reward. Whereupon a second revelation made known to him that his detachment from the world was by no means so complete as he imagined, for that he loved and valued his cat, the sole companion of his solitude, more than St. Gregory loved and valued all his earthly possessions. The Pope on his throne was the truer ascetic of the two.

This little tale conveys to us, in addition to its
excellent moral,—never more needed than at present,—a pleasing truth concerning the lovability of
cats. While they have never attained, and never
deserve to attain, the widespread and somewhat
commonplace popularity of dogs, their fascination
is a more potent and irresistible charm. He who
yields himself to the sweet seductiveness of a cat
is beguiled forever from the simple, honorable friendship of the more generous and open-hearted beast.
The small domestic sphinx whose inscrutable eyes
never soften with affection; the fetich animal that
comes down to us from the far past, adored, hated,
and feared,—a god in wise and silent Egypt, a play-
thing in old Rome, a hunted and unholy creature,
suffering one long martyrdom throughout the half-
seen, dimly-fathomed Middle Ages,—even now this
lovely, uncanny pet is capable of inspiring mingled
sentiments of horror and devotion. Those who are
under its spell rejoice in their thralldom, and, like
M. Champfleury's hermit, grow strangely wedded
to this mute, unsympathetic comradeship. Those
who have inherited the old, half-fearful aversion
render a still finer tribute to the cat's native witchery
and power. I have seen middle-aged women, of
dignified and tranquil aspect, draw back with
unfeigned dismay at the sight of Agrippina, a little
ball of gray and yellow fur, curled up in peaceful
slumber on the hearthrug. And this instinctive
shrinking has nothing in common with the perfectly
reasonable fear we entertain for a terrier snapping
and snarling at our heels, or for a mastiff the size
of a calf, which our friend assures us is as gentle as
a baby, but which looks able and ready to tear us

limb from limb. It may be ignominious to be afraid
of dogs, but the emotion is one which will bear
analysis and explanation; we know exactly what it
is we fear; while the uneasiness with which many
people behold a harmless and perfectly indifferent
cat is a faint reflection of that superstitious terror
which the nineteenth century still borrows occasionally from the ninth. We call it by a different name,
and account for it on purely natural principles, in
deference to progress; but the medieval peasant
·who beheld his cat steal out, like a gray shadow, on
St. John's Eve, to join in unholy rites, felt the same
shuddering abhorrence which we witness and wonder
at to-day. He simplified matters somewhat, and
eased his troubled mind by killing the beast; for
cats that ventured forth on the feast of St. John,
or on Halloween, or on the second Wednesday in
Lent, did so at their peril. Fires blazed for them in
every village, and even quiet stay-at-homes were
too often hunted from their chimney-corners to a
cruel death. There is a receipt signed in 1575 by
one Lucas Pommoreux,—abhorred forever be his
name!—to whom has been paid the sum of a hundred
sols parisis "for having supplied for three years
all the cats required for the fire on St. John's Day;"
and be it remembered that the gracious child, afterwards Louis XIII, interceded with Henry IV for
the lives of these poor animals, sacrificed to wicked
sport and an unreasoning terror.

Girt around with fear, and mystery, and subtle
associations with evil, the cat comes down to us
through the centuries; and from every land fresh
traditions of sorcery claim it for their own. In
Brittany is still whispered the dreadful tale of the

cats that danced with sacrilegious glee around the crucifix until their king was slain; and in Sicily men know that if a black cat serves seven masters in turn he carries the soul of the seventh into hell. In Russia black cats become devils at the end of seven years, and in southern Europe they are merely serving their apprenticeship as witches. Norwegian folk-lore is rich in ghastly stories like that of the wealthy miller whose mill has been twice burned down on Whitsun night, and for whom a traveling tailor offers to keep watch. The tailor chalks a circle on the floor, writes the Lord's Prayer around it, and waits until midnight, when a troop of cats rush in, and hang a great pot of pitch over the fireplace. Again and again they try to overturn this pitch, but every time the tailor frightens them away; and when their leader endeavors stealthily to draw him outside of his magic circle, he cuts off her paw with his knife. Then they all fly howling into the night, and the next morning the miller sees with joy his mill standing whole and unharmed. But the miller's wife cowers under the bedclothes, offering her left hand to the tailor, and hiding as best she can her right arm's bleeding stump.

Finer even than this tale is the well-known story which "Monk" Lewis told to Shelley of a gentle-man who, late one night, went to visit a friend living on the outskirts of a forest in east Germany. He lost his path, and, after wandering aimlessly for some time, beheld at last a light streaming from the windows of an old and ruined abbey. Looking in, he saw a procession of cats lowering into the grave a small coffin with a crown upon it. The sight filled him with horror, and, spurring his horse, he rode away as fast as he could, never stopping until he reached his destination, long after midnight. His friend was still awaiting him, and at once he recounted what had happened; whereupon a cat that lay sleeping by the fire sprang to its feet, cried out, "Then I am the King of the Cats!" and disappeared like a flash up the chimney.

For my part, I consider this the best cat story in all literature, full of suggestiveness and terror, yet picturesque withal, and leaving ample room in the mind for speculation. Why was not the heir apparent bidden to the royal funeral? Was there a disputed succession, and how are such points settled in the mysterious domain of cat-land? The notion that these animals gather in ghost-haunted churches and castles for their nocturnal revels is one common to all parts of Europe. We remember how the little maiden of the "Mountain Idyl" confides to Heine that the innocent-looking cat in the chimney-corner is really a witch, and that at midnight, when the storm is high, she steals away to the ruined keep, where the spirits of the dead wait spellbound for the word that shall waken them. In all scenes of impish revelry cats play a prominent part, although occasionally, by virtue of their dual natures, they serve as barriers against the powers of evil. There is the old story of the witch's cat that was grateful to the good girl who gave it some ham to eat,—I may observe here, parenthetically, that I have never known a cat that would touch ham,—and there is the fine bit of Italian folk-lore about the servant maid who, with no other protector than a black cat, ventures to disturb a procession of ghosts on the dreadful Night of the Dead.

"It is well for you that the cat lies in your arms,"
the angry spirit says to her; "otherwise what I am,
you also would be." The last pale reflex of a universal tradition I found three years ago in London,
where the bad behavior of the Westminster cats—
proverbially the most dissolute and profligate speci-
mens of their race—has given rise to the pleasant
legend of a country house whither these rakish
animals retire for nights of gay festivity, and whence
they return in the early morning, jaded, repentant,
and forlorn.

Of late years there has been a rapid and promising
growth of what disaffected and alliterative critics
call the "cat cult" and poets and painters vie with
one another in celebrating the charms of this long-
neglected pet. Mr. M. H. Spielmann's beautiful
volume in praise of Madame Henriette Ronner and
her pictures is a treasure upon which many an ardent
lover of cats will cast wandering and wistful glances.
It is impossible for even the most disciplined spirit
not to yearn over these little furry darlings, these
gentle, mischievous, lazy, irresistible things. As for
Banjo, that dear and sentimental kitten, with his
head on one side like Lydia Languish, and a de-
corous melancholy suffusing his splendid eyes, let
any obdurate scorner of the race look at his loveliness and be converted. Mrs. Graham R. Tomson's
pretty anthology, *Concerning Cats*, is another
step in the right direction; a dainty volume of selections from French and English verse, where we
may find old favorites like Cowper's "Retired Cat"
and Calverly's "Sad Memories," graceful epitaphs
on departed pussies, some delightful poems from
Baudelaire, and three, no less delightful, from the

pen of Mrs. Tomson herself, whose preface, or
"foreword," is enough to win for her at once the
friendship and sympathy of the elect.   The book,
while it contains a good deal that might well have
been omitted, is necessarily a small one; for poets,
English poets especially, have just begun to sing the
praises of the cat, as they have for generations sung
the praises of the horse and dog.   Nevertheless, all
English literature, and all the literatures of every
land, are full of charming allusions to this friendly
animal,—allusions the brevity of which only en-
hances their value.   Those two delicious lines of
Herrick's, for example,—

> And the brisk mouse may feast herself with crumbs,
> Till that the green-eyed kitling comes,—

are worth the whole of Wordsworth's solemn poem,
"The Kitten and the Falling Leaves."   What did
Wordsworth know of the innate vanity, the affecta-
tion and coquetry, of kittenhood?   He saw the little
beast gamboling on the wall, and he fancied her as
innocent as she looked,—as though any living creature *could* be as innocent as a kitten looks!   With
touching simplicity, he believed her all unconscious
of the admiration she was exciting:—

> What would little Tabby care
> For the plaudits of the crowd?
> Over happy to be proud,
> Over wealthy in the treasure
> Of her own exceeding pleasure!

Ah, the arrant knavery of that kitten!   The tiny
impostor, showing off her best tricks, and feigning
to be occupied exclusively with her own infantile

diversion! We can see her now, prancing and paddling after the leaves, and all the while peeping out of "the tail o' her ee" at the serene poet and philosopher, and waving her naughty tail in glee over his confidence and condescension.

Heine's pretty lines,—

And close beside me the cat sits purring,
  Warming her paws at the cheery gleam;
The flames keep flitting, and flicking, and whirring;
  My mind is wrapped in a realm of dream,—

find their English echo in the letter Shelley writes to Peacock, describing, half wistfully, the shrines of the Penates, "whose hymns are the purring of kittens, the hissing of kettles, the long talks over the past and dead, the laugh of children, the warm wind of summer filling the quiet house, and the pelting storm of winter struggling in vain for entrance." How incomplete would these pictures be, how incomplete is any fireside sketch, without the purring kitten or drowsy cat!

The queen I am o' that cozy place;
As wi' ilka paw I dicht my face,
I sing an' purr wi' mickle grace.

This is the sphinx of the hearthstone, the little god of domesticity, whose presence turns a house into a home. Even the chilly desolation of a hotel may be rendered endurable by these affable and discriminating creatures; for one of them, as we know, once welcomed Sir Walter Scott, and softened for him the unfamiliar and unloved surroundings. "There are no dogs in the hotel where I lodge," he writes to Abbotsford from London, "but a tolerably con-

versable cat *who* eats a mess of cream with me in
the morning." Of course it did, the wise and lynx-
eyed beast! I make no doubt that, day after day
and week after week, that cat had wandered superbly
amid the common throng of lodgers, showing favor
to none, and growing cynical and disillusioned by
constant contact with a crowd. Then, one morning,
it spied the noble, rugged face which neither man
nor beast could look upon without loving, and
forthwith tendered its allegiance on the spot. Only
"tolerably conversable" it was, this reserved and
town-bred animal; less urbane because less happy
than the much-respected retainer at Abbotsford,
Master Hinse of Hinsefeld, whom Sir Walter called
his friend. "Ah, mon grand ami, vous avez tué
mon autre grand ami!" he sighed, when the huge
hound Nimrod ended poor Hinse's placid career.
And if Scott sometimes seems to disparage cats,
as when he unkindly compares Oliver-le-Dain to
one, in *Quentin Durward*, he atones for such indignity by the use of the little pronoun "who" when
writing of the London puss. My own habit is to say
"who" on similar occasions, and I am glad to have
so excellent an authority.

It were an endless though a pleasant task to re-
count all that has been said, and well said, in praise
of the cat by those who have rightly valued her
companionship. M. Loti's Moumoutte Blanche and
Moumoutte Chinoise are well known and widely
beloved, and M. Théophile Gautier's charming pages
are too familiar for comment. Who has not read
with delight of the Black and White Dynasties that
for so long ruled with gentle sway over his hearth
and heart; of Madame Théophile, who thought the

parrot was a green chicken; of Don Pierrot de
Navarre, who deeply resented his master's staying
out late at night; of the graceful and fastidious
Séraphita; the gluttonous Enjolras; the acute Bo-
hemian, Gavroche; the courteous and well-mannered
Eponine, who received M. Gautier's guests in the
drawing-room and dined at his table, taking each
course as it was served, and restraining any rude
distaste for food not to her fancy. "Her place was
laid without a knife and fork, indeed, but with a
glass, and she went regularly through dinner, from
soup to dessert, awaiting her turn to be helped, and
behaving with a quiet propriety which most children
might imitate with advantage. At the first stroke
of the bell she would appear, and when I came into
the dining room she would be at her post, upright
on her chair, her forepaws on the edge of the tablecloth; and she would present her smooth forehead
to be kissed, like a well-bred little girl who was af-
fectionately polite to relatives and old people."

I have read this pretty description several times
to Agrippina, who is extremely wayward and capricious about her food, rejecting plaintively one
day the viands which she has eaten with apparent
enjoyment the day before. In fact, the difficulty of
catering to her is so well understood by tradesmen
that recently, when the housemaid carried her on
an errand to the grocery,—Agrippina is very fond
of these jaunts and of the admiration she excites,—
the grocer, a fatherly man, with cats of his own,
said briskly, "Is this the little lady who eats the
biscuits?" and presented her on the spot with several
choice varieties from which to choose. She is fastidious, too, about the way in which her meals are

served; disliking any other dishes than her own, which are of blue-and-white china; requiring that her meat should be cut up fine and all the fat removed, and that her morning oatmeal should be well sugared and creamed. Milk she holds in scorn. My friends tell me sometimes that it is not the common custom of cats to receive so much attention at table, and that it is my fault Agrippina is so exacting; but such grumblers fail to take into consideration the marked individuality that is the charm of every kindly treated puss. She differs from her sisters as widely as one woman differs from another, and reveals varying characteristics of good and evil, varying powers of intelligence and adaptation. She scales splendid heights of virtue, and, unlike Sir Thomas Browne, is "singular in offenses." Even those primitive instincts which we believe all animals hold in common are lost in acquired ethics and depravity. No heroism could surpass that of the London cat who crawled back five times under the stage of the burning theatre to rescue her litter of kittens, and, having carried four of them to safety, perished devotedly with the fifth. On the other hand, I know of a cat who drowned her three kittens in a water-butt, for no reason, apparently, save to be rid of them, and that she might lie in peace on the hearthrug,—a murder well planned, deliberate, and cruel.

So Tiberius might have sat,
Had Tiberius been a cat.

Only in her grace and beauty, her love of comfort, her dignity of bearing, her courteous reserve, and her independence of character does puss remain immutable and unchanged. These are the traits which win for her the warmest corner by the fire, and the unshaken regard of those who value her friendship and aspire to her affection. These are the traits so subtly suggested by Mrs. Tomson in a sonnet which every true lover of cats feels in his heart *must* have been addressed to his own particular pet:—

Half gentle kindliness, and half disdain,
Thou comest to my call, serenely suave,
With humming speech and gracious gestures grave,
In salutation courtly and urbane;
Yet must I humble me thy grace to gain,
For wiles may win thee, but no arts enslave;
And nowhere gladly thou abidest, save
Where naught disturbs the concord of thy reign.

Sphinx of my quiet hearth! who deign'st to dwell
Friend of my toil, companion of mine ease,
Thine is the lore of Ra and Rameses;
That men forget dost thou remember well,
Beholden still in blinking reveries,
With sombre sea-green gaze inscrutable.

A LIST OF ESSAYS PARTICULARLY ADAPTED FOR USE AS MODELS

Persons

Barrie, James M. *A Day of Her Life*, from *Margaret Ogilvy*, Chapter V. Charles Scribner's Sons.
Dunbar, Olivia Howard. *Portrait of a Family*, in *The Yale Review*, July, 1920.
Kellogg, Charlotte. *Cardinal Mercier—The Passing of the Great Cardinal*, in *The Atlantic Monthly*, May, 1926.
Lamb, Charles. *Captain Jackson*, from *The Last Essays of Elia*.
Lucas, E. V. *A Friend of the Town*, from *Old Lamps for New*. Methuen and Company, Ltd. London.

Lucas, E. V. *A Philosopher that Failed,* from *Character and Comedy.* The Macmillan Company.

Stevenson, Robert Louis. *An Old Scotch Gardener* and *Thomas Stevenson: Civil Engineer,* from *Memories and Portraits.* Charles Scribner's Sons.

Tanner, William M. *Essays and Essay-Writing.* The Atlantic Monthly Press. *Ear-Trumpeting with Friar Juniper* and *The Passing of Emily Ruggles's.*

White, William Allen. *Mary White,* in *Modern Essays, First Series,* selected by Christopher Morley. Harcourt, Brace and Company.

ANIMALS

Dounce, Harry Esty. *Some Nonsense about a Dog,* in *Modern Essays, First Series,* selected by Christopher Morley. Harcourt, Brace and Company.

Gay, Robert M. *Some Stray Notes of a Somewhat Dogged Tendency,* in *The Atlantic Monthly,* June, 1925.

Hudson, W. H. *Geese,* from *Birds and Man.* Alfred A. Knopf. Reprinted in *Modern Essays, Second Series,* selected by Christopher Morley. Harcourt, Brace and ·Company.

Hunt, Leigh. *A Cat by the Fire,* in *Romantic Prose of the Early Nineteenth Century,* edited by Carl H. Grabo. The Modern Student's Library. Charles Scribner's Sons.

McDowall, Arthur. *Cows,* from *Ruminations.* Houghton Mifflin Company.

Repplier, Agnes. *Old World Pets,* from *Essays in Miniature.* Houghton Mifflin Company.

Rhys, Grace. *A Brother of St. Francis,* from *About Many Things.* Methuen and Company, Ltd. London.

Southey, Robert. *Memoir of the Cats of Greta Hall,* in *Romantic Prose of the Early Nineteenth Century.* The Modern Student's Library. Charles Scribner's Sons.

B. Essays on Place

Places have always intrigued the informal essayist. Lamb, falling a prey to their genius, has given us among others *The South Sea House, Christ's Hospital, Oxford in the Vacation,* and, perhaps most charming of all his essays, the exquisite *Blakesmoor in Herefordshire;* Stevenson in his *Essays on Travel* writes of places pleasant and unpleasant; A. Edward Newton and E. V. Lucas take us on delightful excursions through London streets; and Christopher Morley and Simeon Strunsky show us Philadelphia and New York in all moods and seasons.

This type of essay affords the widest possible range to the writer. You may, if you choose, attempt to portray a town or a village as Alexander Smith does in *Dreamthorp,* giving your readers as complete a picture as possible of the place of your choice; you may instead concentrate on one feature of a place as Robert P. Tristram Coffin does in his attempt to show that Iffley is above all else "unspoiled"; you may picture your chosen place at a given time or season as Robert Louis Stevenson does with *Davos in Winter* and as Ludwig Lewissohn does in *The Berlin of the Eighties;* or you may attempt to convey by any means within your power the atmosphere which the place exerts over you yourself, as, in the collection of essays by students, Henry Johnson has so well done in *Ponta Delgata.*

Nor must your place be a town or village, a city or a street. It may be anything under the sun— a river, a pasture, or a vacant lot in which you once played, a cathedral close at twilight, a swimming-hole, a hay-loft, a five- and ten-cent store during the Christmas rush. Or it may be a place which you have never seen save in the recitals of some friend or of some member of your family, but which you long some day to see—a fiord in Norway, a heather-clad moor in Scotland, a village in Italy, an English castle, a German beer-garden. Your essay, in such a case, will give us the place as it exists for you in your imagination and anticipation. Most of us have Carcassones to which we have never been. Again, you may write of a place which once existed but is now no more, a place created for you by legend and history—Nineveh, Carthage, Palmyra, a cliff-town like those depicted by Miss Cather in her beautiful *Death Comes for the Archbishop*. And finally your essay may present a place which exists only in the realm of your imagination—a dream-place which you alone have created for yourself as De Quincey and his brother did when they were children.

Could any field be wider?

DREAMTHORP [1]

BY

Alexander Smith

IT matters not to relate how or when I became a denizen of Dreamthorp; it will be sufficient to say that I am not a born native, but that I came to reside in it a good while ago now. The several towns and villages in which, in my time, I have pitched a tent did not please, for one obscure reason or another: this one was too large, t'other too small; but when, on a summer evening about the hour of eight, I first beheld Dreamthorp, with its westward-looking windows painted by sunset, its children playing in the single straggling street, the mothers knitting at the open doors, the fathers standing about in long white blouses, chatting or smoking; the great tower of the ruined castle rising high into the rosy air, with a whole troop of swallows —by distance made as small as gnats—skimming about its rents and fissures;—when I first beheld all this, I felt instinctively that my knapsack might be taken off my shoulders, that my tired feet might wander no more, that at last, on the planet, I had found a home. From that evening I have dwelt here, and the only journey I am like now to make, is the very inconsiderable one, so far at least as distance is concerned, from the house in which I live to the graveyard beside the ruined castle. There, with the former

---

[1] From *Dreamthorp and Other Essays*, by Alexander Smith.

inhabitants of the place, I trust to sleep quietly enough, and nature will draw over our heads her coverlet of green sod, and tenderly tuck us in, as a mother her sleeping ones, so that no sound from the world shall ever reach us, and no sorrow trouble us any more.

The village stands far inland; and the streams that trot through the soft green valleys all about have as little knowledge of the sea as the three-years' child of the storms and passions of manhood. The surrounding country is smooth and green, full of undulations; and pleasant country roads strike through it in every direction, bound for distant towns and villages, yet in no hurry to reach them. On these roads the lark in summer is continually heard; nests are plentiful in the hedges and dry ditches; and on the grassy banks, and at the feet of the bowed dikes, the blue-eyed speedwell smiles its benison on the passing wayfarer. On these roads you may walk for a year and encounter nothing more remarkable than the country cart, troops of tawny children from the woods, laden with primroses, and at long intervals—for people in this district live to a ripe age—a black funeral creeping in from some remote hamlet; and to this last the people reverently doff their hats and stand aside. Death does not walk about here often, but when he does, he receives as much respect as the squire himself. Everything round one is unhurried, quiet, moss-grown, and orderly. Season follows in the track of season, and one year can hardly be distinguished from another. Time should be measured here by the silent dial, rather than by the ticking clock, or by the chimes of the church. Dream-thorp can boast of a respectable antiquity, and in

it the trade of the builder is unknown. Ever since
I remember, not a single stone has been laid on the
top of another. The castle, inhabited now by jackdaws and starlings, is old; the chapel which adjoins
it is older still; and the lake behind both, and in
which their shadows sleep, is, I suppose, as old as
Adam. A fountain in the market-place, all mouths
and faces and curious arabesques—as dry, however,
as the castle moat—has a tradition connected with
it; and a great noble, riding through the street one
day several hundred years ago, was shot from a
window by a man whom he had injured. The death
of this noble is the chief link which connects the
place with authentic history. The houses are old,
and remote dates may yet be deciphered on the
stones above the doors; the apple-trees are mossed
and ancient; countless generations of sparrows
have bred in the thatched roofs, and thereon have
chirped out their lives. In every room of the place
men have been born, men have died. On Dreamthorp centuries have fallen, and have left no more
trace than have last winter's snowflakes. This
commonplace sequence and flowing on of life is
immeasurably affecting. That winter morning
when Charles lost his head in front of the ban-
queting-hall of his own palace, the icicles hung
from the eaves of the houses here, and the clown
kicked the snowballs from his clouted shoon, and
thought but of his supper when, at three o'clock,
the red sun set in the purple mist. On that Sunday
in June while Waterloo was going on, the gossips,
after morning service, stood on the country roads
discussing agricultural prospects, without the slightest suspicion that the day passing over their heads

would be a famous one in the calendar. Battles
have been fought, kings have died, history has
transacted itself; but, all unheeding and untouched,
Dreamthorp has watched apple-trees redden and
wheat ripen, and smoked its pipe, and quaffed its
mug of beer, and rejoiced over its newborn children
and with proper solemnity carried its dead to the
churchyard. As I gaze on the village of my adop-
tion, I think of many things very far removed, and
seem to get closer to them. The last setting sun
that Shakespeare saw reddened the windows here,
and struck warmly on the faces of the hinds coming
home from the fields. The mighty storm that
raged while Cromwell lay a-dying made all the
oak woods groan round about here, and tore the
thatch from the very roofs I gaze upon. When I
think of this, I can almost, so to speak, lay my hand
on Shakespeare and on Cromwell. These poor
walls were contemporaries of both, and I find something affecting in the thought. The mere soil is,
of course, far older than either, but *it* does not
touch one in the same way. A wall is the creation
of a human hand, the soil is not.

This place suits my whim, and I like it better
year after year. As with everything else, since
I began to love it I find it gradually growing beautiful. Dreamthorp—a castle, a chapel, a lake, a
straggling strip of gray houses, with a blue film of
smoke over all—lies embosomed in emerald. Summer, with its daisies, runs up to every cottage door.
From the little height where I am now sitting, I
see it beneath me. Nothing could be more peaceful.
The wind and the birds fly over it. A passing sunbeam makes brilliant a white gable-end, and brings

out the colors of the blossomed apple-tree beyond,
and disappears. I see figures in the street, but hear
them not. The hands on the church clock
seem always pointing to one hour. Time has fallen
asleep in the afternoon sunshine. I make a frame
of my fingers, and look at my picture. On the
walls of the next Academy's Exhibition will hang
nothing half so beautiful!

My village is, I think, a special favorite of summer's. Every window-sill in it she touches with color
and fragrance; everywhere she wakens the drowsy
murmurs of the hives; every place she scents with
apple-blossom. Traces of her hand are to be seen on
the weir beside the ruined mill; and even the canal,
along which the barges come and go, has a great
white water lily asleep on its olive-colored face.
Never was velvet on a monarch's robe so gorgeous
as the green mosses that beruff the roofs of farm
and cottage, when the sunbeam slants on them and
goes. The old road out towards the common, and
the hoary dikes that might have been built in the
reign of Alfred, have not been forgotten by the generous adorning season; for every fissure has its mossy
cushion, and the old blocks themselves are washed
by the loveliest gray-green lichens in the world, and
the large loose stones lying on the ground have
gathered to themselves the peacefulest mossy cover-
ings. Some of these have not been disturbed for a
century. Summer has adorned my village as gaily,
and taken as much pleasure in the task, as the people
of old, when Elizabeth was queen, took in the adorn-
ment of the Maypole against a summer festival.
And, just think, not only Dreamthorp, but every
English village she has made beautiful after one

fashion or another—making vivid green the hill
slope on which straggling white Welsh hamlets hang
right opposite the sea; drowning in apple-blossom
the red Sussex ones in the fat valley. And think,
once more, every spear of grass in England she has
touched with a livelier green; the crest of every bird
she has burnished; every old wall between the four
seas has received her mossy and licheny attentions;
every nook in every forest she has sown with pale
flowers, every marsh she has dashed with the fires of
the marigold. And in the wonderful night the moon
knows, she hangs—the planet on which so many
millions of us fight, and sin, and agonize, and die—
a sphere of glowworm light.

Having discoursed so long about Dreamthorp, it
is but fair that I should now introduce you to her
lions. These are, for the most part, of a commonplace kind: and I am afraid that, if you wish to find
romance in them, you must bring it with you.   I
might speak of the old church tower, or of the
churchyard beneath it, in which the village holds
its dead, each resting place marked by a simple
stone, on which is inscribed the name and age of the
sleeper, and a Scripture text beneath, in which live
our hopes of immortality. But, on the whole, perhaps it will be better to begin with the canal, which
wears on its olive-colored face the big white water
lily already chronicled. Such a secluded place is
Dreamthorp that the railway does not come near,
and the canal is the only thing that connects it with
the world. It stands high, and from it the undulat-
ing country may be seen stretching away into the
gray of distance, with hills and woods, and stains of
smoke which mark the sites of villages. Every now

and then a horse comes staggering along the towing-path, trailing a sleepy barge filled with merchandise. A quiet, indolent life these bargemen lead in the summer days. One lies stretched at his length on the sun-heated plank; his comrade sits smoking in the little dog hutch, which I suppose he calls a cabin. Silently they come and go; silently the wooden bridge lifts to let them through. The horse stops at the bridge house for a drink, and there I like to talk a little with the men. They serve instead of a newspaper, and retail with great willingness the news they have picked up in their progress from town to town. I am told they sometimes marvel who the old gentleman is who accosts them from beneath a huge umbrella in the sun, and that they think him either very wise or very foolish. Not in the least unnatural! We are great friends, I believe—evidence of which they occasionally exhibit by requesting me to disburse a trifle for drink money. This canal is a great haunt of mine of an evening. The water hardly invites one to bathe in it, and a delicate stomach might suspect the flavor of the eels caught therein; yet, to my thinking, it is not in the least destitute of beauty. A barge trailing up through it in the sunset is a pretty sight; and the heavenly crimsons and purples sleep quite lovingly upon its glossy ripples. Nor does the evening star disdain it, for as I walk along I see it mirrored therein as clearly as in the waters of the Mediterranean itself.

The old castle and chapel already alluded to are, perhaps, to a stranger, the points of attraction in Dreamthorp. Back from the houses is the lake, on the green sloping banks of which, with broken windows and tombs, the ruins stand. As it is noon,

and the weather is warm, let us go and sit on a
turret. Here, on these very steps, as old ballads
tell, a queen sat once, day after day, looking southward for the light of returning spears. I bethink
me that yesterday, no further gone, I went to visit
a consumptive shoemaker; seated here I can single
out his very house, nay, the very window of the
room in which he is lying. On that straw roof might
the raven alight, and flap his sable wings. There,
at this moment, is the supreme tragedy being en-
acted. A woman is weeping there, and little children
are looking on with a sore bewilderment. Before
nightfall the poor peaked face of the bowed artisan
will have gathered its ineffable peace, and the widow
will be led away from the bedside by the tenderness
of neighbors, and the cries of the orphan brood will
be stilled. And yet this present indubitable suffering and loss does not touch me like the sorrow of the
woman of the ballad, the phantom probably of a
minstrel's brain. The shoemaker will be forgotten—
I shall be forgotten; and long after visitors will sit
here and look out on the landscape and murmur the
simple lines. But why do death and dying obtrude
themselves at the present moment? On the turret
opposite, about the distance of a gunshot, is as pretty
a sight as eye could wish to see. Two young people,
strangers apparently, have come to visit the ruin.
Neither the ballad queen, nor the shoemaker down
yonder, whose respirations are getting shorter and
shorter, touches them in the least. They are merry
and happy, and the graybeard turret has not the
heart to thrust a foolish moral upon them. They
would not thank him if he did, I daresay. Perhaps
they could not understand him. Time enough!

Twenty years hence they will be able to sit down at his feet, and count griefs with him, and tell him tale for tale. Human hearts get ruinous in so much less time than stone walls and towers. See, the young man has thrown himself down at the girl's feet on a little space of grass. In her scarlet cloak she looks like a blossom springing out of a crevice on the ruined steps. He gives her a flower, and she bows her face down over it almost to her knees. What did the flower say? Is it to hide a blush? He looks delighted; and I almost fancy I see a proud color on his brow. As I gaze, these young people make for me a perfect idyl. The generous, ungrudging sun, the melancholy ruin, decked, like mad Lear, with the flowers and ivies of forgetfulness and grief, and between them, sweet and evanescent, human truth and love!

Love!—does it yet walk the world, or is it imprisoned in poems and romances? Has not the circulating library become the sole home of the passion? Is love not become the exclusive property of novelists and playwrights, to be used by them only for professional purposes? Surely, if the men I see are lovers, or ever have been lovers, they would be nobler than they are. The knowledge that he is beloved should—*must* make a man tender, gentle, upright, pure. While yet a youngster in a jacket, I can remember falling desperately in love with a young lady several years my senior— after the fashion of youngsters in jackets. Could I have fibbed in these days? Could I have betrayed a comrade? Could I have stolen eggs or callow young from the nest? Could I have stood quietly by and seen the weak or the maimed bullied? Nay, verily! In these absurd days she lighted up the whole world for me. To sit in the same room with her was like the happiness of perpetual holiday; when she asked me to run a message for her, or to do any, the slightest, service for her, I felt as if a patent of nobility were conferred on me. I kept my passion to myself, like a cake, and nibbled it in private. Juliet was several years my senior, and had a lover—was, in point of fact, actually engaged; and, in looking back, I can remember I was too much in love to feel the slightest twinge of jealousy. I remember also seeing Romeo for the first time, and thinking him a greater man than Cæsar or Napoleon. The worth I credited him with, the cleverness, the goodness, the everything! He awed me by his manner and bearing. He accepted that girl's love coolly and as a matter of course; it put him no more about than a crown and scepter puts about a king. What I would have given my life to possess—being only fourteen, it was not much to part with after all—he wore lightly, as he wore his gloves or his cane. It did not seem a bit too good for him. His self-possession appalled me. If I had seen him take the sun out of the sky, and put it into his breeches' pocket, I don't think I should have been in the least degree surprised. Well, years after, when I had discarded my passion with my jacket, I have assisted this middle-aged Romeo home from a roystering wine party, and heard him hiccup out his marital annoyances, with the strangest remembrances of old times, and the strangest deductions therefrom. Did that man with the idiotic laugh and the blurred utterance ever love? Was he ever capable of loving? I protest I have my doubts.

But where are my young people? Gone! So it is always. We begin to moralize and look wise, and Beauty, who is something of a coquette, and of an exacting turn of mind, and likes attentions, gets disgusted with our wisdom or our stupidity, and goes off in a huff. Let the baggage go!

The ruined chapel adjoins the ruined castle on which I am now sitting, and is evidently a building of much older date. It is a mere shell now. It is quite roofless, ivy covers it in part; the stone tracery of the great western window is yet intact, but the colored glass is gone with the splendid vestments of the abbot, the fuming incense, the chanting choirs, and the patient, sad-eyed monks, who muttered *Aves*, shrived guilt, and illuminated missals. Time was when this place breathed actual benedictions, and was a home of active peace. At present it is visited only by the stranger, and delights but the antiquary. The village people have so little respect for it that they do not even consider it haunted. There are several tombs in the interior bearing knights' escutcheons, which time has sadly defaced. The dust you stand upon is noble. Earls have been brought here in dinted mail from battle, and earls' wives from the pangs of childbearing. The last trumpet will break the slumber of a right honorable company. One of the tombs—the most perfect of all in point of preservation—I look at often, and try to conjecture what it commemorates. With all my fancies, I can get no further than the old story of love and death. There, on the slab, the white figures sleep; marble hands, folded in prayer, on marble breasts. And I like to think that he was brave, she beautiful; that although the monument is worn

by time, and sullied by the stains of the weather,
the qualities which it commemorates—husbandly
and wifely affection, courtesy, courage, knightly
scorn of wrong and falsehood, meekness, penitence,
charity—are existing yet somewhere, recognizable
by each other. The man who in this world can keep
the whiteness of his soul, is not likely to lose it in
any other.

In summer I spend a good deal of time floating
about the lake. The landing place to which my
boat is tethered is ruinous, like the chapel and
palace, and my embarkation causes quite a stir
in the sleepy little village. Small boys leave their
games and mud pies, and gather round in silence;
they have seen me get off a hundred times, but
their interest in the matter seems always new.
Not unfrequently an idle cobbler, in red nightcap
and leathern apron, leans on a broken stile, and
honors my proceedings with his attention. I shoot
off, and the human knot dissolves. The lake contains three islands, each with a solitary tree, and
on these islands the swans breed. I feed the birds
daily with bits of bread. See, one comes gliding
towards me, with superbly arched neck, to receive
its customary alms! How wildly beautiful its motions! How haughtily it begs! The green pasture
lands run down to the edge of the water, and into it
in the afternoons the red kine wade and stand knee-
deep in their shadows, surrounded by troops of flies.
Patiently the honest creatures abide the attacks of
their tormentors. Now one swishes itself with its
tail—now its neighbor flaps a huge ear. I draw
my oars alongside, and let my boat float at its own
will. The soft blue heavenly abysses, the wandering

streams of vapor, the long beaches of rippled cloud,
are glassed and repeated in the lake. Dreamthorp
is silent as a picture, the voices of the children
are mute; and the smoke from the houses, the blue
pillars all sloping in one angle, float upward as if in
sleep. Grave and stern the old castle rises from its
emerald banks, which long ago came down to the
lake in terrace on terrace, gay with fruits and flowers,
and with stone nymph and satyrs hid in every nook.
Silent and empty enough to-day! A flock of daws
suddenly bursts out from a turret, and round and
round they wheel, as if in panic. Has some great
scandal exploded? Has a conspiracy been discovered? Has a revolution broken out? The excitement has subsided, and one of them, perched
on the old banner staff, chatters confidentially to
himself as he, sideways, eyes the world beneath
him. Floating about thus, time passes swiftly, for,
before I know where I am, the kine have withdrawn
from the lake to couch on the herbage, while one
on a little height is lowing for the milkmaid and her
pails. Along the road I see the laborers coming
home for supper, while the sun setting behind me
makes the village windows blaze; and so I take out
my oars, and pull leisurely through waters faintly
flushed with evening colors.

I do not think that Mr. Buckle could have written his *History in Civilization* in Dreamthorp
because in it books, conversation, and the other
appurtenances of intellectual life, are not to be
procured. I am acquainted with birds, and the
building of nests—with wild-flowers, and the seasons
in which they blow—but with the big world far
away, with what men and women are thinking,

and doing, and saying, I am acquainted only through the *Times*, and the occasional magazine or review, sent by friends whom I have not looked upon for years, but by whom, it seems, I am not yet forgotten. The village has but few intellectual wants, and the intellectual supply is strictly measured by the demand. Still there is something. Down in the village, and opposite the curiously-carved fountain, is a schoolroom which can accommodate a couple of hundred people on a pinch. There are our public meetings held. Musical entertainments have been given there by a single performer. In that schoolroom last winter an American biologist terrified the villagers, and, to their simple understandings, mingled up the next world with this. Now and again some rare bird of an itinerant lecturer covers dead walls with posters, yellow and blue, and to that schoolroom we flock to hear him. His rounded periods the eloquent gentleman devolves amidst a respectful silence. His audience do not understand him, but they see that the clergyman does, and the doctor does; and so they are content, and look as attentive and wise as possible. Then, in connection with the schoolroom, there is a public library, where books are exchanged once a month. This library is a kind of Greenwich Hospital for disabled novels and romances. Each of these books has been in the wars; some are unquestionable antiques. The tears of three generations have fallen upon their dusky pages. The heroes and the heroines are of another age than ours. Sir Charles Grandison is standing with his hat under his arm. Tom Jones plops from the tree into the water, to the infinite distress of Sophia.

Moses comes home from market with his stock of
shagreen spectacles. Lovers, warriors, and villains—
as dead to the present generation of readers as
Cambyses—are weeping, fighting, and intriguing.
These books, tattered and torn as they are, are
read with delight to-day. The viands are celestial
if set forth on a dingy tablecloth. The gaps and
chasms which occur in pathetic or perilous chapters
are felt to be personal calamities. It is with a
certain feeling of tenderness that I look upon these
books; I think of the dead fingers that have turned
over the leaves, of the dead eyes that have traveled
along the lines. An old novel has a history of its
own. When fresh and new, and before it had
breathed its secret, it lay on my lady's table. She
killed the weary day with it, and when night came
it was placed beneath her pillow. At the sea-side
a couple of foolish heads have bent over it, hands
have touched and tingled, and it has heard vows
and protestations as passionate as any its pages
contained. Coming down in the world, Cinderella
in the kitchen has blubbered over it by the light of
a surreptitious candle, conceiving herself the while
the magnificent Georgiana, and Lord Mordaunt,
Georgiana's lover, the potboy round the corner.
Tied up with many a dingy brother, the auctioneer
knocks the bundle down to the bidder of a few
pence, and it finds its way to the quiet cove of
some village library, where with some difficulty—
as if from want of teeth, and with numerous in-
terruptions—as if from lack of memory, it tells its
old stories, and wakes tears, and blushes, and
laughter as of yore. Thus it spends its age, and in
a few years it will become unintelligible, and then,

in the dust-bin, like poor human mortals in the grave, it will rest from all its labors. It is impossible to estimate the benefit which such books have conferred. How often have they loosed the chain of circumstance! What unfamiliar tears—what unfamiliar laughter they have caused! What chivalry and tenderness they have infused into rustic loves! Of what weary hours they have cheated and beguiled their readers! The big, solemn history books are in excellent preservation; the story-books are defaced and frayed, and their out-of-elbows condition is their pride, and the best justification of their existence. They are tashed, as roses are, by being eagerly handled and smelled. I observe, too, that the most ancient romances are not in every case the most severely worn. It is the pace that tells in horses, men, and books. There are Nestors wonderfully hale; there are juveniles in a state of dilapidation. One of the youngest books, *The Old Curiosity Shop*, is absolutely falling to pieces. That book, like Italy, is possessor of the fatal gift; but happily, in its case, everything can be rectified by a new edition. We have buried warriors and poets, princes and queens, but no one of these was followed to the grave by sincerer mourners than was little Nell.

Besides the itinerant lecturer, and the permanent library, we have the Sunday sermon. These sum up the intellectual aids and furtherances of the whole place. We have a church and a chapel, and I attend both. The Dreamthorp people are Dissenters, for the most part; why, I never could understand, because dissent implies a certain intellectual effort. But Dissenters they are, and

Dissenters they are likely to remain. In an ungainly building, filled with hard gaunt pews, without an organ, without a touch of color in the windows, with nothing to stir the imagination or the devotional sense, the simple people worship. On Sunday, they are put upon a diet of spiritual bread-and-water. Personally, I should desire more generous food. But the laboring people listen attentively, till once they fall asleep, and they wake up to receive the benediction with a feeling of having done their duty. They know they ought to go to chapel, and they go. I go likewise, from habit, although I have long ago lost the power of following a discourse. In my pew, and whilst the clergyman is going on, I think of the strangest things—of the tree at the window, of the congregation of the dead outside, of the wheat fields and the cornfields beyond and all around. And the odd thing is, that it is during sermon only that my mind flies off at a tangent and busies itself with things removed from the place and the circumstances. Whenever it is finished, fancy returns from her wanderings, and I am alive to the objects around me. The clergyman knows my humor, and is good Christian enough to forgive me; and he smiles good-humoredly when I ask him to let me have the chapel keys, that I may enter, when in the mood, and preach a sermon to myself. To my mind, an empty chapel is impressive; a crowded one, comparatively a commonplace affair. Alone, I could choose my own text, and my silent discourse would not be without its practical applications.

An idle life I live in this place, as the world counts it; but then I have the satisfaction of differing from the world as to the meaning of idleness. A windmill twirling its arms all day is admirable only when there is corn to grind. Twirling its arms for the mere barren pleasure of twirling them, or for the sake of looking busy, does not deserve any rapturous pæan of praise. I must be made happy after my own fashion, not after the fashion of other people. Here I can live as I please, here I can throw the reins on the neck of my whim. Here I play with my own thoughts; here I ripen for the grave.

IFFLEY THE UNSPOILED [1]

BY

Robert P. Tristram Coffin

THE only proper way into the Village Unspoiled is along the Thames, through the meadows that Arnold's Scholar Gypsy loved, past fishermen who fish for the joy of the thing and not for fish, who might serve as models for "patience on a monument" save for noses that are perpetually red. One has the consolation of goodly English precedent behind the claw-like hand that reaches forth from the tiny toll house to take the halfpenny which is the price of entering Iffley the ideal way: Roman *denarii*, together with Saxon coins, have been found on the river bottom beneath the bridge. Hard by the toll house are the broken paddles of the mossy waterwheel, and an idle millstone, of the mill that had ground a century of grists in Chaucer's time and that ground on down to a decade ago when fire took it.

Up a cobbled hill and under lime trees the lane winds to a gate beneath a chestnut tree; one is in the heart of England. Here is one of the hundred churchyards within footing distance of Oxford where one may live Gray's *Elegy*. Iffley Church is Norman and is as old as the singing monks sailing by, down stream to Abingdon. The lichens

---

[1] From *Crowns and Cottages*. Reprinted by the kind permission of the author, *The North American Review*, and the Yale University Press.

and the love of eight hundred years are in its walls
rising from the green benediction of graves.   It
must be easy and pleasant to sleep here, with the
earliest snowdrops starring the turf, and roses at
the floodtide of the year.   With its half effaced,
zigzag bordered arches set with beaks of queer
birds from medieval bestiaries, which bite and vex
their own wings to prove their ancient lineage, the
church is as lovely as it is old.   The wide tower
and round-topped windows are full of the naïve
frankness of folk who have found the holiness of
simplicity.   Inside the sunlight carpets the floor
with the same patterns that made beautiful the
feet which rest these centuries under the green
outside.   All the honest and humble prayers of
the devout of many years seem to sweeten the plain
white walls.   One thinks of the long sunbeams
of many children's hair reaching back from to-day
at the ancient carven font into the yesterdays.
Here are holy things time cannot touch, the truce
of God, faith in gold and gray, precepts of happiness,
precepts of peace.

Just beyond the wall of the churchyard is the
rectory, a refectory of monks in other days.   It
bears its seven centuries felicitously on eaves hung
green with moss and tiles of kindly gray.   There
is no better place to read the Church Fathers than
the rector's oaken paneled study, with bees making
the afternoon golden about the pleached pear
trees outside and blue English skies that mind of
forget-me-nots through leaded casements opened
wide.   Chrysostom and the sunlight of summer,
Ambrose and the scent of honey.   Men with gold
and honey in their names are at home here; and the

windows open on a place very like the New Jerusa-
lem. Indeed, below is the great drawing-room with
a gold and blue motto for a border promising

manibus non factam domum
Sempiternam in cœlis.

And there is the rector's wife, whose dearly cherished
Infant Dionysius of too white marble cannot destroy
the atmosphere of ages, pouring the rectory dog
his milk and saying over tea things the happy
things a rector's wife finds to say. And Audrey,
the sporting daughter of the house, the ruddiness of
October beagle hunts on her face, is tapping the
panels to show you where the secret passage is and
perhaps dislodging a pet Dresden shepherdess in
her enthusiasm. Winding passages, mysterious stairs
down which a friar may walk, and the rector with his
puns to take you back with him through the years of
his house. But outside in the rectory gardens is the
heart of England. The sanctity of an enclosure had
never so sweet a demonstration. There are peach
trees standing English fashion, to get the ripening
heat of the stone, like candelabra against walls; Virginia creeper, to tell the passing of the year in red;
ivy, to keep the year immortally green; and beyond
the antique sundial seven terraces go down with urns
and rose arbors to the swallow-haunted Thames. Best
of all, there is a cosy quiet, sounds of village dogs and
boys faint and musical beyond high walls, tea and
talk, talk and tea, and the day's shadows growing
longer on the grass. If a man is ever going to be a
poet, it is in such a place.

But one cannot play the hermit forever. Outside, above the rectory, the hill rises where Haw-

thorne, come three thousand miles to love Oxford, found his view of the city that turns white with all her towers in the sunshine. Beyond hedges of whitethorn on this hill, in a place I know but will not tell you of for fear the Iffley boys would find it, are glades yellow with February primroses, and May comes there with miles of bluebells until they look like smoke under the trees. But you shall turn instead into the long village street by Postmistress Blay's little cottage. Mistress Blay is keeper of the mails and the lone telephone that thrusts but this one finger of a rushing age into this quiet place; the watchful gods of Iffley have palsied this one digit, for it is better to trust in leather soles than in this telephone perpetually out of order. The postmistress could put old-fashioned New England housewives to shame; her arms, *argent;* a scrubbing brush, *or*, rampant; and of chevrons, *sable*, none at all. One could eat off her hearthstones. I honestly believe she scrubs the stamps.

Perhaps, across the street little girls in pinafores and martyred hair and boys with apple cheeks, smooched Eton collars, and sturdy bare knees will be filing into the schoolhouse by their separate doors. Under the thatch of the schoolhouse there is more than numbers and knitting for the boys, numbers and plain sewing for the girls. There are dishes for school teas, a floor for dancing and games. May Day sets forth in fine style from this base, attendants bearing flower wreaths before the May King and Queen who have all the morning on their faces, or at least as much of it as soap can put there.

Nearby the milkman lives in the past, though trafficking in the present. His stoop has the sea shell

which hides the key just as in New England villages;
on the shrine of his parlor table rests his Sunday-
go-to-meeting hat and his prayer book wrapped in a
spotless handkerchief. His delivery man, an ungainly boy in teens, who brings you the buttercups
and marigolds of Iffley meadows mistakenly called
cream, is a poor Hermes to this Zeus. In the village
phrase he is "eleven pence, three farthings," which
means in our speech "not all there." He leaves
the filled crock just where you will upset it when
you open the garden gate. If you chide him, he
will fill your measure without emptying the rain
water out. But the milkman is greater than his
servant, and lives in his clouds.

In the midst of houses of "county" families, a
thatched cottage overgrown with roses and smelling to the skies of sweet lavender is most delightful
of all. Bees make the golden and chocolate thatch-
ing their hive; window geraniums grow best there.
And there is the plumpest and rosiest of boy babies
to make the day complete with his play among the
dainty daisies on the lawn . . . a place of things
that matter in this world.

The houses of village "quality" are pleasant
places, too. The Malt House was once a real malt
house; in the days when good things to eat and
drink, food for holy songs, were still under the
wings of the Church, shaven tonsures bent over the
mash to watch it change into the ale of beatitude.
Stone figures in miter and sanctified attitudes are
dug up among to-day's brussels sprouts. One wishes
to dig in the bed of violas for relics. Rivermead is
Elizabethan and rambling, with carven griffins on
the doors, rooms that run over into the gardens,

and gardens that invade the rooms. And the river alone to keep the gardens from going straight on to the City Delectable. Here a bishop enjoys his valedictory days, after the clouds and mists of Newfoundland. Death can come sweetly to him here; when ears fail, there are roses, and when eyes, the smell of them and the feel of their petals. In the "fourth gentleman's house on the left," as its delightful occupant describes it, the Victorian Age is entrenched. You find scrapbooks and water-colors of Sicilian ruins of the bold wash school affected by all young ladies of yesterday. The chairs wear plush and are stuffed; carved grapes crop out where least expected; inevitably there is that chair that reproduces a scallop of the sea. Doilies are thick as cobwebs on morning grass. The politeness that meant life itself forty years ago becomes the lady of this house exceedingly. Even Billy, her terrier, barks lower than dogs of an un-Victorian school.

The Tree Inn, a rallying place for villagers, has gardens where tables spread under chestnut boughs at which on Sunday splendid workingmen wet their thick mustaches in their ale, while their wives strive to sort their offspring out of masses of struggling boyhood. The Institute, the village clubhouse, need not overawe one with its name; it is only a small cottage done over. But it is a perfect memorial to the men in the late War who have gone Westward forever to a place sweeter even than Iffley. Here their memory keeps green, not in a cold shaft, but in a house where home folks can play the games they loved to play and read the books they left unread. Whist drives bring the Colonel and the postmistress together to clash with Lady John and the village butcher; the tennis court, the rector's daughter and the toffee girl from the village store.

If one is seeking contentment in this life, one would do well to lift the latch of Donnington Cottage at the sign of Teas Provided. If there is balm in Gilead, this is Gilead. If the fallible human be the essence of art, here is a masterpiece. The tiles are crooked, the gables go up, the roof sags down, peeling mortar shows timbering of Shakespeare's day, cracks creep down the walls, casemented windows droop under climbing roses, moss caravans along the drains, the chimney pots lean over. Nasturtiums choke the doorway; the garden has run wild with unbridled japonica. Inside is a kitten, sedate as one of the Pharaohs, and a copper kettle with a song quite its own. Old plates catch the glow of seacoal fire. Each cosy thing goes straight home to the heart. Upstairs in a room with windows full of dewy stars there is such sleep as children have. Worries slip away, with the world, in any room at all. But

nulla rosa sine spina.

The thorn in this rose is the landlady. Through years of living alone she has evolved a code of etiquette in pots and pans that would baffle a Balkan diplomat. Each saucepan has its charter of rights; this must never be set on the flame, this is for water only. Now, though dishes are essential things, one still could manage. But not if one happens to be a man. Disappointed once in the *genus* in the person of her husband, she has sworn herself to hate all the rest. So Donnington, for the sins of man, like Eden, goes tenantless.

There are other inviting houses. The elms of
one estate are haunted with nightingales; over its
lawns of an evening larks go up into a *nunc dimittis*
sky. Another is the home of all the hollyhocks and
wallflowers. A woman and her daughter live there,
too, who brew a tea that makes you say the kindliest
things, that wreathes the evening with garlands of
peace. Their hearth is the benediction for any
golden day. Last of all, there is the Turn, where
Sir George and Lady John with their acres keep out
the jinns of modern suburbandom from Iffley.
Lady John rides her wheel as though her seventy
years were twenty, and the May has never left her
cheeks. If there are kindly things done, she has her
hand in them; she is the village mother, first there
with ointments for burns, last to leave the child with
the aching tooth. If her taste in Old Masters may
be questioned, her house is hung with healing herbs
and charity. To hear Sir George, who is a don at
Jesus, among his fragrant books, is to have a university at its source. He has been everywhere and
done many things well. India and Ireland meet in
his witty wisdom. He can tell equally well the story
he unearthed in the shadow of the Himalayas of
Abraham and the Parsee, or the ending of his recent
visit as a secret conciliatory emissary from Parliament to Belfast and how the Irish students, dyed-
in-the-wool Sinn Feiners all, bade him Godspeed
with cries—"Come back soon, Sir George, and we'll
make you the next President of Ireland!" He
would be a great philosopher if, as Dr. Johnson remarked, cheerfulness were not always breaking in.

It is the greatest charm of Iffley that here one
can see old Dame Human Nature knitting her socks

unhurried by the clanking machines of this age. Simple houses, simple lives.   Picturesque person- alities thrive.   Fitz Clare, with his mountain of a perambulator outgrown by his daughter and used now as a barrow for parcels, will keep you from your ways with philippics well seasoned with peppery profanity on a weather that blights his potatoes; or Miss Duke will gave you intimate details of royalty (she does not go below earls), while Mrs. Graydon's baked beans, a dish you have transplanted three thousand miles, are left burning on the high knees of the gods.   Miss Norris, who is High Church and speaks to no one except Sir George and the rector, goes her withering way through the big estate where she rents one of the smaller cottages with that spirited aloofness which New England has described as "head up, tail over the dashboard." The Iffley babies have a reputation of sunny op- timism even under gray skies, their faces like apple blossoms of Eastertide.   One meets such people as the patriarch carrying waterpails on a yoke; Bill, a "proper poacher," who does not keep his rectitude after sunset when hares come out of burrows and who is afflicted by spirits; a vendor of chrysanthe- mums with spotless apron and shoes as long behind the ankle as in front; the curate in shovel hat with socks flapping over his shoes; the Cowley Father with ankles bare for medieval humility; the girl who fancies and dresses herself as Red Riding Hood; and the philosopher in corduroys strapped below the knees, whose faggots cannot cover the patch- work on his breeches beside which Joseph's coat is as vanity.   The wash lady who "does for" Iffley is a philosopher, too; from her experience with three

husbands she gives you wisdom for marital felicity,
"if you leaves 'em, you loses 'em." Tramps knock
at Iffley doors for hot water to make their tea.
The temperamental baker furnishes human nature
unadulterated. To him the symmetry of a loaf is
as music. He makes music, too, with his bass in
the choir. But he shares the weakness of all artists;
he will punish you for buying loaves in town by
letting you and your tea guests go breadless; he will
come out of the choir to sing his solo, though he
have but two bars to sing.

Old things keep green in Iffley, old customs, old
hearts. The years go by along the London Road,
but miss the turn to the village. One can walk its
middle ways without fear of motors. The carol
singers still lead the Christmas in; December nights
have lanterns with frosty aureoles and the clear
Noel under the starlit skies. Boy mummers gather
pennies from house to house on Twelfth Night,
armed with swords of lath, playing an Oxfordshire
Saint George to a dragon of very broad Oxfordshire
brogue. People pluck their forelocks to Lady John
and address her as "My Lady"; they would resent
being told that such an act betokened servility.
Plodding workmen bid you good night when they
meet you on lanes full of dusk. And old men and
women do not creep away into houses there. They
ride their wheels and play astounding tennis, laugh
and walk abroad for ale and primroses, for the sunshine they may find and the rain in their faces, for
the fountains of youth. Like babies, old folks
flourish there.

It is good to live in Iffley. Somehow, unconsciously, people there seem to have learned the art

of living.   Tending their roses, living as they please
behind their high walls, having their hearts open
to their open fires, getting the singing of teakettles
into their souls, somehow they have learned the
art.   The beauty and ease of it are everywhere.
Old houses long filled with tears and laughter to
live in, chairs hallowed with use by little children,
old ivied stones to love, these help to give felicity.
But the greatest of all their blessedness is simplicity.
They have found out that the deepest and sweetest
things are the little beauties of every day, porridge
in bowls with blue flowers, baby shoes worn over
at the heel, sunlight and firelight on dishes, smiles,
and voices speaking low.   The luxuries of life and
the unessentials do not greatly trouble them.   The
simple, single things that last they have, not motor
cars, not phonographs, not telephones, not cinemas,
not electricity; but in their homes you will find plain
pity and love and grief and mercy and, best of all,
kindliness.   So they are able to talk of happy things,
so they can walk along their fields and share the
joy the skylarks feel, see the way Spring treads,
love sunset and after that the stars.   So they can
play their croquet till every daisy of their hopes
closes gladly with the dusk, and ride their bicycles
right up to the green edge of the grave.

THE STREET [1]

Simeon Strunsky

A FORETASTE of the languor of June is in the
air. The turnstile storm doors in our office-
building, which have been put aside for brief periods
during the first deceptive approaches of spring, only to
come back triumphant from Elba, have been definitely removed. The steel workers pace their girders
twenty floors high almost in mid-season form, and
their pneumatic hammers scold and chatter through
the sultry hours. The soda fountains are bright
with new compounds whose names ingeniously
reflect the world's progress from day to day in
politics, science, and the arts. From my window
I can see the long black steamships pushing down
to the sea, and they raise vague speculations in my
mind about the cost of living in the vicinity of
Sorrento and Fontainebleau. On such a day I am
reminded of my physician's orders, issued last December, to walk a mile every afternoon on leaving
my office. So I stroll up Broadway with the intention of taking my train farther up-town, at
Fourteenth Street.

. . . In the city, where I should swing along
briskly, I lounge. What is there on Broadway to
linger over? On Broadway Nature has used her

[1] From *Belshazzar Court*. By the kind permission of Henry
Holt & Company.

biggest, fattest typeforms. Tall, flat, building fronts, brazen with many windows and ribbed with commercial gilt lettering six feet high; shrieking proclamations of auction sales written in letters of fire on vast canvases; railway posters in scarlet and blue and green; rotatory barber poles striving at the national colors and producing vertigo; banners, escutcheons, crests in all the primary colors— surely none of these things needs poring over. And I know them with my eyes closed. I know the windows where lithe youths in gymnasium dress demonstrate the virtue of home exercises; the windows where other young men do nothing but put on and take off patent reversible near-linen collars; where young women deftly roll cigarettes; where other young women whittle at sticks with miraculously stropped razors. I know these things by heart, yet I linger over them in flagrantly unhygienic attitudes, my shoulders bent forward, and my chest and diaphragm precisely the reverse of that prescribed by the doctor.

Perhaps the thing that makes me linger before these familiar sights is the odd circumstance that in Broadway's shop windows Nature is almost never herself, but is either supernatural or artificial. Nature, for instance, never intended that razors should cut wood and remain sharp; that linen collars should keep on getting cleaner the longer they are worn; that glass should not break; that ink should not stain; that gauze should not tear; that an object worth five dollars should sell for $1.39; but all these things happen in Broadway windows. Williams, whom I meet now and then, who sometimes turns and walks up with me to

Fourteenth Street, pointed out to me the other day how strange a thing it was that the one street which has become a synonym for "real life" to all good suburban Americans, is not real at all, but is crowded either with miracles or with imitations.

The windows on Broadway glow with wax fruits and with flowers of muslin and taffeta drawn by bounteous Nature from her storehouses in Parisian garret workshops. Broadway's ostrich feathers have been plucked in East side tenements. The huge cigars in the tobacconists' windows are of wood. The enormous bottles of champagne in the saloons are of cardboard, and empty. The tall scaffoldings of proprietary medicine bottles in the drug shops are of paper. "Why," said Williams, "even the jewelry sold in the Japanese auction stores is not genuine, and the sellers are not Japanese."

This bustling mart of commerce, as the generation after the Civil War used to say, is only a world of illusion. Artificial flowers, artificial fruits, artificial limbs, tobacco, rubber, silks, woolens, straws, gold, silver. . . . The ladies who smile out of charming morning costumes are obviously of lining and plaster. Their smug Herculean husbands in pajamas preserve their equanimity in the severest weather only because of their wire-and-plaster constitutions. The baby reposing in its beribboned crib is china and excelsior. Illusion everywhere.

But the Broadway crowd is real. You only have to buffet it for five minutes to feel, in eyes and arms and shoulders, how real it is. When I was a boy and was taken to the circus, it was always an amazing thing to me that there should be so many people in the street moving in a direction away from the circus. . . . But on Broadway on a late summer afternoon . . . the natural thing is that the living tide as it presses south shall beat me back, halt me, eddy around me. I know that there are people moving north with me, but I am not acutely aware of them. This onrush of faces converges on me alone. It is I against half the world.

The crowd on lower Broadway is alert and well set up. . . . The men on the sidewalk are young, limber, sharp-faced, almost insolent young men. There are not very many old men in the crowd, though I see any number of gray-haired young men. Seldom do you detect the traditional signs of age, the sagging lines of the face, the relaxed abdominal contour, the tamed spirit. The young, the young-old, the old-young, but rarely quite the old.

I am speaking only of externals. Clean-cut eager faces are very frequently disappointing. A very ordinary mind may be working behind that clear sweep of brow and nose and chin. I have known the shock of young men who look like kings of Wall Street and speak like shoe clerks. They are shoe clerks. But the appearance is there, that athletic carriage which is helped out by our triumphant, ready-made clothing. I suppose I ought to detest the tailor's tricks which iron out all ages and all stations into a uniformity of padded shoulders and trim waistlines and hips. I imagine I ought to despise our habit of wearing elegant shoddy where the European chooses honest, clumsy woolens. But I am concerned only with externals, and in outward appearances a Broadway crowd beats the world. . . .

I still have to speak of the women in the crowd. What an infinitely finer thing is a woman than a man of her class! To see this for yourself you have only to walk up Broadway until the southward-bearing stream breaks off and the tide begins to run from west to east. You have passed out of the commercial district into the region of factories. It is well on toward dark, and the barracks that go by the unlovely name of loft buildings are pouring out their battalions of needle-workers. The crowd has become a mass. The nervous pace of lower Broadway slackens to the steady, patient tramp of a host. It is an army of women, with here and there a flying detachment of the male. . . .

. . . I am now on a different Broadway. The crowd is no longer north and south, but flows in every direction. It is churned up at every corner and spreads itself across the squares and open places. Its appearance has changed. It is no longer a factory population. Women still predominate, but they are the women of the professions and trades which center about Madison Square— business women of independent standing, women from the magazine offices, the publishing houses, the insurance offices. You detect the bachelor girl in the current which sets in toward the home quarters of the undomesticated, the little Bohemias, the foreign eating places, whose fixed *table d'hôte* prices flash out in illumined signs from the side streets. Still farther north and the crowd becomes tinged with the current of that Broadway which the outside world knows best. The idlers begin to mingle with the workers, men appear in English clothes with canes, women desperately corseted

with plumes and jeweled reticules. You catch the
first heart-beat of Little Old New York.

The first stirrings of this gayer Broadway die
down as quickly almost as they manifest themselves.
The idlers and those who minister to them have
heard the call of the dinner hour and have vanished,
into hotel doors, into shabbier quarters by no
means in keeping with the cut of their garments
and their apparent indifference to useful employment. Soon the street is almost empty. It is not
a beautiful Broadway in this garish interval between the last of the matinée and shopping crowd
and the vanguard of the night crowd. The monster
electric sign boards have not begun to gleam and
flash and revolve and confound the eye and the
senses. At night the electric Niagara hides the
squalid fronts of ugly brick, the dark doorways,
the clutter of fire escapes, the rickety wooden
hoardings. Not an imperial street this Broadway
at 6:30 of a summer's afternoon. Cheap jewelry
shops, cheap tobacconists' shops, cheap haber-
dasheries, cheap restaurants, grimy little newspaper agencies and ticket offices, and "demonstration" stores for patent foods, patent waters, patent
razors. . . .

O Gay White Way, you are far from gay in the
fast-fading light, before the magic hand of Edison
wipes the wrinkles from your face and galvanizes
you into hectic vitality; far from alluring with
your tinsel shop windows, with your puffy-faced,
unshaven men leaning against doorposts and chew-
ing pessimistic toothpicks, your sharp-eyed news-
boys wise with the wisdom of the Tenderloin, and
your itinerant women whose eyes flash from side to

side. It is not in this guise that you draw the hearts of millions to yourself, O dingy Gay White Way, O Via Lobsteria Dolorosa!

Well, when a man begins to moralize, it is time to go home. I have walked farther than I intended, and I am soft from lack of exercise, and tired. The romance of the crowd has disappeared. Romance cannot survive that short passage of Longacre Square, where the art of the theater and of the picture postcard flourish in an atmosphere impregnated with gasoline. As I glance into the windows of the automobile salesrooms and catch my own reflection in the enamel of Babylonian limousines, I find myself thinking all at once of the children at home. They expand and fill up the horizon. Broadway disappears. I smile into the face of a painted promenader, but how is she to know that it is not at her I smile, but at the sudden recollection of what the baby said at the breakfast table that morning? Like all good New Yorkers when they enter the subway, I proceed to choke up all my senses against contact with the external world, and thus resolving myself into a state of coma, I dip down into the bowels of the earth, whence in due time I am spewed out two short blocks from Belshazzar Court.

THE BERLIN OF THE EIGHTIES [1]

BY

Ludwig Lewisohn

THE city that I remember, the Berlin of the eighties, was rugged and gray. But it had nothing forbidding in its aspect, rather an air of homely and familiar comfort. There were few private houses, but people lived in their apartments in large airy rooms with tall French windows and neat, white tile ovens. The streets were monotonous in appearance but admirably clean. There were no posters, no public advertisements except upon the pillars erected for that purpose, the traffic of horse cars, omnibuses and cabs was orderly and convenient. The cabs, driven by red-faced, loquacious cabbies in blue-caped coats and top hats, were cheap. My father and mother, though far from rich, used them constantly, and I remember being driven for hours through the black-draped city on that icy day in 1888 on which the old emperor's body lay in state in the cathedral.

My earliest glimpses of beauty are characteristic of the city. One was the windows of the Royal Porcelain Works on the Leipziger Strasse. With all the exquisite sensitiveness of childhood I saw those wonderful little figures and their porcelain veils and draperies and delicately molded forms.

[1] From *Upstream*. By permission of Boni and Liveright, Publishers.

They were so tiny and yet so perfect, and they thrilled me far more than Rauch's equestrian statue of the great Frederic or the chariot of victory over the city gate. The latter were dutifully impressed upon me by my father; my mother let me stand and gaze my fill before the windows of the porcelain shop. . . . But the great sight to me, which I never saw without a lifting of the heart, was a certain public square. One walked or drove through a short street in which villas stood in gardens; at the end of that street one came upon the square quite suddenly. To that moment I always looked forward; the sensation was like the sudden crash of an orchestra. For the square spread out with an airiness, a fine and noble amplitude of shape and proportion, a grace and majesty at once that I despair of rendering into words. I have seen nothing like it since. Perhaps it seemed finer to my childish eyes than it was or is; but I am willing to yield to that old vision as a true one, since the seat of beauty is after all in the beholding mind.

Beyond the square lay the Tiergarten. Thither I was taken on many pleasant afternoons. And I can still see very clearly the statue of Flora surrounded by gorgeous flower beds and the monument of Queen Louise and the "snail hill" swarming with other children and their nursemaids; I can still hear their merry cries; I can still feel the stinging coolness on my heated throat of the milk sold at the famous kiosks of Bolle. But when I was four or five years old I would beg my nurse to take me to the gold-fish pond. It was generally still by the little artificial lake, and I loved the stillness; the dark green foliage was very thick all around

and the dusk fell early there. The mute darting
about of the fishes seemed mysterious and soothing,
the stone benches were cool and strong and bare.
I felt in this spot, without knowing it, the majesty
of places withdrawn from the cries of men. . . .
Another scene of the great park I remember: a
winter scene. Bare trees and the frozen river
around the Rousseau Island and the gay scarfs of
the skaters. And suddenly dusk and a brazen
sun-disc black-barred by trees. Then the swift
early winter night and the gas lamps of the streets
and the warmth and security of home. . . .

But the out-of-door scenes of winter that I recall
are few; another square and the snowflakes falling
thick and my father and I walking across it to a
Vienna café where he played chess on Sunday mornings. This is one scene. And another is our sturdy
maid carrying me from a playmate's house to a cab
through a blinding blizzard. And the third is the
Christmas fair—long since abolished—on the Belle-
Alliance Square. Twinkling lights in the frosty
air, and booths noisy and gay with cheap toys and
cakes, and everywhere the sharp odor of the fir
trees.

I loved spring more than even this—the cool,
virginal, gradual spring of the North. The windows
were opened and children reappeared on the streets
and great boughs of lilacs were sold. Have the
German lilacs a headier and sweeter fragrance
than ours? It seemed to fill the air and the heart:
it meant the winds of spring and people sitting in
gardens and casting aside their cares. For the
Germans, I can recognize now, yield to the natural
moods of the seasons. Spring is to them still the

spring of the folk-songs and they would like to pack a bundle and wander out into the land with lilac blossoms in their hats. . . . My father and mother took a cab on Sunday and drove in the Tiergarten or else went by boat up the river Spree to Treptow and there we sat on pleasant terraces and watched the life on the water. Even then I loved to see men and youths in their skiffs with bare white arms and legs and paddles flashing in the sunlight, and took a deep delight in the strong, silent, virile rhythm of the rise and fall of their oars. . . .

In the summer of my sixth year my father rented a house by a lake in Straussberg near Berlin. The village was still isolated. You took the train and then a stagecoach to reach it. There were swans on the lake and a boat, sheep in the meadows and gooseberry bushes in the garden. Over all a deep, brooding, old-world peace. . . .

Two scenes stand before me which symbolize the character of the social group from which I sprang. This is one: I am sitting in a half-darkened room and my heart beats and my cheeks burn. It is Christmas Eve. I look through the dark pane and across the street. Ah, there, behind an uncurtained window, a tree with candles. Quickly I turn my eyes away. I do not want to taste the glory until it is truly mine. And at last, at last, a bell rings. The folding doors open and there—in the drawing room—stands my own tree in its glimmering splendor and around it the gifts from my parents and my grandmother and my uncles and aunts— charming German toys and books of fairy tales and marchpane from Königsberg. And my mother

takes me by the hand and leads me to the table
and I feel as though I were myself walking straight
into a fairy tale. . . .

And the other scene: It was my grandmother's
custom, in pious remembrance of her husband,
to visit the temple on the chief Jewish holidays—
New Year and the Day of Atonement. And once,
on the day of the great white feast, I was taken
there to see her. The temple was large and rather
splendid; the great seven-branched candelabra were
of shining silver. The rabbi, the cantor and the
large congregation of men were all clad in their
gleaming shrouds and their white silken praying
shawls and had white caps on their heads. I can
still see one venerable old man who read his Hebrew
book through a large magnifying glass. The whiteness of that penitential scene was wonderful and
solemn. Then the first star came out and the
great day was over and in the vestibule I saw my
grandmother reverently saluted by her sons who
wished her a happy holiday.

A LIST OF BOOKS PARTICULARLY ADAPTED FOR
USE AS MODELS

Belloc, Hilaire. *Delft*, from *Hills and the Sea*. Methuen & Co.,
   Ltd., London.
Brooke, Rupert. *Niagara Falls*, from *Letters from America*.
   Charles Scribner's Sons.
Cautela, Guiseppe. *Gravesend Bay*, in *The American Mercury*,
   September, 1925.
Coffin, Robert P. Tristram. *Backwaters of Berkshire*, in *The
   North American Review*, October, 1923.
Guedalla, Philip. *Fez*, from *A Gallery*. G. P. Putnam's Sons.
Hall, Norman. *An Autumn Sojourn in Iceland*, in *Harper's
   Magazine*, January, 1924.

Hawthorne, Nathaniel. *New College Gardens*, from *English Note Books*, Volume VIII.

Hewlett, Maurice. *A Hermitage in Sight*, from *In a Green Shade*. G. Bell & Sons, Ltd., London.

Lamb, Charles. *Blakesmoor in H———shire* and *The Old Margate Hoy*, from *The Last Essays of Elia*.

Lamb, Charles. *Oxford in the Vacation*, from *The Essays of Elia*.

Lucas, E. V. *The Royal Mint and New Scotland Yard* and *The Zoo*, from *More Wanderings in London*. George H. Doran Company.

McFee, William. *The Market*, from *Harbours of Memory*. Doubleday, Page & Company.

Morley, Christopher. *The Enchanted Village* and *South Broad Street*, from *Travels in Philadelphia*. David McKay Company.

Newton, A. Edward. *My Old Lady London*, from *A Magnificent Farce*. The Atlantic Monthly Press.

Thompson, Basil. *Louisiana: (Madame de la Louisiane)*, from *These United States, First Series*. Boni and Liveright.

Stevenson, Robert Louis. *Davos in Winter*, from *Essays of Travel*. Charles Scribner's Sons.

Stevenson, Robert Louis. *On the Enjoyment of Unpleasant Places*, from *Essays of Travel*. Charles Scribner's Sons.

Stevenson, Robert Louis. *Memories of an Islet*, from *Memories and Portraits*. Charles Scribner's Sons.

C. Essays on Authors

The four essays that follow, diverse as even a cursory reading will show them to be, are all essays in appreciation of some author. None of us can hope to emulate James Barrie's touching and whimsical tribute to George Meredith, but all of us can reverently acknowledge the beauty of its workmanship and the charm of its fancy, both of which compelled its inclusion in this book. Christopher Morley's birthday letter to Charles Lamb is perhaps somewhat nearer our abilities. We ourselves, seizing upon his idea, might perchance essay a letter to some one we especially admire in the unbounded realm of letters or of music or of painting. Ethel Wallace Hawkins proves to us the impossibility of drawing fast lines about any type of essays. Is her *Introduced by Mr. Housman* an appreciation of the poet of *A Shropshire Lad* or is it an appreciation of Shropshire and its villages? It is assuredly both, though we feel that after all it is inspired by Mr. Housman rather than by Shropshire; and we include it largely because we wish to draw your attention to the fact that delightful essays may be written about just such a combination. And a careful study of Llewelyn Powy's more formal and thorough *Michel de Montaigne*, himself the first of essayists, will suggest to you the effects gained through the use of concrete detail, of portraiture, and of quotations taken at first hand from the author under consideration.

We would supplement our title of this section by the suggestion that such appreciative essays may well be written about your favorite musicians and painters, in fact about any artist or scientist whose work you admire or whose personality appeals to you. Nor do such essays need to present the man by means of all his work or all his traits of personality. Christopher Morley, you will see, in his letter to Charles Lamb is concerned before all else with banishing the idea, to him fallacious, that his hero was "gentle;" and Eleanor Lincoln in the collection of student essays sees Lewis Carroll first of all as a dreamer.

GEORGE MEREDITH [1]

BY

J. M. Barrie

ALL morning there had been a little gathering of
people outside the gate. It was the day on
which Mr. Meredith was to be, as they say, buried.
He had been, as they say, cremated. The funeral
coach came, and a very small thing was placed in it
and covered with flowers. One plant of the wall-
flower in the garden would have covered it. The
coach, followed by a few others, took the road to
Dorking, where, in familiar phrase, the funeral was
to be, and in a moment or two all seemed silent and
deserted, the cottage, the garden, and Box Hill.

The cottage was not deserted, as they knew who
now trooped into the round in front of it, their
eyes on the closed door. They were the mighty company, his children, Lucy and Clara and Rhoda and
Diana and Rose and old Mel and Roy Richmond
and Adrian and Sir Willoughby and a hundred others,
and they stood in line against the boxwood, waiting
for him to come out. Each of his proud women carried a flower, and the hands of all his men were ready
for the salute.

In the room on the right, in an armchair which had
been his home for years—to many the throne of
letters in this country—sat an old man, like one

[1] Reprinted by the kind permission of Thomas Bird Mosher,
Publisher.

forgotten in an empty house. When the last sound of the coaches had passed away, he moved in his chair. He wore gray clothes and a red tie, and his face was rarely beautiful, but the hair was white and the limbs were feeble, and the wonderful eyes dimmed, and he was hard of hearing. He moved in his chair, for something was happening to him, and it was this, old age was falling from him. This is what is meant by Death to such as he, and the company awaiting knew. His eyes became again those of the eagle, and his hair was brown, and the lustiness of youth was in his frame, but still he wore the red tie. He rose, and not a moment did he remain within the house, for "golden lie the meadows, golden run the streams," and "the fields and the waters shout to him golden shouts." He flung open the door, as they knew he would do who were awaiting him, and he stood there looking at them, a general reviewing his troops. They wore the pretty clothing in which he had loved to drape them; they were not sad like the mourners who had gone, but happy as the forget-me-nots and pansies at their feet and the lilac overhead, for they knew that this was his coronation day. Only one was airily in mourning, as knowing better than the others what fitted the occasion, the Countess de Saldar. He recognized her sense of the fitness of things with a smile and a bow. The men saluted, the women gave their flowers to Dahlia to give to him, so that she, being the most unhappy and therefore by him the most beloved, should have his last word, and he took their offerings and passed on. They did not go with him, these, his splendid progeny, the ladies of the future; they went their ways to tell the whole earth of the new

world for women which he had been the first to
foresee.

Without knowing why, for his work was done,
he turned to the left, passing his famous cherry
blossom, and climbed between apple trees to a
little house of two rooms, whence most of that
noble company had sprung. It is the Chalet,
where he worked, and good and brave men will forever bow proudly before it, but good and brave
women will bow more proudly still. He went there
only because he had gone so often, and this time
the door was locked; he did not know why nor care.
He came swinging down the path, singing lustily,
and calling to his dogs, his dogs of the present and
the past; and they yelped with joy, for they knew
they were once again to breast the hill with him.

He strode up the hill whirling his staff, for which
he had no longer any other use. His hearing was
again so acute that from far away on the Dorking
road he could hear the rumbling of a coach. It had
been disputed whether he should be buried in
Westminster Abbey or in a quiet churchyard, and
there came to him somehow a knowledge (it was
the last he ever knew of little things) that people
had been at variance as to whether a casket of
dust should be laid away in one hole or in another,
and he flung back his head with the old glorious
action, and laughed a laugh "broad as a thousand
beeves at pasture."

Box Hill was no longer deserted. When a great
man dies—and this was one of the greatest since
Shakespeare—the immortals await him at the top
of the nearest hill. He looked up and saw his
peers. They were all young, like himself. He

waved the staff in greeting. One, a mere stripling, "slight unspeakably," R. L. S., detached himself from the others, crying gloriously, "Here's the fellow I have been telling you about!" and ran down the hill to be the first to take his Master's hand. In the meanwhile an empty coach was rolling on to Dorking.

A BIRTHDAY LETTER TO CHARLES LAMB [1]

BY

Christopher Morley

You understood about human weakness, so you will know how it is that I have left writing for your birthday until this last possible moment. I've been looking over some of your old letters. I don't do so often, it is too troublesome to see how some have misfeatured you. Then last night, about bread-and-cheese time—the *wishing* time of the evening you used to call it, when one rather hankers for some friend to drop in (to get between one's self and Eternity)—I began gaping stupidly into the fire, wondering how to light a candle for your cake. It was a different fire from yours; a fire of logs; wood that might have been made into desks. It was silly of me to sit brooding there, for to you of all men a letter should be the unstudied excess of the mind. But it was the distance between us, as snow was sifting, that chilled my fingers. You have said pleasant things about the difficulties of Distant Correspondence; but no letter was ever addressed you from so far as this. I sat there, empty of everything but angry love. I could not write, so in your honor I had some hot water with its Better Adjunct, and went to bed.

[1] From *The Romany Stain* by Christopher Morley; copyright, 1926, by Doubleday, Page and Company.

What can I tell you that would interest you most?
There are still Richardsons about (you remember
him, the fellow who used to keep you waiting for
your holidays? What an uneasy immortality he
got himself thereby); and fellows like Rickman, of
whom you said that he didn't have to be told a
thing twice, are still rare birds. But it is as impossible to be bored on Murray Hill as it was on
Fleet Street. Your old anxieties about abstaining
from tobacco and liquor would be made more meta-
physical here, since the abstention is supposed to
be compulsory. You'd be amused, if you knew
how you are regarded as a gospel for the young,
"studied" in schools, your desperate and special
humor conned as a textbook of "whimsicality."
Yes, they still label you "the gentle." They have
forgotten your letters to S. T. C., imploring him
to substitute drunken, shabby, unshaven, cross-
eyed, stammering, or any other epithet that rang
true in your ear. So endlessly has your "gentle-
ness" been drummed into young ears that there
has been, among our more savage juniors, a kind
of odd blindness as to the real you. Perhaps they
do not know you as you are in your letters. The
rest of you, I must confess, it is long since I read.
I am not a systematic reader, I love to gather my
notions of people from their casual ejaculations
rather than where they open themselves deliberately.
So it is in your letters that I have you and hold
you. There you have taught us, more than a hundred novelists could do, what love means. It suffers
long and is kind. There I see your trouble and
weakness so much greater than many others'
strength. There I see you laughing at solemn apes;

I see your divine silliness and your rich shrewdness. Sometimes, when my self-pitying generation beats its breast, I think of your magnanimous patience. I think of your rockets of absurdity, sent up like sea-signals on a dark sky of loneliness. I think of those last days when you and Mary said that the auction-posters were your playbills. I think of your great love story—yours and Mary's—perhaps the bravest in the world. Then I wonder whether some of us nowadays should not write an *Apologia pro Vita Sua*—an Apology for living in a Sewer.

You could remember "few specialties in your life," you wrote once for some one (a publisher, perhaps?) who wanted a blurb about you. Except, you added, that you "once caught a swallow flying." Indeed you did; the wild fierce bird of laughter with wet eyes. I think that to have known you when you had been walking arm in arm with Barleycorn, and cast no shadow on the pavements of Covent Garden, would have been very close to my idea of religion. I smile, as you did, to remember that the Woodbridge Book Club blackballed your volume. There was something in it—they did not know just what—that was not quite seemly. This implicates me, too, for some of my forbears, I suspect, may have cast a black pellet or so in that matter. I apologize; and neither of us loves them any the less for their genteel simplicity. And indeed that strange fancy of yours, when brightened into flame by understanding intercourse, must have been a lovely and reproachable sight.

We shall receive no letters in the grave, some one said; Doctor Johnson, perhaps. It is just as well, for you would scarcely relish this one. But it had to be written. If there are 150 candles on this cake of yours, they will be put there by the 150 who think of you not as the gentle, but as the tormented, desperate, mad, and tipsy Elia. Still as you said of the *Ancient Mariner*, literature can sting us through sufferings into high pleasure. "I shall never like tripe again." Once you wrote "I never saw a hero; I wonder how they look." Ah, dear Charles, you need not have searched far. Mary could have told you.

INTRODUCED BY MR. HOUSMAN [1]

BY

Ethel Wallace Hawkins

I

THE seed of the desire to see Shropshire was planted by the lyric called "The First of May" —that clear minor melody, never more wistful than through the major ring of the close.

> The orchards half the way
>   From home to Ludlow fair
> Flowered on the first of May
>   In Mays when I was there;
> And seen from stile or turning
>   The plume of smoke would show
> Where fires were burning
>   That went out long ago.
>
> The plum broke forth in green,
>   The pear stood high and snowed,
> My friends and I between
>   Would take the Ludlow road;
> Dressed to the nines and drinking
>   And light in heart and limb,
> And each chap thinking
>   The fair was held for him.

[1] Reprinted by the kind permission of the author and of *The Atlantic Monthly.*

Between the trees in flower
    New friends at fairtime tread
The way where Ludlow tower
    Stands planted on the dead.
Our thoughts, a long while after,
    They think, our words they say;
Theirs now the laughter,
    The fair, the first of May.

Ay, yonder lads are yet
    The fools that we were then;
For oh, the sons we get
    Are still the sons of men.
The sumless tale of sorrow
    Is all unrolled in vain:
May comes to-morrow
    And Ludlow fair again.

Every one knows the risk of seeking out a place around which a glamour has been thrown by verse. It is all too likely that along a macadamized Tewkesbury Road motor cars will be whizzing; that over "dark Tintagil by the Cornish sea" will be scurrying a raucous company for whom a char-à-bancs waits. It is a dangerous thing to use as a guidebook a handful of lyrics into which a poet has put, living, the sunshine and the flowers and the hills of a shire that he loves; and the peril is the greater when the very names of hill and river and town hold an unreasonable charm. Clee Hill, the Wrekin, Wenlock Edge; the Teme, the Corve; "Clunton and Clunbury, Clungunford and Clun"—how could these be matched by the reality?

A dangerous thing—and profane, perhaps. Yet I went to Shropshire.

It was by no means all because of the delicate chiming of "The First of May." For there are those other lyrics of Shropshire that flower on the grim background of Mr. Housman's pessimism as the valerian flowers bright and beautiful and sad on the rugged walls of Ludlow castle. And indeed is there an Englishman alive who equals Mr. Housman as the poet of nostalgia? Mr. Masefield's "West Wind," it is true, aches and cries; but it also flutes a little, almost in the Irish manner. Mr. Housman's lyrics of homesickness are all ache. They have the simplicity of emotion itself; they have the very minimum of decoration, and a matchless brevity.

> 'T is time, I think, by Wenlock Town
>   The golden broom should blow;
> The hawthorn sprinkled up and down
>   Should charge the land with snow.
>
> Spring will not wait the loiterer's time
>   Who keeps so long away;
> So others wear the broom and climb
>   The hedgerows heaped with may.
>
> Oh, tarnish late on Wenlock Edge,
>   Gold that I never see;
> Lie long, high snowdrifts in the hedge
>   That will not shower on me.

Hawthorn and broom were over when we headed for Shropshire; and as our train left London in the most depressing of rains, in the heart of at least one of us—the one who had held out resolutely, not to say obstinately, for a week or two in Ludlow—there was a heavy qualm of apprehension. For while English rain may softly veil some of the traveler's most

charming pictures of English landscape (I myself remember my first English, or, to be quite accurate,
Scotch, robin singing "with treble soft" in a beech
copse at Ardlui in a hearty, chuckling downpour;
and a sunset of unearthly beauty, a pale gold and
pale mauve sunset, seen from Land's End through a
thin shower), this late July rain was of the kind that
dulls landscape and zest alike. But just beyond
Shrewsbury the rain stopped, and the window began
to frame pictures. Fresh greenness lay around us;
cottage gardens were gay. We were slipping into

> The country for easy livers,
> The quietest under the sun.

And as high hills began to spring up on the left and
the right, we saw ahead an evening rainbow laid
across the valley.

The quaint Ludlow that met us at the door of the
little railroad station was not recognizably the Ludlow of the *Shropshire Lad;* the horse-drawn bus was
not, nor the long street that climbed from "the bottom of the town," nor the rare old Feathers Hotel,
with its half-timbered walls, its gabled projections,
and its leaded windows; nor even the extraordinarily
mellow chimes that played, somewhere very near,
"The Bluebells of Scotland" as we ate our Severn
salmon in the low-ceiled dining room with its priceless carving. It was on the next morning, a breezy,
sunny morning, that I found Shropshire of the poems
—the Shropshire I was to keep.

I had walked to "the bottom of the town" and
taken at random a road that wound and mounted,
bordered by hedges, toward rolling hills. Where the
hedgerow was broken by a stile, I stopped to look

back and down—and there indeed, across the meadows, stood the tower which to many a generation of
farm lads has been the sign that they were drawing
near to Ludlow fair. Beautiful and tall it sprang up;
for while the slope of the town is such that from
some points of view the church seems to settle low,
and that at the Feathers Hotel, for example, the
chimes seem to wander casually and companionably
in at the door, from a distance the tower rises dom-
inant. I was to learn the beauty of coming back at
twilight from Much Wenlock or from Craven Arms
and seeing the castle ruins and the tower lifting
solemnly into the violet-gray haze of the evening.

Ludlow castle does not, I think, figure in Mr.
Housman's poems. But it is certain that the Shropshire Lad loved the River Teme; and where is there
a more charming reach of the Teme than the one
that lies below the castle walls, to the west? Is it
better to look down from the window frame in the
west wall that bounds a narrow picture of the stream
winding between its willows down the green valley,
or to drift under those banks where meadow-sweet
grows and dabchicks dive and clatter and large Here-
ford cows snuffle and stare at the navigator, and to
look up at the great walls looming almost overhead?
Of this I am certain: that nowhere on earth has a bit
of small change more purchasing power than here on
the Teme. I forget whether it is sixpence or a shilling that one pays for a very glut of boating. This
part of the river is not navigable for more than a
mile, between a courteously firm sign above and a
weir below; and one may row upstream and drift
down, row up and drift down, with green willows
and green banks to right and left, and green water

under, and store up for a permanent possession pictures of the castle in the sky and Ludlow tower across the meadows.

It is good, too, to stand on the high tower of the castle keep; best of all, perhaps, on such a morning as the one I most remember of many mornings spent in the castle ruins—a day of sunshine and fleet cloud, with a strong, pure wind blowing out of Wales. "Smoke stood up from Ludlow," its plumes flying all one way; the reddish roofs of the town seemed to glow; above them Ludlow tower rose up near and friendly, yet not so near but that half the noon chimes were caught and swept away on the flaws of the wind; and the quarries on Clee Hill sprang out in that indescribable color, neither orange nor gold nor strong yellow, with which they meet certain slants of sunshine. Far, far down, below the steep drop of the castle hill, the little Teme slipped twinkling over the weir, and, backed by the high green slope and the great beeches of Whitcliff Park, ran curving to the fine old Ludford bridge with its three graduated arches. At the foot of the tower lay, outside the castle wall and across the dry moat, the wide spaces of the tiltyard, empty of everything but sunshine and silence; inside, that most lovable ruin, its broken walls darkened here and there, in squares and bars, by their own shadows. And it was down here, not on the windy top of the tower, that one tasted best the true flavor of Ludlow castle—the strong sense of its past, and the quiet present beauty that washes over it. Here one might see the shell of the finely proportioned hall where *Comus* had its première, and might wonder, fruitlessly, at which door the "rout of monsters" rushed in, and where and

how Sabrina rose; or might look up to—not through,
for stairs and flooring are gone—the high windows
from which Prince Arthur must have looked down
on the Teme before he died; or might mount the
winding steps, leading now to nothing but space, up
and down which the Little Princes may have run,
shouting, in the days when their hearts were still
light. Here, too, the sunshine lay warm; the tufts
of valerian stirred in the crevices of the stone; jackdaws dropped their queer notes, so throaty yet so
ringing, from the topmost walls, and now and then
showed their capable little profiles in silhouette
against the sky; and goats cropped the grass in the
courtyard, or stood contemplative in doorway or
window frame of the wonderful little round chapel.
By whose authority, or perhaps by what hereditary
right, these pensioners dwell in Ludlow castle, I
never learned; but their decorative effect was certainly great. Their angular bodies, so dignified yet
so nimble, and their glances, aloof yet ribald, had
the accentuating value that a gargoyle has in the
midst of solemn beauty. There was one of them—
in appearance the oldest—who late in the afternoon
used to lie along a ledge where church dignitaries
must once have sat; his beard up, his horns back,
his eyelids drooped—a picture of rather cynical in-
scrutability and repose. But to establish any social
contact with these decorations was a mistake, as I
found one day when I impulsively offered one a
tablet of Cadbury's chocolate. Instantly the whole
band sprang to life, rushed around me, penned me
in a close, leaping ring, "mounting up . . . like
thin flames," in the manner of the souls seen by the
Blessed Damozel: incredibly tall on their hind legs,

and incredibly light except when in their ardor they
stood on one's foot.   In the end they had to be
quieted, like Gareth's adversaries, "with good
blows."   But the initial indiscretion was mine, not
theirs; and I should be sorry indeed to go back to
Ludlow castle and find those picturesque presences
no longer there.

II

Next to Ludlow, the name of Wenlock had been
set chiming by *A Shropshire Lad* and the lovely
"Fancy's Knell" of the *Last Poems*.   To Much Wenlock we went for its name; and went again for what
we found there.   The road from Ludlow, if without
spectacular beauty, has a peculiar soft charm.   The
different fields of grain through which it ran had no
names, to our agricultural ignorance, but the great
rectangles of straw-yellow, of rich tan, of bronze,
and of willow-green were none the less lovely to the
eye.   Phlox, roses, and hollyhocks brimmed the low-
walled gardens of the little houses along the road.
And no sooner was Clee Hill left behind than far off
to the right Brown Clee flung up its long curve and
seemed to go with us all the way.   In the little
flowery town of Much Wenlock we found two rare
treasures.   One was its guildhall, where the soul of
its ancient dignity and pageantry lives on in the
magnificently carved chamber—a room that wakes
Hawthornesque imaginings of the presences that
must move there of nights, when the door is locked,
and the moonlight falls through the leaded panes,
and sleep is over Much Wenlock.   The other was
the fragmentary abbey ruin, with its roofless but
marvelously preserved Norman chapter house.   One

might stare for hours at the three valerian-tufted
arches of the west wall without fully absorbing their
perfect beauty; or, passing into the chapter house,
might look out through them at the sunny green
garth, with its standard rose bushes like tall red-
flamed lamps, and its box shrubs slipped by a master
hand in the design of hounds chasing a fox. In the
midst of this flying hunt reared up, or rather reeled
back *sur son séant*, with forepaws in a sparring attitude, a small heraldic-looking creature which might
have been an infant dinosaur, and which seemed,
though perhaps not altogether logically, to reconcile
chase and cloister walls.

From Much Wenlock one of us was drawn on an
hour's digression by the haunting picture that is
painted in "Hughley Steeple"—that dark and tender lyric of sunshine and shadow and unforgetting
affection, which begins,—

> The vane on Hughley steeple
>   Veers bright, a far-known sign,
> And there lie Hughley people,
>   And there lie friends of mine.
> Tall in the midst the tower
>   Divides the shade and sun,
> And the clock strikes the hour,
>   And tells the time to none.

Here again was a risk—but a risk that it would
have been a loss not to take. A wooded road dropped
sharply down · from Wenlock Edge, and curved
through a tiny cluster of houses around a sunken
trough where some cows were splashing loudly with
their forefeet and drinking in the snuffling and blowing manner of cows whose thirst has not extinguished

their simple sense of amusement. A few rods beyond, a weather vane flashed; and there, with its trees, and its low enclosing wall, and its sunny tangled graveyard, stood, infinitely reticent, the little square-towered church. Into the silence of its interior fell, from the clock tower, a living sound—the loud slow ticking that is always somewhat awful in a place empty of humanity. Outside were sunshine and wild greenness and peace, and once the rich solemn tone of the clock striking the hour. It was impossible to feel that the matter of trimming and clipping was of much importance in a churchyard where a poet's loyal remembering flowered, invisibly but with such beauty.

The loveliest thing of all about our day in Much Wenlock, however, was the drive back to Ludlow in the early evening. In the slight dampness, the smell of the gardens and of the freshly cut hay was piercingly sweet. The sun, very low, shone through a thin haze. To the east, the meadows lay in a silvery light, and the hills beyond them were blue; the quarries on Clee Hill and Brown Clee flushed silver-rose. To the west, the stirring feathery fields were brushed by a metallic color that one might despair of phrasing. But Mr. Housman has done it:—

> On acres of the seeded grasses
> The changing burnish heaves.

As we drove, all colors imperceptibly merged in violet-gray; and presently Ludlow tower and the castle loomed softly ahead.

III

I do not remember whether it was in the Bull Ring, the commercial center of Ludlow, or in Harp Lane, close by, and also, incongruously, commercial, that we found on a wall the poster which divided our small party in two; or, more accurately, caused an ardent remnant to stay on in Shropshire when the others made for the east, where were Ely Cathedral and Will Rogers.

LUDLOW
AGRICULTURAL SOCIETY
75TH MEETING
ON
Monday, 2nd August, 1926

said the poster. Ludlow fair! Not, of course, the great fair of the first of May; not, indeed, to be pedantic, a fair at all—rather an exhibition. But, to one who would have it so, Ludlow fair for all that. Surely one of the sharpest of the mutually exclusive human divisions is the one between those who have, and those who have not, the true passion for animals. To those who have this passion the lack of it seems as bleak a limitation as color blindness or tone deafness; to those who have it not it seems a silly puerility. I could only hope—against hope—that my valued friends felt as respectfully toward my beeves and sheep as I felt toward their cathedral and their comedian, as I waved them a temporary farewell and fell to counting days and hours. On the night of August first, I dozed happily off with

May comes to-morrow
And Ludlow fair again

singing through my head, in defiance of the calendar; and early in the morning heard, with ineffable satisfaction, the *clap-clap* of an army of small hooves passing by the Feathers Hotel.

It was a fine, sunny day. It may no longer be true that "the lads in their hundreds to Ludlow come in for the fair"; but by ten o'clock High Street and Broad Street and the Bull Ring were relatively thronged, the tide setting toward Ludford bridge, beyond which the fairground lay. I had my first taste of the fair here on Ludford bridge, where, between the rows of observers leaning on the parapets, two men were leading, with difficulty, a monstrous and reluctant bull. He had quite the most bored, snobbish, and stupid expression that I have ever seen on the face of a quadruped; his enormous bulk advanced laboriously, inch by inch almost, on small straddling legs. Yet there was a magnificence about him, and more than any of the human beings watching him he seemed in harmony with the ancient bridge. He might have been, to an unknowing eye, four hundred years old, instead of the four that the official program, as I learned later, gave him. I felt, not altogether tenably, a strong personal pride when in the afternoon he marched ponderously at the head of the prize winners' parade.

The fairground was a great green oblong, designed by nature for cattle shows. Three sides were walled by trees; the fourth sloped softly up to the sky. On this slope moved all day an irregular, shifting pattern of horses. Now a hunter would canter along the ridge; now mighty cart mares, with little whickering foals, stood on the incline waiting their turn to go down and be judged. On the opposite side of the field, close to the twinkling screen of poplars behind which the Teme gurgled now and then, a long row of cattle of high degree stood in makeshift pens; and from one of these shot at irregular intervals an indomitable little red bull calf, who intended to see, between captures, as much as he could of what was going on. Flocks of sheep poured through the entrance gateway, and were crowded into little enclosures of hurdles. At one moment a running flame seemed to go over the grass; this was the advance of a flock drenched with Sunset Orange powder— "the brightest made," said proudly the advertisement in the program. A shepherd undertook my education in the matter of lambs and ewes, and, being a thorough man, pulled open many mouths that I might learn lore by observing teeth. Later in the day I was delighted to find prize tickets tied on his hurdles, and himself vivid with elation. "And there," he cried, pointing to a singularly torpid ram prone in an adjacent pen, "is the fortunate father!"

It would have been a satisfaction to see parading a flock whose teeth one knew all about; better still, perhaps to see the Sunset Orange company stream around the ring. But the sheep were not permitted to parade—and indeed one must grant that as marchers sheep are rather incalculable—any more than the fancy pigeons with feathers to the very tips of their toes. To the inexpert eye of one spectator the great moments of the Parade of Stock were two. The first was when the mighty bull of the Ludford bridge straddled slowly and scornfully around the ring, while the Ludlow Town Band played *con brio*. The other was when a group passed that might have come to life from a Greek

frieze. A young man, bright-haired, broad-shoul-
dered, slim-hipped, glittering with triumph, who
looked as Phœbus must have looked when he served
Admetus, led along—master of her, though half
lifted off his feet by her—a magnificent cart mare,
rather wild with the excitement of the show and the
clash of the band. When she pranced, it was as if
the mountains skipped, and as she planted each
great hoof she shook the earth. Her dark coat
shone, her powerful neck arched gloriously. At her
side, head up, a foal sprang along, light as a bubble.
This group of three, on fire with life, was the picture
still in my mind when all the winners of the morning
had gone glorying around the ring; and the splendid
hunters had taken their hurdles and their water
jump; and cattle and sheep—mildly puzzled, perhaps, but as to that, who shall say?—streamed out
through the gateway, toward home; and those of
us who flung away our privilege of crowding into
the big tea tent streamed out likewise, crossed Ludford bridge again, and climbed the long street to
the town, where Ludlow tower was chiming late
afternoon.

IV

But the best, perhaps, of all my hours in Shropshire
was spent neither in Ludlow nor in Much Wenlock,
but near Church Stretton, at sunset, on the Caradoc.
One may believe or not, as one chooses, that here
Caractacus made his last stand (and certainly around
the summit run shadowy trenches soft with heather);
but in the austere, high solitude it is easy to feel
that Roman ghosts are blowing by on the hill wind.
I risk the assertion that if one is to drink the full

flavor of the Caradoc it is best to be there alone, in a gusty, red-gold sunset, with the vast shadow of the Longmynd swallowing, league after league, the brightness of the valley. "Fancy's Knell" has it: if not the exact topography, yet the very air and the spaciousness.

> Wenlock Edge was umbered,
>   And bright was Abdon Burf,
> And warm between them slumbered
>   The smooth green miles of turf;
> Until from grass and clover
>   The upshot beam would fade,
> And England over
>   Advanced the lofty shade.

With the sinking of the sun behind the Longmynd, the wind dropped, and the silence became a limitless living presence. A kestrel hung perfectly motionless against the amber sky. The still fields so far below took on the strange, intense green that comes between sunset and twilight. And presently the deep bowl of the valley was brimmed with dimness; the Wrekin, to the north, was softened to mystery; in some wood far away, owls had begun to call. It was time to come down from Caer Caradoc, before the infinitely light whispering of the heather should turn too eerie under the stars.

It would be an arrogant spirit indeed who, knowing Mr. Housman's poems, should indulge too strong a sense of possessorship in Shropshire. For, however much the stranger may love that quiet, unspoiled beauty, he knows that it has been loved better. Back in his own land, he will not presume to appropriate the lines that set his wistfulness to music:—

Into my heart an air that kills
  From yon far country blows:
What are those blue remembered hills,
  What spires, what farms are those?

That is the land of lost content,
  I see it shining plain,
The happy highways where I went
  And cannot come again.

But for me, as doubtless for others, it is not only humility that makes me refrain from taking these verses to myself; it is also the fact that they do not— at least I trust they do not—wholly fit my case. For I hope to come again. If, contrary to all legend, one has indeed found the rainbow's end, and found it pure gold, what shall hold one away forever? For me, I hope to go again where the solemn shadow of the Longmynd creeps to Caer Caradoc; where the willows dip and the dabchicks dive in the green Teme below Ludlow castle; where Clee Hill and Brown Clee burn silver-rose at sunset, and hay smells sweet in the evening on the road to Much Wenlock.

MICHEL DE MONTAIGNE [1]

BY

Llewelyn Powys

O N a lichen-covered wall of an ancient château
which for long ages had stood "amid the fat
noonday Gascon scenery," these words, carved
deeply in the crumbling masonry, were to be read
by the curious for many generations: "In the year
of our Lord, 1571, at the age of thirty-eight, on the
last day of February, being the anniversary of his
birth, Monsieur de Montaigne, long weary of the
service of the Court and of public employments,
while still in his full vigor, betook himself to the
bosom of the nine learned virgins." Could anything have been more significant of the character,
tastes, and sturdy Epicurean aplomb of the man
to whom they owed their origin?

In every sense that the gracious phrase implies,
Montaigne was first and last "a good European"
and not one inclined to set aside the true values of
life. A generous lover of leisure, of spiritual and
physical well-being, of curious meditations, of quaint
erudition, he was by no means a man to suffer his
days to slide by unnoticed because of an overzealous
preoccupation with the illusive activities that belong
to everyday life. It is said that Montaigne was
an eleven months' child, and indeed in his shrewd,

[1] From *Thirteen Worthies*. Used by permission of the publishers, Harcourt, Brace & Company.

slow-moving constitution—so full of a mature sanity
—there is something that goes to suggest a longer
time in the making than is granted to most mortal
men.

He was born in a turbulent and unsettled age, an
age as bewildered with difficulties and confusions as
is our own, and yet was able to reach to an adjust-
ment with life which for civilized poise has scarcely
been surpassed before or since. He was fortunate
in his upbringing. He owed his lifelong enthusiasm
"for the greatness of old Greek and Roman life" to
the eccentric theories of his father, who, while Michel
was a child, would have no word spoken in the
château, not even by the servants, except it was
Latin. Indeed, so thoroughly was the rule kept
that a hundred years later certain Latin nouns were
found to have lingered on in the mouths of the plow-
men and vine tenders employed about the eighteen
farms that constituted the broad estates of the
castle.

It has been remarked that another refining influence invaded the spirit of the sun-tanned, broad-
mouthed *seigneur*—his meeting with Estienne de la
Boëtie. It happened, so it always seemed to Montaigne, "by some secret appointment of Heaven,"
and without doubt it did more than anything else
in his life to impart to his jocund, earth-bound nature a suspicion that there might be, possibly, after
all, abroad in the world an unutterable something
above and beyond what his eager and insatiable
senses saw and felt. The memory of his dead friend
was never out of his mind. Twenty years later, he
tells us, when he was bathing in the waters of Lucca,
the thought of the irremediable loss he had sustained

by this death swept suddenly over his soul with un-
rebated bitterness. It was the one experience of his
life that perplexed and astounded the old skeptic,
the one experience capable of endowing his style
with a new tone of passionate inspiration. There
is a certain pathos in observing how rattled and put
about the old egoist was by this tragic and unexpected revelation—the old red fox caught at last
in the gin of the absolute! Craftily he scans the
familiar landscape of his mind. How could this be?
The explanation of this! what was it? "Because
it was he, because it was I" is all that he, the master
"idealclast," finds it in him to say.

For the most part, however, he was able to survey
the grotesque panorama of human life with a mas-
sive and indelible satisfaction. It pleased him might-
ily to hold discourse with two aboriginals from the
New World whom he lit upon in Rouen. They had
come, he tells us, "to learn the wisdom of Europe"
and were "men of dignity, although they wore no
breeches." He liked to note the fact that "tortoises
and ostriches hatch their eggs with only looking on
them, which infers that their eyes have in them ejac-
ulative virtue," that "Xerxes was a coxcombical
blockhead," that "Carneades was so besotted with
knowledge that he would not find time so much as
to comb his head or to pare his nails," and that
there existed a certain nation that fed on spiders—
"Yea, made provision of them and fed them for
their tables, as also they did grasshoppers, mice,
lizards, and bats; and in a time of a scarcity of such
delicacies a toad was sold for six crowns, all which
they cook and dish up with several sauces." It
amused him to observe that when the vines of his

village were nipped with frost "his parish priest presently concluded that the indignation of God is gone out against *all the human race.*"

But his interests were by no means confined to such objective observations. There was nothing that diverted him so much as to mark down his own peculiar tastes and idiosyncrasies, whether at home in his cheerful, sunlit tower, or abroad on horseback, wrapped about in the dark, threadbare mantle that had belonged to his father, "because it seemed to envelop me in him."

Nobody prognosticated that I should be wicked, but only useless; they foresaw idleness, but no malice; and I find it falls out accordingly.

I never inquire, when I am to take a footman, if he be chaste, but if he be diligent; and am not solicitous if my muleteer be given to gaming, as if he be strong and able, or if my cook be a swearer, if he be a good cook.

For table-talk, I prefer the pleasant and witty before the learned and grave; in bed, beauty before goodness.

The generality of more solid sort of men look upon abundance of children as a great blessing; I and some others think it a great benefit to be without them.

I love stout expressions amongst gentlemen and to have them speak as they think.

I love rain and to dabble in the dirt as well as ducks do.

I give great authority to my propensions and desires. To be subject to the stone and subject to abstention from eating oysters are two evils instead of one.

I have ever loved to repose myself whether sitting or lying, with my heels as high or higher than my seat.

I do not remember that I ever had the itch, and yet scratching is one of nature's sweetest gratifications. . . . I use it most on my ears, which are often apt to itch.

We have in us notions that are inconsistent and for

which no reason can be given; for example, I found radishes first grateful to my stomach, since that nauseous, and now again grateful.

At the little jerks of oars, stealing the vessel from under me, I find, I know not how, both my head and my stomach disordered.

'Tis indecent, beside the hurt it does to one's health and even to the pleasure of eating, to eat so greedily as I do. I often bite my tongue and sometimes my fingers, in my haste.

To the end that even sleep itself should not so stupidly escape from me, I have formerly caused myself to be disturbed in my sleep, so that I might the better and more sensibly relish and taste it.

I have never put myself to great pains to curb the desires by the which I have found myself beset. My virtue is a virtue, or rather an innocence, which is purely random and accidental.

From these and similar utterances what a vivid picture is evoked of the genial, philosophic old aristocrat. His short, thickset figure, tough and individual as one of his own gnarled vine stumps, is never out of our sight as we review the various events of his life. There he stands superintending the construction of the lighthouse at Bordeaux for the better direction of the mariners returning from that New World which had so intrigued his imagination; there he sits, goose quill in hand, composing the letter in which he proffered his resignation from the mayoralty of the city, for no better reason, forsooth, than the personal apprehension that he felt with regard to the plague. "For my part, I am of the mind that if a man can by any means avoid danger, though by creeping under a calf's skin, I am one that would not be ashamed of the shift." We see him on his travels observing how ill-favored were the faces of German women, buying a new fur hat at Augsburg, or rating a Swiss tavern keeper because his table was ill provided with crayfish! We see him at Rome attending Christmas Mass, or walking the streets, which through his reading were as familiar to him as those of Paris, impatient sometimes of the Renaissance buildings which cluttered up the monumental foundations that were so dear to his heart. They resemble, he thinks, the martins' and jackdaws' nests that adhere to the shattered fragments of the churches in France which had been brought to ruin by the ravages of the Huguenots.

Two volumes of his *Essays* were found in his trunks and fell into the hands of the ecclesiastical censor. He was brought to task by Pope Gregory. He himself willingly enough condemns them beforehand, out of hand, "if so be anything should be found in his rhapsodies contrary to the holy resolutions and prescriptions of the Catholic Apostolic and Roman Church into which I was born and in which I shall die," and then returns to France to publish from the safe retreat of his castle the very passages to which exception has been taken. He visit. the unfortunate Tasso in his convent at Ferrara, and in the papal library peers curiously at the writing of St. Thomas Aquinas, which he observes to be even more illegible than his own. "I cannot even write properly myself, so that when I have finished a scrawl I had rather rewrite it than give myself the trouble of deciphering it." He makes friends with Anthony Bacon, a

brother of the great Francis, and embarks upon
a correspondence with him. His zest for life is
insatiable. He indulges the fancy of being given
the full citizenship of Rome. To be a Roman citizen! One can understand how of all others he
would covet that distinction. He pursues his
purpose "with all his five natural senses" and is
accorded the honor. He goes about glancing now
at this damsel, now at that, never failing to allow
due credit for beauty and charm.

But, of course, it is at home, in his serene and
hospitable château of St. Michel de Montaigne,
that we are able to envisage him best. Here, within
those cool, stone-flagged courtyards, the gates of
which stood ever open to welcome king or beggar,
"having no other guard than my porter, no other
sentinel than the stars," his extraordinary personality, "virgin from all law suits" and "harbor-
ing but a perplexed and uncertain knowledge about
his money," found full scope for placid, unhampered
development. Alternately, to and fro across the
neighboring countryside, the warring factions passed,
devastating all that came in their way. But it would
seem that both Catholic and Huguenot felt a strange
reluctance to trouble the residence of the old, indulgent, philosophic opportunist, who, as he himself
declares, would be as ready, at a pinch, to carry a
taper "before the Dragon as before St. George."
Decade followed decade, and still the château of
Montaigne remained intact on its green eminence, a
symbol of civilized humanism and happy tolerance
amid a crazed and distracted world.

In the famous room of his tower, surrounded by
a library of over a thousand folios, Montaigne

passed his days in peace, disturbed only by the
reverberating echoes of the great bell above him
as it was rung morning and evening for the Ave
Marias to be held in the castle chapel below. Here
it was that the stout, good-natured, weather-
beaten philosopher, crossing himself, as he tells us,
whenever he yawned, composed his essays, played
with his cat, or interviewed that honest lad that he
had to his tailor, "whom I never knew guilty of
one truth," or ate his bread without salt, or drank
the wine "that they mix in the buttery two or three
hours before 'tis brought in," and even then, old
hedonist that he was, "not willingly out of common
glass, but in those that are clear and transparent."

We are made to see the passing of his easy, indolent days almost as clearly as if we ourselves had
shared with Henry of Navarre the privilege of
being his guest. Sometimes, when the mood was
upon him, he would go down into the great hall
and play cards with his wife and daughter, or take
a stroll in his secluded orchard. Then, again, with
whimsical, incredulous eye, he would stand watching his long-suffering lady busying herself with her
aromatic simples and medicinal herbs, or the in-
expedient ways of the governess with his daughter,
Léonore. Tired of this, he would go riding abroad
over his lands, and although, as he confesses, he
had "no manner of complacency for husbandry,"
he would while away his time talking to this or
that familiar rustic, for he always, as he tells us,
"had an inclination towards the meaner sort of
people." Wherever he went there beat under his
doublet a spleenless and generous heart, a heart
unexpectedly tender, as, for instance, when he

assures us he could with difficulty watch a chicken being killed or hear the cries of a hare in her agony when the dogs had got her. Always simply enough dressed in black and white "in imitation of my father," he would return from such homely excursions to the perusal of his Plutarch or even to the reading of Cicero, though he remarks that an hour with this latter formal stylist "was a great deal for him."

Little enough is known of his wife, the Lady Françoise de la Chassaigne. It is apparent that Montaigne's attitude towards her was one of indulgent tolerance not unmingled with contempt.

Feminine policy has a mysterious course and we must e'en let them go on their own way.

There is a natural feud, a fray, between us and women; the closest agreement that we have with them is more or less turbulent and stormy.

I see and I am vexed to see, in several families I know, Monsieur about dinner time comes home all jaded and ruffled about his affairs when Madame is still pouncing and tricking up herself, forsooth, in her closet. This is for queens to do, and that's a question too; 'tis ridiculous and unjust that the laziness of our wives should be maintained with our sweat and labor.

The pains of childbearing, said by the physicians and by God himself to be very great, *and which our women keep such a clutter about*—there are whole nations that make nothing of them.

I for my part went ever the plain way to work.

I love to lie hard and alone, yea, even without my wife, as kings do.

And as great a libertine as I am taken to be, I have in truth more strictly observed the laws of marriage than I either promised or expected.

Who for seeing me one while cold and presently very
fond towards my wife, believes the one or the other to be
counterfeited is an ass.

There have been many who have had it in them
to dispute Montaigne's claim to be considered as
a serious philosopher. They are mistaken. If
wisdom is philosophy, what a rich store of it is
contained in these quaint, closely written pages.
It is a Shakespearean wisdom, a wisdom that is
simple and that springs as naturally from the
pasture-land and parks of Warwickshire as from
the vineyards of Guyenne. When we loiter near
some place full of suggestions of age-long human
usages—a graveyard perhaps, or a sheep-shearing
barton, or a blacksmith's forge when horseshoeing
is in progress—and overhear some pithy comment
that seems to have the very sap of life in it, we are
listening to the voice of Montaigne. John Cowper
Powys, in his *Suspended Judgments*, has after his
poetic manner expressed this most excellently:

The wisdom of Montaigne is the wisdom of lazy noons
in spacious corn-fields, of dewy mornings in misty lanes
and moss-grown paths; of dreamy shadows in deep grass
when the apple boughs hang heavily earthward, and long
nights of autumn rain have left amber-colored pools in
the hollow places of the trees and in the mud trodden by
the cattle. . . . It is the wisdom of the earth itself;
shrewd, friendly, full of unaccountable instincts; obstinate and capricious, given up to irrational and inexplicable superstitions, sluggish, suspicious, cautious, hos-
tile to theory, enamored of inconsistencies, humorously
critical of all ideals, realistic, empirical, wayward.

Montaigne himself affirmed that there should be
"nothing more airy, more gay, more frolic, and I

had like to have said more wanton, than philosophy"; and certainly if one takes some of his
utterances at random one is astounded at the deep,
lætificant sagacity which they reveal. In the mean,
famished period in which we live, wherein ill-bred
industrial commercialism masquerades as civilized
life, how consoling, how infinitely restorative they
are, as it were like great dripping combs of
golden honey gathered from I know not what distant blossoms!

Man (in good earnest) is a marvelous, vain, fickle, and
unstable subject, and one on whom it is very hard to form
a certain and uniform judgment.

I would always have a man to be doing . . . and then
let death take me planting my cabbages, indifferent to him
and still less of my garden's not being finished.

They begin to teach us to live when we have almost
done living. A hundred students have gotten the pox
before they have come to read Aristotle's lecture on
temperance.

There is indeed a certain low and moderate sort of
poetry, that a man may well enough judge by certain
rules of art; but the true supreme and divine poetry is
above all rules and reason . . . it does not exercise but
ravishes and overwhelms our judgments.

All whimsies as are in use amongst us deserve at least a
hearing.

A young man should often plunge even into excesses,
otherwise the least vice will ruin him, and he also is apt to
become tiresome and *inconvenient in conversation.*

Women are not in the wrong when they refuse the rules
of life obtaining in the world; it is the man who made
these laws without them.

The for and the against are both possible.

I am a man and nothing human is alien to me.

So taken was Montaigne himself with the last two sentences that he caused them to be engraved upon the ceiling of his tower. It seems he was often in doubt concerning the intrinsic value of his writings, though he never allowed such misgivings to ruffle his accustomed equanimity. "I do not, nevertheless, always believe myself; I often hazard sallies of mine own wit, wherein I very much suspect myself and shake my ears; but I let them go at a venture." After all, what did it matter? "If I should have a long life my memory is so bad that I believe I shall forget my own name. So greatly do I excel in forgetfulness that even my writings are forgotten. The public dealeth me blows about them, and I do not feel them." Should his papers eventually be used as wrappers he makes little of it: "I shall at least keep some pats of butter from melting in the market."

Montaigne died at his château in his sixtieth year. The grapes that covered so closely those sun-drenched, hand-cultivated slopes had already been harvested, and already the trees that held with so firm a root to the opulent soil of his broad acres were changing color. "In the last piece between death and you there is no pretending; you must speak French."

On 13 September, 1592, Michel de Montaigne, having distributed certain legacies to his servants, summoned his parish priest to his bedside, and there in his curious room with the swallows already gathering on the leaden gutters outside, he heard Mass said for the last time in the company of certain of his neighbors. With due solemnity the blessed sacrament was elevated, and at the very moment that

this good heretical Catholic and Catholic heretic
(unmindful for once of his nine learned virgins) was
raising his arms in seemly devotion toward the sacred
morsel which in its essence—*que sçais-je*—might, or
might not, contain a subtle and crafty secret, he fell
back dead.

A LIST OF ESSAYS PARTICULARLY ADAPTED FOR USE AS MODELS

Birrell, Augustine. *Charles Lamb*, from *Obiter Dicta, Second Series*. Charles Scribner's Sons.

Bradford, Gamaliel. *The Soul of Samuel Pepys*, especially Chapter IV. Houghton Mifflin Company.

Crothers, Samuel McChord. *Education in Pursuit of Henry Adams*, from *The Dame School of Experience*. Houghton Mifflin Company.

Ford, R. Clyde. *Modestine's Shoes*. The *Atlantic Monthly*, April, 1926.

Matthews, Brander. *Rab's Friend*, from *Adventures among Books*. Longmans, Green & Co.

Matthews, Brander. *Thomas de Quincey*, from *Hours with Men and Books*. S. C. Griggs and Company.

More, Paul Elmer. *A Hermit's Notes on Thoreau*, from *Shelburne Essays, First Series*. G. P. Putnam's Sons.

Newton, A. Edward. *The Ghosts of Gough Square*. The *Atlantic Monthly*, June, 1925.

Newton, A. Edward. *Shakespeare and the "Old Vic,"* from *The Greatest Book in the World*. Little, Brown, and Company.

Newton, A. Edward. *What Might Have Been*, from *The Amenities of Book-Collecting*. The Atlantic Monthly Press.

Repplier, Agnes. *Three Famous Old Maids*, from *Essays in Miniature*. Houghton Mifflin Company.

Smith, Alexander. *Chaucer* and *William Dunbar*, from *Dreamthorp*. Thomas B. Mosher, Publisher.

Wiggin, Kate Douglas. *A Child's Journey with Dickens*, from *My Garden of Memory*. Houghton Mifflin Company.

D. Essays on Books

It is quite safe to say that no other one subject has claimed such attention from informal essayists as that of books. Hazlitt, Lamb, Leigh Hunt, and Stevenson, writing in the last century, have all recorded for our delectation their thoughts on this intriguing subject, and each in his own way. Hazlitt hates to read new books; Lamb is annoyed by narrative but loves biography; Leigh Hunt wards off melancholy by a glance at his Spenser and wishes to die with his head upon a book; Stevenson has had few living friends who have influenced him as have Hamlet or Rosalind. In our own day we are by no means impoverished by any lack of such essays. A. Edward Newton, A. C. Benson, Andrew Lang, Agnes Repplier, Zephine Humphrey, H. M. Tomlinson, Stark Young, G. K. Chesterton—these are but a few names of that great number who have had a delightful word to say about books. Let us then, following, like the little page of good King Wencelas, in their footprints, see what we can find to say about the books which we hold most dear or about those which, perchance, have displeased us.

There are many ways to go about an essay of this sort. The models given suggest but a few of them. It may be that like George Gissing you will choose to "survey your bookshelves" and recall the occasions and circumstances of your acquisition of certain favorite volumes. It may be that you will rather take a hint from Miss Repplier's humorous arraignment of certain highly-esteemed volumes, or decide like Mr. Chesterton to defend a book or a type of writing which others have frowned upon. Happy indeed you will be if, having chosen a subject, you can use it as a point of departure for such reflections and perceptions as those of H. M. Tomlinson in *Bed Books and Night Lights*.

There are dozens of other ways also to go about an essay of this sort. One of the simplest and yet best is to concentrate on some one especially loved book, perhaps one of your childhood, recalling the time and occasion of your possession of it, its appearance, the incidents and characters that early claimed your attention, its influence on your thought and play. Some years ago in one of our large cities the school children were asked to vote on their favorite story. Johanna Spryri's *Heidi* led by a vast majority. An informal essay written in appreciation of *Heidi* should make good reading! Again perhaps the characters of books live with you longer than their incidents. They obviously do with Ruth Carlson who uses her remembrance of them to such good advantage in *Husbands Black and White*, reprinted in the student essays. Nor do the books need to be fiction or poetry, biography or drama, to engage the essayist's attention. Delightful essays have been written on an arithmetic, on drug store pamphlets, on almanacs, on telephone directories, on . . .?

MY BOOKS [1]

BY

George Gissing

As often as I survey my bookshelves I am reminded of Lamb's "ragged veterans." Not that all my volumes came from the second-hand stall; many of them were neat enough in new covers, some were even stately in fragrant bindings, when they passed into my hands. But so often have I removed, so rough has been the treatment of my little library at each change of place, and, to tell the truth, so little care have I given to its well-being at normal times (for in all practical matters I am idle and inept), that even the comeliest of my books show the results of unfair usage. More than one has been foully injured by a great nail driven into a packing-case—this but the extreme instance of the wrongs they have undergone. Now that I have leisure and peace of mind, I find myself growing more careful—an illustration of the great truth that virtue is made easy by circumstance. But I confess that, so long as a volume hold together, I am not much troubled as to its outer appearance.

I know men who say they had as lief read any book in a library copy as in one from their own shelf. To me that is unintelligible. For one thing, I know every book of mine by its *scent*, and I have but to put my nose between the pages to be reminded

[1] From *The Private Papers of Henry Ryecroft* by George Gissing.

of all sorts of things. My Gibbon, for example,
my well-bound eight-volume Milman edition, which
I have read and read and read again for more
than thirty years—never do I open it but the scent
of the noble page restores to me all the exultant
happiness of that moment when I received it as a
prize. Or my Shakespeare, the great Cambridge
Shakespeare—it has an odor which carries me yet
further back in life; for these volumes belonged
to my father, and before I was old enough to read
them with understanding it was often permitted
me, as a treat, to take down one of them from the
bookcase, and reverently to turn the leaves. The
volumes smell exactly as they did in that old time,
and what a strange tenderness comes upon me when
I hold one of them in hand. For that reason I do
not often read Shakespeare in this edition. My
eyes being good as ever, I take the Globe volume,
which I bought in days when such a purchase was
something more than an extravagance; wherefore
I regard the book with that peculiar affection which
results from sacrifice.

Sacrifice—in no drawing-room sense of the word.
Dozens of my books were purchased with money
which ought to have been spent upon what are
called the necessaries of life. Many a time I have
stood before a stall, or a bookseller's window, torn
by conflict of intellectual desire and bodily need.
At the very hour of dinner, when my stomach
clamored for food, I have been stopped by sight of
a volume so long coveted, and marked at so ad-
vantageous a price, that I *could* not let it go; yet
to buy it meant pangs of famine. My Heyne's
Tibullus was grasped at such a moment. It lay on

the stall of the old bookshop in Goodge Street—a
stall where now and then one found an excellent
thing among quantities of rubbish. Sixpence was
the price—sixpence! At that time I used to eat my
midday meal (of course, my dinner) at a coffee shop
in Oxford Street, one of the real old coffee shops,
such as now, I suppose, can hardly be found. Sixpence was all I had—yes, all I had in the world:
it would purchase a plate of meat and vegetables.
But I did not dare to hope that the *Tibullus* would
wait until the morrow, when a certain small sum fell
due to me. I paced the pavement, fingering the cop-
pers in my pocket, eyeing the stall, two appetites
at combat within me. The book was bought and I
went home with it, and as I made a dinner of bread
and butter I gloated over the pages.

In this *Tibullus* I found pencilled on the last page;
"Perlegi, Oct. 4, 1792." Who was that possessor of
the book, nearly a hundred years ago? There was no
other inscription. I like to imagine some poor
scholar, poor and eager as I myself, who bought the
volume with drops of his blood, and enjoyed the reading of it even as I did. How much *that* was I could
not easily say. Gentle-hearted Tibullus!—of whom
there remains to us a poet's portrait more delightful,
I think, than anything of the kind in Roman literature.

> *An tacitum silvas inter reptare salubres,*
> *Curantem quidquid dignum sapiente bonoque est?*

So with many another book on the thronged
shelves. To take them down is to recall, how vividly,
a struggle and a triumph. In those days money
represented nothing to me, nothing I cared to think

about, but the acquisition of books. There were
books of which I had passionate need, books more
necessary to me than bodily nourishment. I could
see them, of course, at the British Museum, but
that was not at all the same thing as having and
holding them, my own property, on my own shelf.
Now and then I bought a volume of the raggedest
and wretchedest aspect, dishonored with foolish
scribbling, torn, blotted—no matter, I liked better
to read out of that than out of a copy that was not
mine. But I was guilty at times of mere self-indulgence; a book tempted me, a book which was not
one of those for which I really craved, a luxury which
prudence might bid me forego. As, for instance, my
Jung-Stilling. It caught my eye in Holywell Street;
the name was familiar to me in *Wahrheit und Dich-
tung*, and curiosity grew as I glanced over the pages.
But that day I resisted; in truth, I could not afford
the eighteenpence, which means that just then I was
poor indeed. Twice again did I pass, each time
assuring myself that *Jung-Stilling* had found no
purchaser. There came a day when I was in funds.
I see myself hastening to Holywell Street (in those
days my habitual pace was five miles an hour), I
see the little gray old man with whom I transacted
my business—what was his name?—the bookseller
who had been, I believe, a Catholic priest, and still
has a certain priestly dignity about him. He took
the volume, opened it, mused for a moment, then,
with a glance at me, said, as if thinking aloud: "Yes,
I wish I had time to read it."

Sometimes I added the labor of a porter to my
fasting endured for the sake of books. At the little
shop near Portland Road Station I came upon a

first edition of Gibbon, the price an absurdity—I
think it was a shilling a volume. To possess those
clean-paged quartos I would have sold my coat. As
it happened, I had not money enough with me, but
sufficient at home. I was living at Islington. Having spoken with the bookseller, I walked home, took
the cash, walked back again, and—carried the tomes
from the west end of Euston Road to a street in
Islington far beyond the *Angel*. I did it in two journeys—this being the only time of my life when I
thought of Gibbon in avoirdupois. Twice—three
times, reckoning the walk for the money—did I de-
scend Euston Road and climb Pentonville on that
occasion. Of the season and the weather I have no
recollection; my joy in the purchase I had made
drove out every other thought. Except, indeed, of
the weight. I had infinite energy, but not much
muscular strength, and the end of the last journey
saw me upon a chair, perspiring, flaccid, aching—
exultant!

The well-to-do person would hear this story with
astonishment. Why did I not get the bookseller to
send me the volumes? Or, if I could not wait, was
there no omnibus along that London highway? How
could I make the well-to-do person understand that
I did not feel able to afford, that day, one penny
more than I spent on the books? No, no, such
labor-saving expenditure did not come within my
scope; whatever I enjoyed I earned it, literally, by
the sweat of my brow. In those days I hardly knew
what it was to travel by omnibus. I have walked
London streets for twelve and fifteen hours together
without ever a thought of saving my legs, or my time,
by paying for waftage. Being poor as poor can be,

there were certain things I had to renounce, and this was one of them.

Years after, I sold my first edition of Gibbon for even less than it cost me; it went with a great many other fine books in folio and quarto, which I could not drag about with me in my constant removals; the man who bought them spoke of them as "tombstones." Why has Gibbon no market value? Often has my heart ached with regret for those quartos. The joy of reading the *Decline and Fall* in that fine type! The page was appropriate to the dignity of the subject; the mere sight of it tuned one's mind. I suppose I could easily get another copy now; but it would not be to me what that other was, with its memory of dust and toil.

BOOKS THAT HAVE HINDERED ME [1]

BY

Agnes Repplier

So many grateful and impetuous spirits have recently come forward to tell to an approving world how they have been benefited by their early reading, and by their wisely chosen favorites in literature, that the trustful listener begins to think, against his own rueful experience, that all books must be pleasant and profitable companions. Those who have honored us with confidence in this matter seem to have found their letters, as Sir Thomas Browne found his religion, "all pure profit." Edward E. Hale, for instance, has been "helped" by every imaginable writer, from Marcus Aurelius to the amiable authoress of *The Wide, Wide World*. Moncure D. Conway acknowledges his obligations to an infinite variety of sources. William T. Harris has been happy enough to seize instinctively upon those works which aroused his "latent energies to industry and self-activity"; and Edward Eggleston has gathered intellectual sustenance from the most unexpected quarters,—the Rollo Books, and Lindley Murray's Reader. Only Andrew Lang and Augustus Jessopp are disposed, with an untimely levity, to confess that they have read for amusement rather

[1] From *Points of View* by Agnes Repplier. By permission of and by arrangement with Houghton Mifflin Company, the authorized publishers.

than for self-instruction, and that they have not
found it so easily attainable.

Now when a man tells us that he has been really
"helped" by certain books, we naturally conclude
that the condition reached by their assistance is,
in some measure, gratifying to himself; and, by the
same token, I am disposed to argue that my own
unsatisfactory development may be the result of
less discreetly selected reading,—reading for which,
in many cases, I was wholly irresponsible. I notice
particularly that several persons who have been
helped acknowledge a very pleasing debt of gratitude
to their early spellingbooks, to Webster's Elemen-
tary, and to those modest volumes which first im-
parted to them the mysteries of the alphabet. It
was not so with me. I learned my letters, at the
cost of infinite tribulation, out of a horrible little
book called *Reading Without Tears*, which I trust
has long since been banished from all Christian
nurseries. It was a brown book, and had on its
cover a deceptive picture of two stout and unclothed
Cupids holding the volume open between them, and
making an ostentatious pretense of enjoyment.
Young as I was, I grew cynical over that title and
that picture, for the torrents of tears that I shed
blotted them both daily from my sight. It might
have been possible for Cupids, who needed no ward-
robes and sat comfortably on clouds, to like such
lessons, but for an ordinary little girl in frock and
pinafore they were simply heart-breaking. Had it
only been my good fortune to be born twenty years
later, spelling would have been left out of my early
discipline, and I should have found congenial occu-
pation in sticking pins or punching mysterious bits

of clay at a kindergarten. But when I was young, the world was still sadly unenlightened in these matters; the plain duty of every child was to learn how to read; and the more hopelessly dull I showed myself to be, the more imperative became the need of forcing some information into me,—information which I received as responsibly as does a Strasbourg goose its daily share of provender. For two bitter years I had for my constant companion that hated reader, which began with such isolated statements as "Ann has a cat," and ended with a dismal story about a little African boy named Sam; Mr. Rider Haggard not having then instructed us as to what truly remarkable titles little African boys enjoy. If, to this day, I am disposed to underrate the advantages of education, and to think but poorly of compulsory school laws and the march of mind, it is because of the unhappy nature of my own early experiences.

Having at last struggled into some acquaintanceship with print, the next book to which I can trace a moral downfall is *Sandford and Merton*, left on the nursery shelves by an elder brother, and read many times, not because I especially liked it, but because I had so little to choose from. Those were not days when a glut of juvenile literature had produced a corresponding indifference, and a spirit of languid hypercriticism. The few volumes we possessed, even those of a severely didactic order, were read and reread, until we knew them well by heart. Now up to a certain age I was, as all healthy children are, essentially democratic, with a decided preference for low company, and a secret affinity for the least desirable little girls in the neighborhood. But *Sand-*

ford and Merton wrought a pitiable change. I do
not think I ever went so far as to dislike the Rev.
Mr. Barlow after the very cordial and hearty fashion
in which Dickens disliked him, and I know I should
have been scandalized by Mr. Burnand's cheerful
mockery; but, pondering over the matter with the
stolid gravity of a child, I reached some highly unsatisfactory conclusions. It did not seem to me then,
and it does not seem to me now, exactly fair in the
estimable clergyman to have refused the board which
Mr. Merton was anxious to pay, and then have re-
proached poor Tommy so coldly with eating the
bread of dependence; neither did it seem worth
while for a wealthy little boy to spend his time in
doing—very inefficiently, I am sure—the work of
an under-gardener. Harry's contempt for riches, and
his supreme satisfaction with a piece of bread for
dinner, struck me as overdrawn; Tommy's mishaps
were more numerous than need be, even if he did
have the misfortune to be a gentleman's son; and
the complacency with which Mr. Barlow permitted
him to give away a whole suit of clothes—clothes
which, according to my childish system of ethics,
belonged, not to him, but to his mother—contrasted
but poorly with the anxiety manifested by the rev-
erend mentor over his own pitiful loaf of bread.
Altogether, *Sandford and Merton* affected me
the wrong way; and for the first time my soul revolted from the pretentious virtues of honest poverty.
It is to the malign influence of that tale that I owe
my sneaking preference for the drones and butter-
flies of earth. I do not now believe that men are
born equal; I do not love universal suffrage; I mis-
trust all popular agitators, all intrusive legislation,

all philanthropic fads, all friends of the people and benefactors of their race. I cannot even sympathize with the noble theory that every man and woman should do their share of the world's work; I would gladly shirk my own if I could. And this lamentable, unworthy view of life and its responsibilities is due to the subtle poison instilled into my youthful mind by the too strenuous counter-teaching of *Sandford and Merton*.

A third pitfall was dug for my unwary feet when, as a school-girl of fifteen, I read, sorely against my will, Milton's *Areopagitica*. I believe this is a work highly esteemed by critics, and I have even heard people in private life, who might say what they pleased without scandal, speak quite enthusi-astically of its manly spirit and sonorous rhetoric. Perhaps they had the privilege of reading it skip-pingly to themselves, and not as I did, aloud, para-graph after paragraph, each weighted with mighty sentences, cumbrous, involved, majestic, and, so far as my narrow comprehension went, almost unin-telligible. Never can I forget the aspect of those pages, bristling all over with mysterious allusions to unknown people and places, and with an armed phalanx of Greek and Roman names which were presumably familiar to my instructed mind, but which were really dug out bodily from my Classical Dictionary, at the cost of much time and temper. I have counted in one paragraph, and that a mod-erately short one, forty-five of these stumbling-blocks, ranging all the way from the "libertine school of Cyrene," about which I knew nothing, to the no less libertine songs of Naso, about which I know nothing now. Neither was it easy to trace the exact

connection between the question at issue, "the freedom of unlicenc'd printing," and such far-off matters
as the gods of Egypt and the comedies of Plau-
tus, Isaiah's prophecies and the Carthaginian coun-
cils.   Erudition, like a bloodhound, is a charming
thing when held firmly in leash, but it is not so at-
tractive when turned loose upon a defenseless and
unerudite public.   Lady Harriet Ashburton used
to say that, when Macaulay talked, she was not
only inundated with learning, but she positively
stood in the slops.   In reading Milton, I waded
knee-deep, utterly out of my element, and deeply
resentful of the experience.   The liberty of the
press was, to my American notions, so much a
matter of course, that the only way I could account
for the continued withholding of so commonplace
a privilege was by supposing that some unwary
members of Parliament read the *Areopagitica*
and were forthwith hardened into tyranny forever.
I own I felt a savage glee in reflecting that Lords
and Commons had received this oppressive bit of
literature in the same aggrieved spirit that I had
myself, and that its immediate result was to put
incautious patriots in a more ticklish position than
before.   If truth now seems to me a sadly over-
rated virtue; if plain-speaking is sure to affront me;
if the vigorous personalities of the journalist and
the amiable indecencies of the novel writer vex
my illiberal soul, and if the superficial precautions
of a paternal government appear estimable in my
eyes, to what can I trace this alien and unprogres-
sive attitude, if not to the *Areopagitica,* and its
adverse influence over my rebellious and suffering
girlhood?

As these youthful reminiscences are of too mournful a nature to be profitably prolonged, I will add only two more to the list of books which have hindered my moral and intellectual development. When I was seventeen, I read, at the earnest solicitation of some well-meaning friends, *The Heir of Redclyffe*, and my carefully guarded theories of life shivered and broke before the baneful lesson it conveyed. Brought up on a comfortable and wholesome diet of Miss Edgeworth's pleasant stories, I had unconsciously absorbed the genial doctrine that virtue is its own reward, and that additional rewards are sure to be forthcoming; that happiness awaits the good and affable little girl, and that well-merited misfortunes dog the footsteps of her who inclines to evil ways. I trusted implicitly to those shadowy mills where the impartial gods grind out our just deserts; and the admirable songs in *Patience* about Gentle Jane and Teasing Tom inadequately express the rigidity of my views and the boundless nature of my confidence. *The Heir of Redclyffe* destroyed, at once and forever, this cheerful delusion, and with it a powerful stimulus to rectitude. Here are Sir Guy Morville and poor little Amy, both of them virtuous to a degree which would have put Miss Edgeworth's most exemplary characters to the blush; yet Guy, after being bullied and badgered through the greater part of his short life, dies of the very fever which should properly have carried off Philip; and Amy, besides being left widowed and heart-broken, gives birth to a daughter instead of a son, and so forfeits the inheritance of Redclyffe. On the other hand, Philip, the most intolerable of

prigs and mischief makers, whose cruel suspicions
play havoc with the happiness of everybody in the
story, and whose obstinate folly brings about the
final disaster,—Philip, who is little better than his
cousin's murderer, succeeds to the estate, marries
that very stilted and unpleasant young person,
Laura (who is after all a world too good for him),
and is left in a blaze of glory, a wealthy, honored,
and distinguished man. It is true that Miss Yonge,
whose conscience must have pricked her a little
at bringing about this unwarranted and unjustifiable
conclusion, would have us believe that he was sorry
for his misbehavior, and that his regret was sufficient to equalize the perfidious scales of justice;
but even at seventeen I was not guileless enough
to credit the lasting quality of Philip's contrition.
A very few years would suffice to reconcile him to
Guy's death, and to convince him that his own
succession was a mere survival of the fittest, an
admirable intervention on the part of Destiny to
remedy her former blunders, and exalt him to his
proper station in the world. But to me this triumph
of guilt meant the downfall of my early creed, the
destruction of my most cherished convictions.
Never again might I look forward with hopeful
heart to the inevitable righting of all wrong things:
never again might I trust with old-time confidence
to the final readjustment of a closing chapter.
Even Emerson's essay on *Compensation* has
failed to restore to me the full measure of all that
I lost through the *The Heir of Redclyffe*.

The last work to injure me seriously as a girl,
and to root up the good seed sown in long years of
righteous education, was *Uncle Tom's Cabin*, which

I read from cover to cover with the innocent credulity of youth; and, when I had finished, the awful conviction forced itself upon me that the thirteenth amendment was a ghastly error, and that the war had been fought in vain. Slavery, which had seemed to me before undeviatingly wicked, now shone in a new and alluring light. All things must be judged by their results, and if the result of slavery was to produce a race so infinitely superior to common humanity; if it bred strong, capable, self-restrained men like George, beautiful, courageous, tender-hearted women like Eliza, visions of innocent loveliness like Emmeline; marvels of acute intelligence like Cassy, children of surpassing precocity and charm like little Harry, mothers and wives of patient, simple goodness like Aunt Chloe, and, finally, models of all known chivalry and virtue like Uncle Tom himself,—then slavery was the most ennobling institution in the world, and we had committed a grievous crime in degrading a whole heroic race to our narrower, viler level. It was but too apparent, even to my immature mind, that the negroes whom I knew, or knew about, were very little better than white people; that they shared in all the manifold failings of humanity, and were not marked by any higher intelligence than their Caucasian neighbors. Even in the matters of physical beauty and mechanical ingenuity there had plainly been some degeneracy, some falling off from the high standard of old slavery days. Reluctantly I concluded that what had seemed so right had all been wrong indeed, and that the only people who stood pre-eminent for virtue, intellect, and nobility had been destroyed by our rash act, had sunk under the enervating influence of freedom to a range of lower feeling, to baser aspirations and content. It was the greatest shock of all, and the last.

I will pursue the subject no further. Those who read these simple statements may not, I fear, find them as edifying or as stimulating as the happier recollections of more favored souls; but it is barely possible that they may see in them the unvarnished reflection of some of their own youthful experiences.

A DEFENSE OF NONSENSE [1]

BY

G. K. Chesterton

THERE are two equal and eternal ways of looking at this twilight world of ours: we may see it as the twilight of evening or the twilight of morning; we may think of anything, down to a fallen acorn, as a descendant or as an ancestor. There are times when we are almost crushed, not so much with the load of the evil as with the load of the goodness of humanity, when we feel that we are nothing but the inheritors of a humiliating splendor. But there are other times when everything seems primitive, when the ancient stars are only sparks blown from a boy's bonfire, when the whole earth seems so young and experimental that even the white hair of the aged, in the fine biblical phrase, is like almond-trees that blossom, like the white hawthorn grown in May. That it is good for a man to realize that he is "the heir of all the ages" is pretty commonly admitted; it is a less popular but equally important point that it is good for him sometimes to realize that he is not only an ancestor, but an ancestor of primal antiquity; it is good for him to wonder whether he is not a hero, and to experience ennobling doubts as to whether he is not a solar myth.

[1] From *Fancies Versus Fads* by G. K. Chesterton. By permission of the author and of Dodd, Mead & Company, Inc.

The matters which most thoroughly evoke this sense of the abiding childhood of the world are those which are really fresh, abrupt and inventive in any age; and if we were asked what was the best proof of this adventurous youth in the nineteenth century we should say, with all respect to its portentous sciences and philosophies, that it was to be found in the rhymes of Mr. Edward Lear and in the literature of nonsense. "The Dong with the Luminous Nose," at least, is original, as the first ship and the first plough were original.

It is true in a certain sense that some of the greatest writers the world has seen—Aristophanes, Rabelais and Sterne—have written nonsense; but unless we are mistaken, it is in a widely different sense. The nonsense of these men was satiric—that is to say, symbolic; it was a kind of exuberant capering round a discovered truth. There is all the difference in the world between the instinct of satire, which, seeing in the Kaiser's mustaches something typical of him, draws them continually larger and larger; and the instinct of nonsense which, for no reason whatever, imagines what those mustaches would look like on the present Archbishop of Canterbury if he grew them in a fit of absence of mind. We incline to think that no age except our own could have understood that the Quangle-Wangle meant absolutely nothing, and the Lands of the Jumblies were absolutely nowhere. We fancy that if the account of the knave's trial in *Alice in Wonderland* had been published in the seventeenth century it would have been bracketed with Bunyan's Trial of Faithful as a parody on the State prosecutions of the time.

We fancy that if "The Dong with the Luminous Nose" had appeared in the same period every one would have called it a dull satire on Oliver Cromwell.

It is altogether advisedly that we quote chiefly from Mr. Lear's "Nonsense Rhymes." To our mind he is both chronologically and essentially the father of nonsense; we think him superior to Lewis Carroll. In one sense, indeed, Lewis Carroll has a great advantage. We know what Lewis Carroll was in daily life: he was a singularly serious and conventional don, universally respected, but very much of a pedant and something of a Philistine. Thus his strange double life in earth and in dreamland emphasizes the idea that lies at the back of nonsense—the idea of *escape*, of escape into a world where things are not fixed horribly in an eternal appropriateness, where apples grow on pear trees, and any odd man you meet may have three legs. Lewis Carroll, living one life in which he would have thundered morally against any one who walked on the wrong plot of grass, and another life in which he would cheerfully call the sun green and the moon blue, was, by his very divided nature, his one foot on both worlds, a perfect type of the position of modern nonsense. His Wonderland is a country populated by insane mathematicians. We feel the whole is an escape into a world of masquerade; we feel that if we could pierce their disguises, we might discover that Humpty Dumpty and the March Hare were Professors and Doctors of Divinity enjoying a mental holiday. This sense of escape is certainly less emphatic in Edward Lear, because of the completeness of his citizenship in the

world of unreason.   We do not know his prosaic
biography as we know Lewis Carroll's. We accept
him as a purely fabulous figure, on his own description of himself:

> His body is perfectly spherical,
> He weareth a runcible hat.

While Lewis Carroll's Wonderland is purely intellectual, Lear introduces quite another element—
the element of the poetical and even emotional.
Carroll works by the pure reason, but this is not
so strong a contrast; for, after all, mankind in the
main has always regarded reason as a bit of a joke.
Lear introduces his unmeaning words and his
amorphous creatures not with the pomp of reason,
but with the romantic prelude of rich hues and
haunting rhythms.

> Far and few, far and few,
> Are the lands where the Jumblies live,

is an entirely different type of poetry to that ex-
hibited in "Jabberwocky."   Carroll, with a sense
of mathematical neatness, makes his whole poem
a mosaic of new and mysterious words.   But Edward Lear, with more subtle and placid effrontery,
is always introducing scraps of his own elvish
dialect into the middle of simple and rational statements, until we are almost stunned into admitting
that we know what they mean.   There is a genial
ring of common sense about such lines as,

> For his aunt Jobiska said "Every one knows
> That a Pobble is better without his toes,"

which is beyond the reach of Carroll. The poet seems so easy on the matter that we are almost driven to pretend that we see his meaning, that we know the peculiar difficulties of a Pobble, that we are as old travelers in the "Gromboolian Plain" as he is.

Our claim that nonsense is a new literature (we might almost say a new sense) would be quite indefensible if nonsense were nothing more than a mere æsthetic fancy. Nothing sublimely artistic has ever arisen out of mere art, any more than anything essentially reasonable has ever arisen out of the pure reason. There must always be a rich moral soil for any great æsthetic growth. The principle of *art for art's sake* is a very good principle if it means that there is a vital distinction between the earth and the tree that has its roots in the earth; but it is a very bad principle if it means that the tree could grow just as well with its roots in the air. Every great literature has always been allegorical—allegorical of some view of the whole universe. The *Iliad* is only great because all life is a battle, the *Odyssey* because all life is a journey, the *Book of Job* because all life is a riddle. There is one attitude in which we think that all existence is summed up in the word "ghosts"; another, and somewhat better one, in which we think it is summed up in the words "A Midsummer Night's Dream." Even the vulgarest melodrama or detective story can be good if it expresses something of the delight in sinister possibilities—the healthy lust for darkness and terror which may come on us any night in walking down a dark lane. If, therefore, nonsense is really to be the literature of the

future, it must have its own version of the Cosmos
to offer; the world must not only be the tragic,
romantic, and religious, it must be nonsensical
also.   And here we fancy that nonsense will, in a
very unexpected way, come to the aid of the spiritual view of things.   Religion has for centuries
been trying to make men exult in the "wonders"
of creation, but it has forgotten that a thing cannot
be completely wonderful so long as it remains sensible.   So long as we regard a tree as an obvious
thing, naturally and reasonably created for a giraffe
to eat, we cannot properly wonder at it.   It is when
we consider it as a prodigious wave of the living
soil sprawling up to the skies for no reason in particular that we take off our hats, to the astonishment of the park keeper.   Everything has in fact
another side to it, like the moon, the patroness of
nonsense.   Viewed from that other side, a bird is
a blossom broken loose from its chain of stalk, a
man a quadruped begging on its hind legs, a house
a gigantesque hat to cover a man from the sun, a
chair an apparatus of four wooden legs for a cripple
with only two.

This is the side of things which tends most truly
to spiritual wonder.   It is significant that in the
greatest religious poem existent, the *Book of Job*,
the argument which convinces the infidel is not
(as has been represented by the merely rational
religionism of the eighteenth century) a picture of
the ordered beneficence of the Creation; but, on the
contrary, a picture of the huge and undecipherable
unreason of it.   "Hast Thou sent the rain upon
the desert where no man is?"   This simple sense
of wonder at the shapes of things, and at their

exuberant independence of our intellectual stand-
ards and our trivial definitions, is the basis of spirit-
uality as it is the basis of nonsense. Nonsense and
faith (strange as the conjunction may seem) are
the two supreme symbolic assertions of the truth
that to draw out the soul of things with a syllogism
is as impossible as to draw out Leviathan with a
hook. The well-meaning person who, by merely
studying the logical side of things, has decided
that "faith is nonsense," does not know how truly
he speaks; later it may come back to him in the
form that nonsense is faith.

BED–BOOKS AND NIGHT–LIGHTS [1]

BY

H. M. Tomlinson

THE rain flashed across the midnight window with a myriad feet. There was a groan in outer darkness, the voice of all nameless dreads. The nervous candle flame shuddered by my bedside. The groaning rose to a shriek, and the little flame jumped in a panic, and nearly left its white column. Out of the corners of the room swarmed the released shadows. Black specters danced in ecstasy over my bed. I love fresh air, but I cannot allow it to slay the shining and delicate body of my little friend the candle flame, the comrade who ventures with me into the solitudes beyond midnight. I shut the window.

They talk of the candle power of an electric bulb. What do they mean? It cannot have the faintest glimmer of the real power of my candle. It would be as right to express, in the same inverted and foolish comparison, the worth of "those delicate sisters, the Pleiades." That pinch of star dust, the Pleiades, exquisitely remote in deepest night, in the profound where light all but fails, has not the power of a sulphur match; yet, still apprehensive to the mind though dimmering on the limit of vision,

[1] Reprinted from *Old Junk* by H. M. Tomlinson, by permission of and special arrangement with Alfred A. Knopf, Inc., authorized publishers.

and sometimes even vanishing, it brings into distinction those distant and difficult tints, hidden far behind all our verified thoughts, which we rarely properly view. I should like to know of any great arc lamp which could do that. So the starlike candle for me. No other light follows so intimately an author's most ghostly suggestion. We sit, the candle and I, in the midst of the shades we are conquering, and sometimes look up from the lucent page to contemplate the dark hosts of the enemy with a smile before they overwhelm us—as they will, of course. Like me, the candle is mortal; it will burn out.

As the bed-book itself should be a sort of night-light, to assist its illumination coarse lamps are useless. They would douse the book. The light for such a book must accord with it. It must be, like the book, a limited, personal, mellow, and companionable glow; the solitary taper beside the only worshiper in a sanctuary. That is why nothing can compare with the intimacy of candlelight for a bed-book. It is a living heart, bright and warm in central night, burning for us alone, holding the gaunt and towering shadows at bay. There the monstrous specters stand in our midnight room, the advance guard of the darkness of the world, held off by our valiant little glim, but ready to flood instantly and founder us in original gloom.

The wind moans without; ancient evils are at large and wandering in torment. The rain shrieks across the window. For a moment, for just a moment, the sentinel candle is shaken, and burns blue with terror. The shadows leap out instantly. The little flame recovers, and merely looks at its foe the darkness, and back to its own place goes the old enemy of light and man. The candle for me, tiny, mortal, warm, and brave, a golden lily on a silver stem!

"Almost any book does for a bed-book," a woman once said to me. I nearly replied in a hurry that almost any woman would do for a wife; but that is not the way to bring people to conviction of sin. Her idea was that the bed-book is a soporific, and for that reason she even advocated the reading of political speeches. That would be a dissolute act. Certainly you would go to sleep; but in what frame of mind! You would enter into sleep with your eyes shut. It would be like dying, not only unshriven, but in the act of guilt.

What book shall it shine upon? Think of Plato, or Dante, or Tolstoy, or a Blue Book, for such an occasion! I cannot. They will not do—they are no good to me. I am not writing about you. I know those men I have named are transcendent, the greater lights. But I am bound to confess at times they bore me. Though their feet are clay and on earth, just as ours, their stellar brows are sometimes dim in remote clouds. For my part, they are too big for bedfellows. I cannot see myself, carrying my feeble and restricted glim, following—in pajamas—the statuesque figure of the Florentine where it stalks, aloof in its garb of austere pity, the sonorous deeps of Hades. Hades! Not for me; not after midnight! Let those go who like it.

As for the Russian, vast and disquieting, I refuse to leave all, including the blankets and the pillow, to follow him into the gelid tranquillity of the upper air where even the colors are prismatic spicules of

ice, to brood upon the erratic orbit of the poor
mud ball below called earth. I know it is my world
also; but I cannot help that. It is too late, after
a busy day, and at that hour, to begin overtime
on fashioning a new and better planet out of cosmic
dust. By breakfast time nothing useful would
have been accomplished. We should all be where
we were the night before. The job is far too long,
once the pillow is nicely set.

For the truth is, there are times when we are too
weary to remain attentive and thankful under the
improving eye, kindly but severe, of the seers. There
are times when we do not wish to be any better
than we are. We do not wish to be elevated and
improved. At midnight, away with such books!
As for the literary pundits, the high priests of the
Temple of Letters, it is interesting and helpful
occasionally for an acolyte to swinge them a good
hard one with an incense burner, and cut and run,
for a change, to something outside their rubrics.
Midnight is the time when one can recall, with
ribald delight, the names of all the Great Works
which every gentleman ought to have read, but
which some of us have not. For there is almost as
much clotted nonsense written about literature as
there is about theology.

There are few books which go with midnight,
solitude, and a candle. It is much easier to say
what does not please us then than what is exactly
right. The book must be, anyhow, something
benedictory by a sinning fellow man. Cleverness
would be repellent at such an hour. Cleverness,
anyhow, is the level of mediocrity to-day; we are
all too infernally clever. The first witty and perverse

paradox blows out the candle. Only the sick in mind crave cleverness, as a morbid body turns to drink. The late candle throws its beams a great distance; and its rays make transparent much that seemed massy and important. The mind at rest beside that light, when the house is asleep, and the consequential affairs of the urgent world have diminished to their right proportions because we see them distantly from another and a more tranquil place in the heavens where duty, honor, witty arguments, controversial logic on great questions, appear such as will leave hardly a trace of fossil in the indurated mud which presently will cover them— the mind then certainly smiles at cleverness.

For though at that hour the body may be dog-tired, the mind is white and lucid, like that of a man from whom a fever has abated. It is bare of illusions. It has a sharp focus, small and starlike, as a clear and lonely flame left burning by the altar of a shrine from which all have gone but one. A book which approaches that light in the privacy of that place must come, as it were, with honest and open pages.

I like Heine then, though. His mockery of the grave and great, in those sentences which are as brave as pennants in a breeze, is comfortable and sedative. One's own secret and awkward convictions, never expressed because not lawful and because it is hard to get words to bear them lightly, seem then to be heard aloud in the mild, easy, and confident diction of an immortal whose voice has the blitheness of one who has watched, amused and irreverent, the high gods in eager and secret debate on the best way to keep the gilt and trappings on the body of the evil they have created.

That first-rate explorer, Gulliver, is also fine in the light of the intimate candle. Have you read lately again his "Voyage to the Houyhnhnms"? Try it alone again in quiet. Swift knew all about our contemporary troubles. He has got it all down. Why was he called a misanthrope? Reading that last voyage of Gulliver in the select intimacy of midnight, I am forced to wonder, not at Swift's hatred of mankind, not at his satire of his fellows, not at the strange and terrible nature of this genius who thought that much of us, but how it is that after such a wise and sorrowful revealing of the things we insist on doing, and our reasons for doing them, and what happens after we have done them, men do not change. It does seem impossible that society could remain unaltered, after the surprise its appearance should have caused it as it saw its face in that ruthless mirror. We point instead to the fact that Swift lost his mind in the end. Well, that is not a matter for surprise.

Such books, and France's *Isle of Penguins*, are not disturbing as bed-books. They resolve one's agitated and outraged soul, relieving it with some free expression for the accusing and questioning thoughts engendered by the day's affairs. But they do not rest immediately to hand on the bookshelf by the bed. They depend on the kind of day one has had. Sterne is closer. One would rather be transported as far as possible from all the disturbance of earth's envelope of clouds, and *Tristram Shandy* is sure to be found in the sun.

But best of all books for midnight are travel books. Once I was lost every night for months with Doughty in the *Arabia Deserta*. He is a craggy author. A long course of the ordinary facile stuff, such as one gets in the press every day, thinking it is English, sends one thoughtless and headlong among the bitter herbs and stark bowlders of Doughty's burning and spacious expanse; only to get bewildered, and the shins broken, and a great fatigue at first, in a strange land of fierce sun, hunger, glittering spar, ancient plutonic rock, and very Adam himself. But once you are acclimatized and know the language,—it takes time,—there is no more London after dark, till, a wanderer returned from a forgotten land, you emerge from the interior of Arabia on the Red Sea coast again, feeling as though you had lost touch with the world you used to know. And if that doesn't mean good writing, I know of no other test.

Because once there was a father whose habit it was to read with his boys nightly some chapters of the Bible,—and cordially they hated that habit of his,—I have that Book too, though I fear I have it for no reason that he, the rigid old faithful, would be pleased to hear about. He thought of the future when he read the Bible; I read it for the past. The familiar names, the familiar rhythm of its words, its wonderful well-remembered stories of things long past,—like that of Esther, one of the best in English,—the eloquent anger of the prophets for the people then who looked as though they were alive but were really dead at heart, all is solace and home to me. And now I think of it, it is our home and solace that we want in a bed-book.

A LIST OF ESSAYS PARTICULARLY ADAPTED FOR USE AS MODELS

Benson, A. C. *Books*, from *A College Window*. G. P. Putnam's Sons.

Bistand, Elizabeth. *The Child in Literature* and *At the Sign of the Hobby Horse*, from *Common or Garden Books*. Houghton Mifflin Company.

Dobson, Austin. *Steele's Letters*, from *Eighteenth Century Vignettes*. Dodd, Mead and Company.

Hazlitt, William. *On Reading Old Books*, from *Table Talk*.

Humphrey, Zephine. *On Re-Reading the Bible*, in *The Saturday Review of Literature*, July 4, 1925.

Hunt, Leigh. *My Books*, in *Romantic Prose of the Early Nineteenth Century*. Modern Student's Library. Charles Scribner's Sons.

Lamb, Charles. *Detached Thoughts on Books and Reading*, from *The Last Essay of Elia*.

Lang, Andrew. *Adventures among Books*, any chapter. Longmans, Green & Co.

Matthews, Brander. *The Confessions of Saint Augustine*, from *Adventures among Books*. Longmans, Green & Co.

Newton, A. Edward. *Book-Collecting Abroad* and *Book-Collecting at Home*, from *The Amenities of Book Collecting*. The Atlantic Monthly Press.

Pearson, Edmund Lester. *The Cary Girls*, from *Books in Black and Red*. The Macmillan Company.

Repplier, Agnes. *English Railway Fiction*, from *Points of View*. Houghton Mifflin Company.

Repplier, Agnes. *A Short Defence of Villains*, from *Essays in Miniature*. Houghton Mifflin Company.

Smith, Alexander. *A Shelf in My Bookcase*, from *Dreamthorp*. Thomas B. Mosher, Publisher.

Stevenson, Robert Louis. *Books which Have Influenced Me* and *A Gossip on Romance*, from *Essays*. Charles Scribner's Sons.

Young, Stark. *Mad Money*, from *Encaustics*. New Republic, Inc.

CHAPTER II

THE OCCASIONAL ESSAY

As a kind of bridge between the objective and the subjective essay (and here again one must remember that we are using most elastic terms) one may place the essay written around and about some occasion. Often more subjective than those types of essays which here precede it in that it frequently includes more of the author, it is yet objective in that it more easily provides material and stimulates thought than does the essay which largely relies upon ideas.

Essayists have always indulged themselves in writing about occasions. Lamb's wistful *New Year's Eve* is no less delightful than his rollicking *All Fools' Day* or than his charming welcome to the fourteenth of February which we quote here. Miss Mitford, that quaint essayist of the last century, writes of an English Whitsun Eve, and Irving's portrayal of Christmas at Bracebridge Hall will always stay in our minds.

Nor is the essay limited to the common festivities of the year. It may well include accounts of religious observances such as that which Stark Young has given us in his *Blessing of the Animals* and with which older countries are now alone peculiarly graced. Meredith Nicholson makes an occasion of breakfast as does Maurice Hewlett of summer. Percy Lubbock, the English essayist and critic, makes an occasion of the morning prayers at Earlham, his somewhat idealized home; and Hardy's beautiful description of the sheep shearing in *Far from the Madding Crowd* is such an essay in itself.

Surely in your own life there has been or is some custom or practice which through long repetition and accumulative sentiment may rightly be termed an occasion. Spring housecleaning is an occasion still in too many families and an evening reading hour in too few. An intriguing essay has been written on such a prosaic occurrence as the Saturday night bath before the omnipresence of modern plumbing. Some of us might use the inevitable Sunday morning codfish balls as a point of departure, others Norwegian cakes on Christmas Eve, and still others the weekly washing of a recalcitrant dog or the detestation of January or the impossibility of banishing from our midst the July Sunday School picnic.

VALENTINE'S DAY [1]

BY

Charles Lamb

HAIL to thy returning festival, old Bishop Valentine! Great is thy name in the rubric, thou venerable Archflamen of Hymen! Immortal Gobetween; who and what manner of person art thou? Art thou but a *name*, typifying the restless principle which impels poor humans to seek perfection in union? or wert thou indeed a mortal prelate, with thy tippet and thy rochet, thy apron on, and decent lawn sleeves? Mysterious personage! Like unto thee, assuredly, there is no other mitered father in the calendar; not Jerome, nor Ambrose, nor Cyril; nor the consigner of undipped infants to eternal torments, Austin, whom all mothers hate; nor he who hated all mothers, Origen; nor Bishop Bull, nor Archbishop Parker, nor Whitgift. Thou comest attended with thousands and ten thousands of little Loves, and the air is

> Brush'd with the hiss of rustling wings.

Singing Cupids are thy choristers and thy precentors; and instead of the crosier, the mystical arrow is borne before thee.

In other words, this is the day on which those charming little missives, ycleped Valentines, cross

[1] From *Essays of Elia* by Charles Lamb.

and intercross each other at every street and turn-
ing. The weary and all forspent twopenny postman sinks beneath a load of delicate embarrass-
ments, not his own. It is scarcely credible to what
an extent this ephemeral courtship is carried on in
this loving town, to the great enrichment of porters,
and detriment of knockers and bell-wires. In these
little visual interpretations, no emblem is so common as the *heart*—that little three-cornered ex-
ponent of all our hopes and fears—the bestuck and
bleeding heart; it is twisted and tortured into more
allegories and affectations than an opera hat. What
authority we have in history or mythology for
placing the headquarters and metropolis of god
Cupid in this anatomical seat rather than in any
other, is not very clear; but we have got it, and it
will serve as well as any other. Else we might
easily imagine, upon some other system which
might have prevailed for anything which our pa-
thology knows to the contrary, a lover addressing
his mistress, in perfect simplicity of feeling, "Madam,
my *liver* and fortune are entirely at your dis-
posal;" or putting a delicate question, "Amanda,
have you a *midriff* to bestow?" But custom has
settled these things, and awarded the seat of sentiment to the aforesaid triangle, while its less fortunate neighbors wait at animal and anatomical
distance.

Not many sounds in life, and I include all urban and
all rural sounds, exceed in interest a *knock at the door*.
It "gives a very echo to the throne where hope is
seated." But its issues seldom answer to this
oracle within. It is so seldom that just the person
we want to see comes. But of all the clamorous

visitations the welcomest in expectation is the
sound that ushers in, or seems to usher in, a Valentine.   As the raven himself was hoarse that announced the fatal entrance of Duncan, so the knock
of the postman on this day is light, airy, confident,
and befitting one that bringeth good tidings.   It
is less mechanical than on other days; you will say,
"That is not the post, I am sure."   Visions of Love,
of Cupids, of Hymens!—delightful eternal common-
places, which "having been will always be;" which
no schoolboy nor schoolman can write away; having
your irreversible throne in the fancy and affections—
what are your transports, when the happy maiden,
opening with careful finger, careful not to break
the emblematic seal, bursts upon the sight of some
well-designed allegory, some type, some youthful
fancy, not without verses—

> Lovers all,
> A madrigal,

or some such device, not overabundant in sense—
young love disclaims it—and not quite silly—something between wind and water, a chorus where the
sheep might almost join the shepherd, as they
did, or as I apprehend they did, in Arcadia.
   All Valentines are not foolish; and I shall not
easily forget thine, my kind friend (if I may have
leave to call you so) E. B——.   E. B. lived opposite
a young maiden whom he had often seen; unseen,
from his parlor window in C——e Street.   She was
all joyousness and innocence, and just of an age
to enjoy receiving a Valentine, and just of a temper
to bear the disappointment of missing one with
good humor.   E. B. is an artist of no common

powers; in the fancy parts of designing, perhaps
inferior to none; his name is known at the bottom
of many a well-executed vignette in the way of
his profession, but no further; for E. B. is modest,
and the world meets nobody half way.   E. B. meditated how he could repay this young maiden for
many a favor which she had done him unknown;
for when a kindly face greets us, though but passing
by, and never knows us again, nor we it, we should
feel it as an obligation; and E. B. did.   This good
artist set himself at work to please the damsel.   It
was just before Valentine's day three years since.
He wrought, unseen and unsuspected, a wondrous
work.   We need not say it was on the finest gilt
paper with borders, full, not of common hearts
and heartless allegory, but all the prettiest stories
of love from Ovid, and older poets than Ovid (for
E. B. is a scholar).   There was Pyramus and Thisbe,
and be sure Dido was not forgot, nor Hero and
Leander, and swans more than sang in Cayster,
with mottoes and fanciful devices, such as be-
seemed—a work, in short, of magic.   Iris dipped
the woof.   This on Valentine's eve he commended
to the all-swallowing indiscriminate orifice (O
ignoble trust!) of the common post; but the humble
medium did its duty, and from his watchful stand
the next morning he saw the cheerful messenger
knock, and by-and-by the precious charge delivered.
He saw, unseen, the happy girl unfold the Valentine,
dance about, clap her hands, as one after one the
pretty emblems unfolded themselves.   She danced
about, not with light love, or foolish expectations,
for she had no lover; or, if she had, none she knew
that could have created those bright images which

delighted her. It was more like some fairy present;
a God-send, as our familiarly pious ancestors termed
a benefit received where the benefactor was unknown. It would do her no harm. It would do her
good forever after. It is good to love the unknown.
I only give this as a specimen of E. B. and his
modest way of doing a concealed kindness.

Good-morrow to my Valentine, sings poor Ophe-
lia; and no better wish, but with better auspices,
we wish to all faithful lovers, who are not too wise
to despise old legends, but are content to rank
themselves humble diocesans of old Bishop Valentine and his true church.

THE BLESSING OF THE ANIMALS [1]

BY

Stark Young

FOR this seventeenth of January, along toward four in the afternoon, there is a commotion at the little church of San Felipe de Jesus. From all over San Antonio, from out by Zazamora Street and the district of the Corpus Christi road, people have brought their favorite animals, parrots, dogs, cats, hens, birds, in their arms, in cages and baskets or on leash, to be blessed. This is the ceremony of the blessing of the animals, the feast of San Antonio de Abad.

On the steps of the church stand three little boys with puppies and a solemn flutter of little girls with puppies and birds and cats. There are men and women, mostly poor people, with parrots and dogs and chickens. The men have off their hats, the women wear bright skirts and have black ribosos over their heads. One woman with a dark blunt face under her riboso has three animals to be blessed; from her right hand hangs a large rush cage with a green parrot in it; on her left arm rests a small cage of canaries, and from it swings a long barrel-like cage of Spanish doves, who huddle together in the midst of such a concourse of men and beasts and before the shine, no doubt, of those white

[1] From *Encaustics* by Stark Young. Reprinted by kind permission of the author.

174

forms that emerge from the church and down the steps to the people under the trees—the Spanish father with his book and the acolytes with the cross and swinging censer.

In the road just outside there is a doubting Thomas in the form of a lady who sits in her motor-car, her dog on her lap. She has chanced by at the moment very likely and has stopped; the regard that she bends on the crowd is cool; you can see that she finds these Mexicans a poor lot. She and her dog enjoy the advantages of a superior civiliza-tion; these animals about to be blessed eat any-thing they can get hold of; she has dog-biscuit. The priest lifts his hand, the service begins. From the silver censer the smoke rises past the bare boughs toward the clear bright sky.

San Antonio de Abad, in whose memory this day opens its loving heart to the dumb creatures here, was an African saint of the fourth or fifth century. I am somewhat unfamiliar with this San Antonio, but my neighbor in the crowd, a little old señor, brown and dried up and kind, tells me something of him. In Egypt he lived, and for many years only in desert places, where he con-sorted with all animals, gentle and ferocious, tam-ing lions and wild bears and living in brotherhood with all that has wings. Through the long stretch of sixty years he was fed by a raven who brought him every day half a loaf of bread; we know it be-cause this raven on one occasion when St. Paul the Hermit paid Saint Anthony a visit, brought them a whole loaf. If Saint Anthony of Padua preached to the fishes after Saint Francis of Assisi had preached to the birds; Saint Jerome drew the thorn from the lion's foot; Saint Isidore tamed wild beasts; San Antonio de Abad was a greater lover still of wild creatures. His constant companion was a pig, even when he was—quite as you can see him sometimes in the pictures—carrying fire in his hands, which showed that he could cure the Sacred Fire, meaning erysipelas, you see. Sometimes when the devil wished to tempt San Antonio he appeared in the form of an animal, but the sign of the cross soon settled that.

The señor gives his terrier a smack for wanting to bark at the smoking incense. Little old women are scattered here and there hugging their cages of pets to them like bright bits of life. The señor points out one of them with a golden brown hen in one hand; she holds by the other a nanny goat's halter. Getting blessed can do the goat no harm, and if you left her at home the neighbors would steal in and milk her. The priest is raising his hand again and the gentle blessing descends on all creatures there.

THE CHEERFUL BREAKFAST TABLE [1]

BY

Meredith Nicholson

A good, honest, wholesome, hungry breakfast.
—*The Compleat Angler.*

"ONE fine morning in the full London season, Major Arthur Pendennis came over from his lodgings, according to his custom, to breakfast at a certain club in Pall Mall, of which he was a chief ornament." This has always seemed to me the noblest possible opening for a tale. The zest of a fine morning in London, the deliberation of a gentleman taking his ease in his club and fortifying himself against the day's events with a satisfying breakfast, are communicated to the reader in a manner that at once inspires confidence and arouses the liveliest expectations. I shall not go the length of saying that all novels should begin with breakfast, but where the disclosures are to be of moment, and we are to be urged upon adventures calculated to tax our emotions or our staying powers, a breakfast table serves admirably as a point of departure. We thus begin the imaginary day where the natural day begins, and we form the acquaintance of the characters at an hour when human nature is most satisfactorily and profitably studied.

[1] From *The Man in the Street.* By permission of Charles Scribner's Sons.

It is only a superstition that night alone affords the proper atmosphere for romance, and that the curtain must fall upon the first scene with the dead face of the king's messenger upturned to the moon and the landlord bawling from an upper window to know what it's all about. Morning is the beginning of all things. Its hours breathe life and hope. "Pistols and coffee!" The phrase whets the appetite both for the encounter and the cheering cup. The duel, to be sure, is no longer in favor, and it is not for me to lament its passing; but I mention it as an affair of dewy mornings, indelibly associated with hours when the hand is steady and courage runs high.

It may be said with all assurance that breakfast has fallen into sad neglect, due to the haste and rush of modern life—the commuter's anxiety touching the 8.27, the city man's fear that he may not be able to absorb the day's news before his car is at the door. Breakfast has become a negligible item of the day's schedule. An increasing number of American citizens are unfit to be seen at the breakfast hour; and a man, woman, or child who cannot present a cheery countenance at breakfast is living an unhealthy life upon the brink of disaster. A hasty visit to the table, the gulping of coffee, the vicious snapping of teeth upon food scarcely looked at, and a wild rush to keep the first appointment noted on the calendar, is the poorest possible preparation for a day of honest work. The man who follows this practice is a terror to his business associates. Reports that "the boss isn't feeling well this morning" pass about the office, with a disturbance of the morale that does not make for the

efficiency of the establishment. The wife who
reaches the table disheveled and fretful, under
compulsion of her conscience, with the idea that
the lord of the house should not be permitted to
fare forth without her benediction, would do better
to keep her bed. If the eggs are overdone or the
coffee is cold and flavorless, her panicky entrance
at the last moment will not save the situation. A
growl from behind the screening newspaper is a
poor return for her wifely self-denial, but she de-
serves it. There is guilt upon her soul; if she had
not insisted on taking the Smiths to supper after
the theater the night before, he would have got
the amount of sleep essential to his well-being and
the curtaining paper would not be camouflaging
a face to which the good-by kiss at the front door
is an affront, not a caress.

"Have the children come down yet?" the lone
breakfaster growlingly demands. The maid replies
indifferently that the children have severally and
separately partaken of their porridge and departed.
Her manner of imparting this information sig-
nifies rebellion against a system which makes necessary the repeated offering of breakfast to persons
who accept only that they may complain of it. No
happier is the matutinal meal in humbler estab-
lishments where the wife prepares and serves the
food, and buttons up Susie's clothes or sews a button on Johnny's jacket while the kettle boils. If
the husband met a bootlegger in the alley the
previous night, it is the wife's disagreeable duty to
rouse him from his protracted slumbers; and if,
when she has produced him at the table, he is displeased with the menu, his resentment, unchecked

by those restraints presupposed of a higher culture, is manifested in the playful distribution of the tableware in the general direction of wife and offspring. The family cluster fearfully at the door as the head of the house, with surly resignation, departs for the scene of his daily servitude with the smoke of his pipe trailing behind him, animated by no love for the human race but only by a firm resolution not to lift his hand until the last echoes of the whistle have died away.

It is foreign to my purpose to indict a whole profession, much less the medical fraternity, which is so sadly harassed by a generation of Americans who demand in pills and serums what its progenitors found in the plough handle and the axe, and yet I cannot refrain from laying at the doors of the doctors some burden of responsibility for the destruction of the breakfast table. The astute and diplomatic physician, perfectly aware that he is dealing with an outraged stomach and that the internal discomfort is due to overindulgence, is nevertheless anxious to impose the slightest tax upon the patient's self-denial. Breakfast, he reflects, is no great shakes anyhow, and he suggests that it be curtailed, or prescribes creamless coffee or offers some other hint equally banal. This is wholly satisfactory to Jones, who says with a sigh of relief that he never cared much for breakfast, and that he can very easily do without it.

About twenty-five years ago some one started a boom for the breakfastless day as conducive to longevity. I know persons who have clung stubbornly to this absurdity. The despicable habit contributes to domestic unsociability and is, I am

convinced by my own experiments, detrimental to
health. The chief business of the world is transacted in the morning hours, and I am reluctant to
believe that it is most successfully done on empty
stomachs. Fasting as a spiritual discipline is, of
course, quite another thing; but fasting by a tired
business man under medical compulsion can hardly
be lifted to the plane of things spiritual. To delete
breakfast from the day's program is sheer cowardice,
a confession of invalidism which is well calculated
to reduce the powers of resistance. The man who
begins the day with a proscription that sets him
apart from his neighbors may venture into the
open jauntily, persuading himself that his ab-
stinence proves his superior qualities; but in his
heart, to say nothing of his stomach, he knows
that he has been guilty of a sneaking evasion. If
he were a normal, healthy being, he would not be
skulking out of the house breakfastless. Early
rising, a prompt response to the breakfast bell,
a joyous breaking of the night's fast is a rite not
to be despised in civilized homes.

Old age rises early and calls for breakfast and the
day's news. Grandfather is entitled to his breakfast at any hour he demands it. He is at an age
when every hour stolen from the night is fairly
plucked from oblivion, and to offer him breakfast
in bed as more convenient to the household, or with
a well-meant intention of easing the day for him,
is merely to wound his feelings. There is something
finely appealing in the thought of a veteran cam-
paigner in the army of life who doesn't wait for
the bugle to sound reveille, but kindles his fire and
eats his ration before his young comrades are awake.

The failure of breakfast, its growing ill repute and disfavor are not, however, wholly attributable to the imperfections of our social or economic system. There is no more reason why the homes of the humble should be illumined by a happy breakfast table than that the morning scene in abodes of comfort and luxury should express cheer and a confident faith in human destiny. Snobbishness must not enter into this matter of breakfast reform; rich and poor alike must be persuaded that the morning meal is deserving of all respect, that it is the first act of the day's drama, not to be performed in a slipshod fashion to spoil the rest of the play. It is the first chapter of a story, and every one who has dallied with the art of fiction knows that not merely the first chapter but the first line must stir the reader's imagination.

It is a common complaint of restrospective elderly persons that the family life, as our grandparents knew it, has been destroyed by the haste and worry incident to modern conditions. Breakfast—a leisurely, jolly affair as I would have it, with every member of the household present on the stroke of the gong—is unequalled as a unifying force. The plea that everybody is in a hurry in the morning is no excuse; if there is any hour when haste is unprofitable it is that first morning hour.

A day should not be "jumped into," but approached tranquilly and with respect and enlivened by every element of joy that can be communicated to it. At noon we are in the midst of conflict; at nightfall we have won or lost battles; but in the morning "all is possible and all unknown." If we have slept like honest folk, and are not afraid of a dash of cold water, we meet the day blithely and with high expectation. If the day dawn brightly, there is good reason for sharing its promise with those who live under the same roof; if it be dark and rain beats upon the pane, even greater is the need of family communion, that every member may be strengthened for valiant wrestling with the day's tasks.

As against the tendency, so destructive of good health and mental and moral efficiency, to slight breakfast, the food manufacturers have set themselves with praiseworthy determination to preserve and dignify the meal. One has but to peruse the advertising pages of the periodicals to learn of the many tempting preparations that are offered to grace the breakfast table. The obtuse, inured to hasty snatches, nibbles, and sips, are assisted to a proper appreciation of these preparations by the most enchanting illustrations. The art of publicity has spent itself lavishly to lure the world to an orderly and contemplative breakfast with an infinite variety of cereals that have been subjected to processes which make them a boon to mankind. When I hear of an addition to the long list, I fly at once to the grocer to obtain one of the crisp packages, and hurry home to deposit it with the cook for early experiment. The adventurous sense is roused not only by the seductive advertisement but by the neatness of the container, the ears of corn or the wheat sheaf so vividly depicted on the wrapper, or the contagious smile of a radiant child brandishing a spoon and demanding more.

Only a slouchy and unimaginative housewife will repeat monotonously a breakfast schedule.

A wise rotation, a continual surprise in the food offered, does much to brighten the table. The damnable iteration of ham and eggs has cracked the pillars of many a happy home. There should be no ground for cavil; the various items should not only be well-chosen, but each dish should be fashioned as for a feast of high ceremony. Gluttony is a grievous sin; breakfast, I repeat, should be a spiritual repast. If fruit is all that the soul craves, well enough; but let it be of paradisaical perfection. If coffee and a roll satisfy the stomach's craving, let the one be clear and not so bitter as to keep the imbiber's heart protesting all day, and the other hot enough to melt butter and of ethereal lightness. The egg is the most sinned against of all foods. It would seem that no one could or would wantonly ruin an egg, a thing so useful, so inoffensive; and yet the proper cooking of an egg is one of the most difficult of all culinary arts. Millions of eggs are ruined every year in American kitchens. Better that the whole annual output should be cast into the sea than that one egg should offend the eye and the palate of the expectant breakfaster.

It grieves me to be obliged to confess that in hotels and on dining cars, particularly west of Pittsburgh, many of my fellow citizens are weak before the temptation of hot cakes, drenched in syrup. I have visited homes where the griddle is an implement frequently invoked through the winter months, and I have at times, in my own house, met the buckwheat cake and the syrup jug and meekly fallen before their combined assault; but the sight of a man eating hot cakes on a flying train, after a night in a sleeper, fills me with a sense of desolation. Verily it is not alone the drama that the tired business man has brought to low estate!

Sausage and buckwheat cakes have never appealed to me as an inevitable combination like ham and eggs. Beefsteak and onions at the breakfast hour are only for those who expect to devote the remainder of the day to crime or wood chopping. The scent in itself is not the incense for rosy-fingered morn; and steak at breakfast, particularly in these times of perpendicular prices, speaks for vulgar display rather than generosity.

The history of breakfast, the many forms that it has known, the customs of various tribes and nations, assist little in any attempt to reëstablish the meal in public confidence. Plato may have done his loftiest thinking on an empty stomach; I incline to the belief that Sophocles was at all times a light breakfaster; Horace must regret that he passed into the Elysian Fields without knowing the refreshing qualities of a grapefruit. If my postmortem terminal were less problematical, I should like to carry him a grapefruit—a specimen not chilled to death in cold storage—and divide it with him, perhaps adding a splash of Falernian for memory's sake. But the habits of the good and great of olden times are not of the slightest importance to us of twentieth-century America. Still, not to ignore wholly the familiar literary associations suggested by my subject, Samuel Rogers and his weakness for entertaining at breakfast shall have honorable mention. Rogers's breakfasts, one of his contemporaries hinted, were a cunning test of the fitness of the guests to be promoted to the host's dinner table—a process I should have reversed, on the theory that the qualifications for breakfast guests are far more exacting than those for a dinner company. We have testimony that Rogers's breakfasts, informal and with every one at ease, were much more successful than his dinners. Wordsworth, Coleridge, Byron and Moore, Southey and Macaulay, the Duke of Wellington and Lord John Russell were fellows to make a lively breakfast table. At one of these functions Coleridge talked for three hours on poetry, an occasion on which, we may assume, the variety or quality of the food didn't matter greatly.

Breakfast as a social medium has never flourished in America, chiefly because of our lack of leisure. Where recognized at all it is thrown into the middle of the day where it becomes an anomaly, an impudent intrusion. A breakfast that is a luncheon is not a breakfast, but a concession to the Philistines. Once, with considerable difficulty, I persuaded a lady of my acquaintance to undertake to popularize breakfast by asking a company, few and fit, for eight o'clock. The first party was delightful, and the second, moved along to nine, was equally successful. But the hostess was so pleased with her success that she increased the number of guests to a dozen and then to fifteen, and advanced the hour to noon, with the result that the felicity of the earlier hours was lost. One must have a concrete program to be of service in these reforms, and I shall say quite fearlessly that a round table set for six is the ideal arrangement.

A breakfast must be planned with greatest care. It should never be resorted to as a means of paying

social debts, but arranged with the utmost independence. Where a wife is a desirable guest
and the husband is not, there is no reason why a
plate should be wasted. On the other hand, I should
as rigidly exclude the wife who is socially a non-
conductor. The talk at a breakfast table must be
spirited, and it will not be otherwise if the company is well chosen. It's an absurd idea that candlelight is essential to sociability and that wit will
not sparkle in the early morning. Some of the
best talk I ever listened to has been at breakfast
tables, where the guests conversed freely under
the inspiration of a mounting sun. Doctor Holmes
clearly believed the breakfast hour appropriate for
the disclosure of the sprightliest philosophy.

An American novelist once explained that he
did his writing in the afternoon because he couldn't
make love in the morning. Not make love in the
morning! The thought is barbarous. Morning
is of sentiment all compact. Morning to the lover
who possesses a soul is washed with Olympian dews.
The world is all before him where to choose and his
heart is his only guide. Love is not love that fears
the morning light. . . . There was a house by the
sea, whence a girl used to dart forth every morning
for a run over the rocks. We used to watch her
from our windows, admiring the lightness of her
step, her unconscious grace as she was silhouetted
on some high point of the shore against the blue
of the sea and sky. It was to think of him, her
lover, in the free sanctuary of the new, clean day
that she ran that morning race with her own spirits.
And he, perhaps knowing that she was thus pre-
paring herself for their first meeting, would fly

after her, and they would come running back, hand in hand, and appear with glowing cheeks and shining eyes at the breakfast table, to communicate to the rest of us the joy of youth.

There are houses in which participation in the family breakfast is frankly denied to the guest, who is informed that by pressing a button in his room coffee will appear at any hour that pleases his fancy. Let us consider this a little. The ideal guest is rare; the number of persons one really enjoys having about, free to penetrate the domestic arcana, is small indeed. This I say who am not an inhospitable soul. That a master and mistress should keep the morning free is, however, no sign of unfriendliness: the shoving of breakfast into a room does not argue necessarily for churlishness, and I have never so interpreted it. A hostess has her own affairs to look after, and the despatch of trays upstairs enables her to guard her morning from invasion. Still, in a country house, a guest is entitled to a fair shot at the morning. The day is happier when the household assembles at a fixed hour not to be trifled with by a lazy and inconsiderate guest.

Moreover, we are entitled to know what our fellows look like in the morning hours. I have spoken of lovers, and there is no sterner test of the affections than a breakfast-table inspection. Is a yawn unbecoming? We have a right to know with what manner of yawn we are to spend our lives. Is it painful to listen to the crunching of toast in the mouth of the adored? Is the wit laggard in the morning hours when it should be at its nimblest? These are grave matters not lightly to be brushed aside. At breakfast the blemish in the damask cheek publishes itself shamelessly; an evil temper that is subdued by candlelight will betray itself over the morning coffee. At breakfast we are what we are, and not what we may make ourselves for good or ill before the stars twinkle.

I protest against breakfast in bed as not only unsocial but unbecoming in the children of democracy. I have never succumbed to this temptation without experiencing a feeling of humiliation and cowardice. A proper punishment for such self-indulgence is inflicted by the stray crumbs that lodge between the sheets unless one be highly skilled in the handling of breakfast trays. Crumbs in bed! Procrustes missed a chance here. The presence of emptied dishes in a bedroom is disheartening in itself; the sight of them brings to a sensitive soul a conviction of incompetence and defeat. You cannot evade their significance; they are the wreck of a battle lost before you have buckled on your armor or fired an arrow at the foe. My experiments have been chiefly in hotels, where I have shrunk from appearing in a vast hall built for banqueting and wholly unsuitable for breakfasting; but better suffer this gloomy isolating experience than huddle between covers and balance a tray on stubborn knees that rebel at the indignity.

The club breakfast is an infamous device designed to relieve the mind of what should be the pleasant privilege of selection. I am uninformed as to who invented this iniquity of numbered alternatives, but I unhesitatingly pronounce him an enemy of mankind. Already too many forces are operating to beat down the imagination. I charge this monstrosity upon the propagandists of realism; certainly no romanticist in the full possession of his powers would tolerate a thing so deadly to the play of fancy. I want neither the No. 7 nor the No. 9 prescribed on the card; and the waiter's index finger wabbling down the margin in an attempt to assist me is an affront, an impudence. Breakfast should be an affair between man and his own soul; a business for the initiative, not the referendum.

Breakfast out of doors is the ideal arrangement, or in winter under an ample screen of glass. My own taste is for a perspective of sea or lake; but a lusty young river at the elbow is not to be despised. The camper, of course, has always the best of it; a breakfast of fresh-caught trout with an Indian for company serves to quicken such vestiges of the primitive as remain in us. But we do not, if we are wise, wait for ideal conditions. It is a part of the great game of life to make the best of what we have, particularly in a day that finds the world spinning madly "down the ringing grooves of change."

The breakfast table must be made a safe place for humanity, an inspirational center of democracy. A land whose people drowsily turn over for another nap at eight o'clock, or languidly ring for coffee at eleven, is doomed to destruction. Of such laziness is unpreparedness born—the vanguard of the enemy already howling at the postern; treason rampant in the citadel; wailing in the court. Breakfast, a sensible meal at a seasonable hour; sausage or beefsteak if you are capable of such atrocities; or only a juicy orange if your appetite be dainty; but breakfast, a cheerful breakfast with family or friends, no matter how great the day's pressure. This, partaken of in a mood of kindliness and tolerance toward all the world, is a definite accomplishment. By so much we are victors, and whether the gulfs wash us down or we sight the happy isles we have set sail with flags flying and to the stirring roll of drums.

SUMMER [1]

BY

Maurice Hewlett

IF, like me, you are more interested in seeing things
happen than in seeing them when they have
happened, you will not be such an advocate of
Summer as of other, any other, seasons. For
Summer is the one time of year when practically
nothing happens outdoors. From about the middle
of May—I speak of the south parts—to the middle
of September Nature sits with her hands in her
lap and a pleasantly tired face. There, my children,
she says, I have done my job. I hope you like it.
Most of us, I own, do like it very much, and signify
the same in the usual manner by vigorous ball-
exercise and liquid refreshment, much of it of an
explosive and delusive kind. When the Summer
is over, somewhere round about Michaelmas day,
Nature rolls up her sleeves and begins again. Properly speaking, there are only two seasons—Spring
and Summer. The people therefore who, like me,
prefer the Spring to the Summer, have more time
in which to exhibit or dissemble their love—and
a good deal of it, I confess, uncommonly beastly in
the matter of weather.

The people who like everything are the people to
envy. Children, for example, love the Winter just

[1] From *Last Essays*. By permission of Charles Scribner's Sons.

as much as the Summer. They whistle as they
jump their feet, or flack their arms across their
bodies; and whistling is one of the sure signs of
contented youth. I remember that we used to
think it rare sport to find the sponge a solid globe
of ice, or to be able to get off cleaning our teeth on
the ground that the tooth water was frozen in the
bottle. I don't believe I ever had cold feet in bed,
and am sure that if I did I had something much
more exciting to think about. There might be
skating to-morrow, or we could finish the snow man,
or go tobogganing with the tea tray; or it was
Christmas; or we were going to the pantomime.
All seasons were alike to us; each had its delights.
That of Summer, undoubtedly, was going to the
seaside. We always had a month of that, and then
a month in some country place or other which my
father did not know. That was done for his sake,
because the seaside bored him so much that even
his children noticed it. It was nothing to us, of
course, as we lived in the country, and did not, as
he did, poor man, spend most days of the year in
London; but equally of course we weren't bored.
I never heard of a child being bored, and can imagine few things more tragic in a small way. No:
it was always interesting to live in some one else's
house, learn something of their ways, chance upon
a family photograph, or a discarded toy, or a dog's
grave in the shrubbery; or to read their books and
guess what bits they had liked—any little things
like that. And, of course, it was comfortable to
know that one's father wasn't always smothering
a gape, or trying to escape from nigger-minstrels.
As for the sea—a very different thing from the sea-

side—I don't believe he ever looked at it. I am
certain that I never saw him on the sands. The
sands are no place for you unless you had rather
be barefoot than not. Now, it is a fact that I never
saw my father's feet.

At the same time, I don't know where else one
could be in August, except at the seaside. Really,
there is very little to say for the country in that
month. The trees are as near black as makes no
matter, the hills are dust-color, the rivers are running dry. True, the harvest is going on; but the
harvest is not what it used to be. You had, indeed,
"A field full of folk" (in old Langland's words)
in former days. All hands were at it, and the women
following the men, building the hiles, as we call
them, and the children beside them, twisting up
the straw ties as fast as they could twist. And then
the bread and cheese and cider—or it might be home-
brewed beer—in the shade! But bless me—last year
I saw the harvesting of a hundred-acre field—our
fields run very big down here; and the whole thing
was being done by one man on a machine! The
Solitary Reaper, forsooth! The man was reaper,
tyer and binder all in one; you never saw so desolate
a spectacle. So the harvest is not what it was. It
may have attractions for the farmer, but for nobody
else that I can think of. Go north for your Summer
and you may do better. August is wet, generally, in
Scotland, but when you are in Scotland you won't
mind rain, or had better not. You can catch trout
in the rain in Scotland, and with a fly too; that is the
extraordinary part of it. And the Scottish summer
twilights are things to remember. They are overdone in Norway, where they go on all night; where

the sun may go behind the hill for five minutes
and begin the day before you have thought of going
to bed. You can't keep that up—but it is exciting
enough at first. The great charm of the Norwegian
Summer to me is that it includes what we call Spring.
The other season in that country is Winter, which
begins in September and ends with May. Then,
immediately Summer begins; the grass grows and
is ready for the scythe, the cherries flower and get
ripe and are eaten—all at once. You get those
amazing contrasts there which you only have in
mountainous countries; which I remember most
vividly crossing the Cevennes from Le Puy to
Alais. On the watershed I was picking daffodils,
only just ready to be picked; in the valley of the
Ardeche they were making hay, and roses were
dusty in the hedges. I slid from March into June—
in twenty minutes. You will not be so piqued in
England; yet if your taste lies in the way of strawberries for instance, you can do pretty work even
in England.. You can begin in Cornwall, or Scilly,
and have your first dish in early May, or late April,
with clotted cream, of course. Then you can eat
your way through the western shires to Hampshire,
and make yourself very ill somewhere about Fare-
ham, in June. When you are able to stand the
journey, you can go on to the Fens and find them
ready for you in early July. In August you will
find them at their best in Cumberland, and in
October, weather permitting, you will have them
on your table in Scotland. After that, if you are
alive, and really care for strawberries, you must
leave this kingdom, and perhaps go to California.
I don't know.

The Summer will give you better berries than the strawberry, in my opinion. It will give you the *wild* strawberry, which, if you can find somebody to pick them for you, and then eat them with sugar and white wine, is a dish for Olympians, ambrosial food. Then there is the bilberry, which wants cream and a great deal of toothbrush afterwards, and the blaeberry, which grows in Cumberland above the 2,000 foot mark, just where the Stagshorn moss begins; and the wild raspberry which here is found on the tops of the hills, and in Scotland at the bottoms. I declare the wild raspberry to be one of the most delicious fruits God Almighty ever made. In Norway you will have the cranberry and the saeter-berry; but in Norway you will want nothing so long as there are cherries. I know Kent very well—but its cherries are not so good as those of Norway.

I had no intention, when I began, to talk about eating all the time. It is a bad sign when one begins that, though as a matter of fact we do think a great deal of our food in the country—because we are hungry, and it is so awfully good; and (as I dare say the Londoner thinks) because we have nothing else to think about. That is a mistake, and the Summer is the time to correct it, by spending it in the country and trying to understand us. Let me be bold enough to suggest to the Londoner who takes the prime of Summer to learn the ways of the country in it, that he would prove a more teachable disciple if he did not bring his own ways with him. He is rather apt to do that. He expects, for example, his golf, and always has his toys with him for the purpose. Well, he should not. Golf

is a suburban game, handy for the townsman in
his off hours. Country people don't play golf.
They have too much to do. The char-à-bancs is
another town institution, to be used like a stagecoach. Nothing of the country can be learned by
streaming over moor and mountain in one of them.
The Oreads hide from them; Pan and old Sylvanus
treat them as natural process, scourges to be endured,
like snowstorms or foot-and-mouth disease. The
country is veiled from char-à-bancs, partly in dust,
partly in disgust. For we don't understand hunting
in gangs. The herd instinct which such things
involve and imply is not a country instinct. We
are self-sufficient here, still, in spite of all invita-
tion, individuals.

A LIST OF ESSAYS PARTICULARLY ADAPTED FOR USE AS MODELS

Baldwin, Charles Sears. *Salad*, from *Essays out of Hours*.
  Longmans, Green & Co.
Birrell, Augustine. *Book-Buying*, from *Obiter Dicta, Second
  Series*. Charles Scribner's Sons.
Hearn, Lafcadio. *Morning in Matsue*, from *Glimpses of Un-
  familiar Japan*. Houghton Mifflin Company.
Irving, Washington. *Christmas Eve*, from *The Sketch Book*.
Lamb, Charles. *All Fools' Day* and *New Year's Eve*, from *The
  Essays of Elia*.
Lubbock, Percy. *Earlham*, pages 1-4. Jonathan Cape, Lon-
  don.
Lucas, E. V. *The Town Week*, from *Fireside and Sunshine*.
  Methuen & Co., Ltd., London.
Lynd, Robert. *Afternoon Tea*, from *The Blue Lion*. Methuen
  & Co., Ltd., London, and George H. Doran Company.
Matthews, Brander. *Book-Buying*, from *Hours with Men and
  Books*. S. C. Griggs and Company.

Matthews, Brander. *Spring in a Side Street* and *Sunday in Central Park*, from *Vignettes of Manhattan*. Harper & Brothers.

Milne, A. A. *A Word for Autumn*, from *Not That It Matters*. E. P. Dutton & Co.

Mitford, Mary Russell. *Whitsun-Eve*, from *Our Village*. The Macmillan Company.

Scheffauer, Herman. *The Black Fog*. *The Atlantic Monthly*, February, 1908.

Smith, Alexander. *Christmas*, from *Dreamthorp*. Thomas B. Mosher, Publisher.

Tanner, William M. *Essays and Essay-Writing*. The Atlantic Monthly Press. *The Saturday-Night Bath*.

Thomas, Edward. *Rain*, from *Roseacre Papers*. Duckworth & Company, London.

Warner, Frances Lester. *Driftwood Fire*, from *Endicott and I*. Houghton Mifflin Company.

Warner, Frances Lester. *"Is There Any Mail?"* and *When Syrup Spins a Thread*, from *Surprising the Family*. Houghton Mifflin Company.

CHAPTER III

THE SUBJECTIVE ESSAY

THIS title is also, strictly speaking, a misnomer. The very word "essay" suggests a personal and subjective quality. Needless to say, the adjective is employed only as a means of distinction just as the seemingly arbitrary divisions which follow serve to separate only by faint lines one type of essay from another. Reminiscence may be and often is employed in an essay on nature, confessions are not infrequently included with opinions, personal experience and perception sometimes go hand in hand. And yet we have found some such division as given here of great help to the student in the sorting and sifting of essay material.

There is, after all, only one requirement exacted of the writer of the more personal essay. Having that, he may with comparative safety ignore divisions, precepts, suggestions; lacking it, no suggestion under heaven can help him. *He must have something to say.* And that broadly interpreted means that he must have learned to value and to evaluate his own experience and environment and those of others, to discriminate between what may be of general and what of special interest, to laugh at himself, to seize upon the ideas of others, and, through reading, observation, and thought, to nurture at least the possibility of conceiving some of his own.

It will be encouraging but surprising if at the outset he can do as well with an essay on nature or

with one based on some stray notion or perception
as he can with a personal experience, a defense, or
a confession.   From our experience we have come
to the inevitable conclusion that such a student and
such capabilities are rare.   Hence the division into
types and the accompanying suggestions.

A. Personal Experiences, Reminiscences, and Confessions

The essay of personal experience often seems
nothing more or less than narrative; but more
thoughtful reading will prove it to be far more than
that.   It is the work of the essayist to retell the
given experience in such a way that the story itself
is only contributory to the comment or observation
on life which he wishes to make.   Thus *Bibles at
Hell Gate*, though its method is largely narrative,
serves better than any comment in itself could do
to show the lack of humor evident in "certain good
persons" of an "admirable society" which sought
to save the boys, the incongruity of their gift, and
the lovely absurdity of the "fleet of fifty floating
Bibles" "drifting in single column toward Hell
Gate."   These are the essay materials which tran-
scend the mere story.

The same situation is often seen in the reminiscent essay.   Reminiscence in itself is not an essay,
but reminiscence which serves to illustrate a common
experience and through that experience to touch
a common emotion is of the very stuff of which the
best essays are made.   The boy in Kenneth Grahame's essay who found the secret drawer was suddenly transported from his need of money and
quickly taken on a wistful and bewildering journey

across a "void stretch of years" to the strange
sense of the mutability of time.   There are few
children who have not experienced in one way or
another the pain of that revelation.   In Helen
Foot's reminiscent essay such a mundane thing
as a kitchen stove treated humorously throughout
becomes almost Platonic in its larger significance.

The essay in the form of a confession is one of
the most delightful.   In this the author may chat
on at will as do Robert Lynd and Christopher
Morley, the one acknowledging his passion for
patent medicine, the other ruminating on the joys
of smoking.   The tone of essays such as these, conciliatory, frank, good natured, confidential, engages
at once the sympathetic attention of the reader;
and the literary references, particularly in Mr.
Morley's, engender an atmosphere of far wider
range than that at first suggested by the title.

Essays such as these, based on your own experience, will form an excellent starting point for
your never-ending and delightful journey through
the wide fields of the subjective essay.

BIBLES AT HELL GATE [1]

BY

Felix Riesenberg

SCHOOLSHIPS (and what finer place for a school than on board a ship?) have had a rather bad name in days past on this little island of Manhattan. Very old citizens may remember the *Mercury*, filled with really bad boys. This old hulk for many years cast a shadow of reproach over the schoolship *St. Mary's*, on which the New York Nautical School began its great career in 1875. People, even as far along as 1896, referred to the old *St. Mary's* as a reform school.

But any school worthy of the name must be somewhat of a reform school, of character and perhaps also of ideas. The *St. Mary's*, a wooden sloop of war, ship rigged, built at Washington in 1844, of live oak framing and white oak planking, fastened with mighty bolts and spikes of red copper, had wrought into her ribs and keel a strength and durability unknown to the steel ships of to-day. This old craft housed a hundred boys, more or less bad, many from the crowded slums, and a large proportion from the respectable comfort of plain homes. She even held a few wild spirits cast off, or run away, from luxurious moorings. Let us admit that the old ship was a tough packet.

[1] From *Vignettes of the Sea*. Used by permission of the publishers, Harcourt, Brace & Company, and of the author.

Built as a slave chaser, her underbody had the sharp lines of a yacht. Her copper sheathing, her tall spars, her great spread of sail, filled the youth upon her clean white decks with a spirit of romantic abandon that obtuse persons often interpreted as vicious. Of course there were a great many fights on board, conducted regularly forward of the mast. Loose talk always led to blows. There was very little disturbance in the way of vocal bickering under this system. But the stern rule on board gave the hard-fisted youth an exaggerated air of piratical importance. They were tough as hell and liked to show it.

Something must be done to save these boys. It was the duty of certain good persons to care for their souls. A consignment of fifty Bibles was sent on board, the idea being that the Bibles would work watch and watch, as the youngsters did, four on and four off, when at sea. A spirit of commendable economy divided the good books on this system and also caused them to be stamped in a dozen different places with the name of the society, to prevent loss by theft.

These Bibles had reposed under a large locker in the little cubbyhole of the ship's library, down on the berth deck, for many years. The writer's literary career began as librarian on the old *St. Mary's*. Being librarian carried with it many great privileges. Not the least of these was the discreet use of the snug cabin itself. A small round port light pierced the thick oak sides of the hull, not more than two feet above the water line, and on the inside of the ship's skin a huge "dagger knee," a broad diagonal brace of oak, was providentially set below the

light. The librarian often reclined on this wide
hook of oak, the light over his left shoulder, a book
in hand, enjoying such ease and comfort as even
the captain might have envied. Of course this
secret pleasure was unknown to the executive officer
and first lieutenant.

The cabin also had other secret advantages. It
was small, lined with shelves, and might be used for
the modest stowage of private provisions behind
the upper rows of books. Just previous to the
starting of the foreign cruise, while anchored in the
East River off Twenty-third Street, a large box of
groceries was received on board, a consignment from
the mother of the librarian. This contraband had to
be hidden from the searching eye of the executive.
Deposited in the library, after a great deal of ma-
neuvering, a problem presented itself. Where might
the dozens of jars and cans of potted chicken, mar-
malade, pickles, and so forth, be stowed?

The one locker, under the dagger knee, was filled
with the fifty Bibles—musty, soggy, unread Bibles,
Bibles marred by great red stamps of an admirable
society. These Bibles were below the water line of
the hull. They had been there in dank confinement
for nearly twenty years.

On the deck, on top of the locker, and all about,
were cans and bottles and jars filled with seductive
jellies, sparkling, enticing juices, and mouth-water-
ing condiments. Outside was the entrance to the
wardroom country, the sacred habitat of officers.
On deck one of these lordly beings walked back
and forth between the gangway and the horse block.
It was late forenoon of a Saturday. The wash-
down was over. Liberty would be granted after

dinner, and at Sunday morning inspection the library door would be opened and the librarian, cap in hand, would stand by while the captain, the executive, and the surgeon peered into the ordered neatness of the den of books.

The huge consignment (only a mother can do these things largely) must be hidden. A great resolve, a huge wrench, half conscience lifting from its moorings, half relief, and the port light was unscrewed. The locker was quickly opened, and Bibles began to drop through the open port.

Suddenly there was a rap at the door. The last Bible had been pushed out into the waters.

"What in the name of blankety blank are you doing?" a voice called through the lattice. I opened cautiously. It was my chum, Dick Rush.

"Come up on deck, quick!"

We gained the spar deck and stepped to the port gangway. A few feet from the ship and drifting up the East River with the flood tide was a fleet of fifty floating Bibles, stretching a quarter mile and drifting in single column towards Hell Gate.

"My God, Dick! I thought they would sink," I exclaimed.

For a half hour we stood breathless, lest the officer of the deck walk to port and sight the slowly departing flotilla of the Gospel.

Then we went below and stowed the empty locker with the delights of the flesh and ate unwholesome quantities of jam and pickles.

THE SECRET DRAWER [1]

BY

Kenneth Grahame

IT must surely have served as a boudoir for the
ladies of old time, this little-used, rarely-entered
chamber where the neglected old bureau stood.
There was something very feminine in the faint
hues of its faded brocades, in the rose and blue of
such bits of china as yet remained, and in the
delicate, old-world fragrance of potpourri from the
great bowl—blue and white, with funny holes in
its cover—that stood on the bureau's flat top.
Modern aunts disdained this out-of-the-way, back-
water, upstairs room, preferring to do their accounts and grapple with their correspondence in
some central position more in the whirl of things,
whence one eye could be kept on the carriage-drive,
while the other was alert for malingering servants
and marauding children. Those aunts of a former
generation—I sometimes felt—would have suited
our habits better. But even by us children, to
whom few places were private or reserved, the
room was visited but rarely. To be sure, there was
nothing in particular in it that we coveted or required—only a few spindle-legged, gilt-backed chairs;
an old harp on which, so the legend ran, Aunt
Eliza herself used once to play in years remote,

[1] From *The Golden Age* by Kenneth Grahame. By permission
of Dodd, Mead & Company, Inc.

unchronicled; a corner cupboard with a few pieces of china; and the old bureau. But one other thing the room possessed peculiar to itself: a certain sense of privacy—a power of making the intruder feel that he *was* intruding—perhaps even a faculty of hinting that some one might have been sitting on those chairs, writing at the bureau, or fingering the china just a second before one entered. No such violent word as "haunted" could possibly apply to this pleasant old-fashioned chamber, which indeed we all rather liked; but there was no doubt it was reserved and stand-offish, keeping itself to itself.

Uncle Thomas was the first to draw my attention to the possibilities of the old bureau. He was pottering about the house one afternoon, having ordered me to keep at his heels for company—he was a man who hated to be left one minute alone—when his eye fell on it. "H'm! Sheraton!" he remarked. (He had a smattering of most things, this uncle, especially the vocabularies.) Then he let down the flap, and examined the empty pigeonholes and dusty panelling. "Fine bit of inlay," he went on; "good work, all of it. I know the sort. There's a secret drawer in there somewhere." Then, as I breathlessly drew near, he suddenly exclaimed, "By Jove, I do want to smoke!" And wheeling round, he abruptly fled for the garden, leaving me with the cup dashed from my lips. What a strange thing, I mused, was this smoking, that takes a man suddenly—be he in the court, the camp, or the grove—grips him like an Afreet, and whirls him off to do its imperious behests! Would it be even so with myself, I wondered, in those unknown grown-up years to come?

But I had no time to waste in vain speculations. My whole being was still vibrating to those magic syllables "secret drawer"; and that particular chord had been touched that never fails to thrill responsive to such words as *cave, trap-door, sliding-panel, bullion, ingots,* or *Spanish dollars.* For, besides its own special bliss, who ever heard of a secret drawer with nothing in it? And oh, I did want money so badly! I mentally ran over the list of demands which were pressing me the most imperiously.

First, there was the pipe I wanted to give George Jannaway. George, who was Martha's young man, was a shepherd, and a great ally of mine; and the last fair he was at, when he bought his sweetheart fairings, as a right-minded shepherd should, he had purchased a lovely snake expressly for me—one of the wooden sort, with joints, waggling deliciously in the hand; with yellow spots on a green ground, sticky and strong-smelling, as a fresh-painted snake ought to be; and with a red-flannel tongue pasted cunningly into its jaws. I loved it much, and took it to bed with me every night till what time its spinal cord was loosed and it fell apart, and went the way of all mortal joys. I thought it very nice of George to think of me at the fair, and that's why I wanted to give him a pipe. When the young year was chill and lambing-time was on, George inhabited a little wooden house on wheels, far out on the wintry downs, and saw no faces but such as were sheepish and woolly and mute; and when he and Martha were married, she was going to carry his dinner out to him every day, two miles; and after it, perhaps he would smoke

my pipe. It seemed an idyllic sort of existence for
both the parties concerned; but a pipe of quality,
a pipe fitted to be part of such a life as this, could
not be procured (so Martha informed me) for a
smaller sum than eighteenpence. And meantime—

Then there was the fourpence I owed Edward;
not that he was bothering me for it, but I knew
he was in need of it himself to pay back Selina,
who wanted it to make up a sum of two shillings to
buy Harold an ironclad for his approaching birthday—H.M.S. *Majestic*, now lying uselessly careened
in the toy-shop window, just when her country had
such sore need of her.

And then there was that boy in the village who
had caught a young squirrel, and I had never
possessed one; and he wanted a shilling for it, but
I knew that for ninepence in cash— But what was
the good of these sorry, threadbare reflections?
I had wants enough to exhaust any possible find
of bullion, even if it amount to half a sovereign.
My only hope now lay in the magic drawer; and
here I was, standing and letting the precious minutes
slip by! Whether "findings" of this sort could,
morally speaking, be considered "keepings" was a
point that did not occur to me.

The room was very still as I approached the
bureau; possessed, it seemed to be, by a sort of
hush of expectation. The faint odor of orris root
that floated forth as I let down the flap seemed to
identify itself with the yellows and browns of the
old wood, till hue and scent were of one quality
and interchangeable. Even so, ere this, the potpourri had mixed itself with the tints of the old
brocade, and brocade and potpourri had long

been one. With expectant fingers I explored the empty pigeonholes and sounded the depths of the softly-sliding drawers. No books that I knew of gave any general recipe for a request like this; but the glory, should I succeed unaided, would be all the greater.

To him who is destined to arrive, the fates never fail to afford on the way their small encouragements. In less than two minutes I had come across a rusty buttonhook. This was truly magnificent. In the nursery there existed, indeed, a general buttonhook, common to either sex; but none of us possessed a private and special buttonhook, to lend or to refuse, as suited the high humor of the moment. I pocketed the treasure carefully, and proceeded. At the back of another drawer three old foreign stamps told me I was surely on the highroad to fortune.

Following on these bracing incentives came a dull, blank period of unrewarded search. In vain I removed all the drawers and felt over every inch of the smooth surfaces from front to back. Never a knob, spring, or projection met the thrilling finger-tips; unyielding the old bureau stood, stoutly guarding its secret, if secret it really had. I began to grow weary and disheartened. This was not the first time that Uncle Thomas had proved shallow, uninformed—a guide into blind alleys where the echoes mocked you. Was it any good persisting longer? Was anything any good whatever? In my mind I began to review past disappointments, and life seemed one long record of failure and of non-arrival. Disillusioned and depressed I left my work and went to the window. The light was ebbing from the room, and seemed outside to be collecting itself on the horizon for its concentrated effort of sunset. Far down in the garden, Uncle Thomas was holding Edward in the air reversed, and smacking him. Edward, gurgling hysterically, was striking blind fists in the direction where he judged his uncle's stomach should rightly be; the contents of his pockets—a motley show—were strewing the lawn. Somehow, though I had been put through a similar performance myself an hour or two ago, it all seemed very far away and cut off from me.

Westwards, the clouds were massing themselves in a low violet bank; below them, to north and south, as far round as eye could reach, a narrow streak of gold ran out and stretched away, straight along the horizon. Somewhere very far off a horn was blowing, clear and thin; it sounded like the golden streak grown audible, while the gold seemed the visible sound. It pricked my ebbing courage, this blended strain of music and color. I turned for a last effort; and Fortune thereupon, as if half ashamed of the unworthy game she had been playing with me, relented, opening her clenched fist. Hardly had I put my hand once more to the obdurate wood, when with a sort of small sigh, almost a sob—as it were—of relief, the secret drawer sprang open.

I drew it out and carried it to the window, to examine it in the failing light. Too hopeless had I gradually grown in my dispiriting search to expect very much and yet at a glance I saw that my basket of glass lay in shivers at my feet. No ingots or dollars were here, to crown me the little Monte

Cristo of a week. Outside, the distant horn had ceased its gnat song, the gold was paling to primrose, and everything was lonely and still. Within, my confident little castles were tumbling down like so many card houses, leaving me stripped of estate, both real and personal, and dominated by the depressing reaction.

And yet, as I looked again at the small collection that lay within that drawer of disillusions, some warmth crept back to my heart as I recognized that a kindred spirit to my own had been at the making of it. Two tarnished gilt buttons—naval, apparently; a portrait of a monarch unknown to me, cut from some antique print and deftly colored by hand in just my own bold style of brushwork; some foreign copper coins, thicker and clumsier of make than those I hoarded myself; and a list of birds' eggs, with names of the places where they had been found. Also a ferret's muzzle, and a twist of tarry string, still faintly aromatic! It was a real boy's hoard, then, that I had happened upon. He, too, had found out the secret drawer, this happy-starred young person; and here he had stowed away his treasures, one by one, and had cherished them secretly awhile; and then—what? Well, one would never know now the reason why these priceless possessions lay still here unreclaimed; but across the void stretch of years I seemed to touch hands a moment with my little comrade of seasons—how many seasons?—long since dead.

I restored the drawer, with its contents, to the trusty bureau, and heard the spring click with a certain satisfaction. Some other boy, perhaps, would some day release that spring again. I trusted

he would be equally appreciative. As I opened
the door to go, I could hear, from the nursery at
the end of the passage, shouts and yells, telling
that the hunt was up. Bears, apparently, or bandits,
were on the evening bill of fare, judging by the
character of the noises. In another minute I would
be in the thick of it, in all the warmth and light
and laughter. And yet—what a long way off it
all seemed, both in space and time, to me yet lingering on the threshold of that old-world chamber!

IN DEFENSE OF PATENT MEDICINES [1]

BY

Robert Lynd

How few people there are who are fair in their attitude to patent medicines! Almost everybody takes them, but scarcely anybody speaks of them without derision. If a man likes—nay, loves—roast duckling, he will confess his taste to the world as though it were something to boast about. If he enjoys tobacco or red wine, he will talk about them by the hour to anyone for whom he really cares. The conversation will come and go in little warm waves of happy understanding that meet and leap as they cross each other, so much is to be said on these great subjects. But if you speak in praise of a patent medicine in company, you will only invite ridicule. Everybody will pretend to be incredulous, and even the quiet little man in the corner who says nothing and makes a note in his mind to go round to the chemist's in the morning and buy a bottle will pretend to join in the laugh with the rest. This is surely not quite honest. If men were all really skeptics about patent medicines, it would obviously not pay to advertise pills and potions day after day in the newspapers, and chemists would not be so much commoner than booksellers. It is a moderate estimate that fifty people

[1] From *The Peal of Bells* by Robert Lynd. Reprinted by kind permission of the author.

buy patent medicines for one who buys books.
Yet a man can praise Mr. Conrad in talk without
raising a smile, whereas, if he goes about trying to
persuade everybody to use Zang, the great cure
for pains in the shoulders, he will soon get the
reputation of an odd creature.

I, for one, having little reputation to lose, intend
henceforth to be bold about the matter, and I
herewith confess myself a devoted adherent of
patent medicines. The taste, I think, is inherited.
I grew up in an environment of shelves of books
and shelves of medicine bottles, and I found myself
at an early age stretching up a tiny hand for the
treasures of both. I do not know which I learned
to love first—Hans Andersen's *Ugly Duckling* or
sugar-coated pills. I remember that I had to
stand on a chair to reach either of the n, for Hans
Andersen was, as luck had it, on a top shelf, which
may have made him the more desirable. The pills,
however, were not only on a top shelf, but in a cupboard with a glass door, and that, too, was attrac-
tive. There they stood, pretty, shining and tempting, charming as eggs that had been laid under the
rafters of Noah's Ark, and delicious as sweetmeats,
huddled together in a little flat circular box that had
itself the air of a toy. I fancy the eye of a child is
attracted by almost anything that is small and round.
How we loved pellets of shot, making little crooked
courses for them in the school desks and becoming
so absorbed in the journeys on which we sent them
racing that the arithmetic master could recall our
attention only with a shout that made us jump!

It was the same passion for the small and the
round that made many of us in childhood, when a

whole cod was on the dinner table, ask humbly and hopefully for one or both of the fish's eyes. There may be men who have never known what a pleasure it is to sit looking at the eye of a dead fish on the edge of the plate through a course at dinner. I have heard a nurse reproving small children for so disgusting a taste, and I was shocked as though she were giving them a first lesson in atheism. For the love of the round is the love of perfection; and the earth and the stars, which are shaped like a fish's eye, incite us to it. I cannot say that it was religious enthusiasm that primarily led me to half carry and half push the chair over to the medicine cupboard and to stand up on it and peer into the secrets of the pill box. But I am sure, if the pills had been shaped less like the worlds that were created during the first week, if they had been flat or square or conical, I should not have unlidded the boxes that contained them so eagerly or so often.

Even then I did not all at once go so far as to "take" the pills. I had always looked on this as a dangerous procedure which women and children had better leave alone. My aunt used to gaze on my uncle with awe whenever he took a pill, swallowing it with the merest sip of water, and she often told me that she did not know how he did it, giving me the impression that it was a scarcely less heroic exploit than that of my theological uncle when he fought the tinker. We did not dare to speak while the pill was being swallowed. We watched till it was safely down, almost rigid with apprehension, as those spectators must have felt who saw Blondin crossing Niagara on a tight rope. To this day I cannot swallow a pill without a moment of excited doubt whether it is in my throat or my windpipe.

Naturally, then, I began experimenting with pills only in the timidest fashion. Those that were blackish I did not even taste, but one day I must have put one of the white globes into my mouth and found that in its first flavor it resembled a sugar almond. But after it had been in the mouth for a minute or so, what a sudden change! I have grown fond of bitter medicine since those days, but even now I can scarcely forbear making a face when I remember my disgust on first discovering what a pill tasted like when the sugar had been sucked through. I do not know what may be the flavors of gall and wormwood, but I fancy they must be something like the inside of that first pill. Practice makes perfect, however, and I became so cunning, in my later raids on my uncle's medicine shelves, that I was in time able to suck all—or nearly all— the sugar off his pills without more than a faint hint on the tongue of the bitterness concealed within.

As I always threw the rest of the pill out of the window, you might think that my uncle would before long have noticed the depletion of his boxes and have made perilous inquiries. Like all true devotees of patent medicines, however, he bought a great many more pills and bottles than one man could consume. You will have observed that, if a man is fond of books, he is constantly buying books that at the time he intends to read but in fact never does read. In the same way the lover of medicines is constantly being lured into the purchase of cure-alls, of which, after the first dose, he forgets the very existence on his shelves. I have seen in my uncle's study a volume still uncut after a dozen years, and he accumulated medicines with the same generous carelessness and pleasure in the mere purchase. After all, the ordinary man who is in fairly good health changes his opinion from day to day as to the disease with which he is most desperately threatened. The bottle that he buys to-day for heart disease will be of no use to-morrow when he decides that something is wrong with his liver. I myself remember buying a bottle of Swamp-root, but, long before there was time to get through it, I had completely forgotten the illness that I had supposed myself to be suffering from and was off on the track of some other disease, much rarer and more dangerous. I can also remember going into a chemist's for a bottle of Warner's Safe Cure, but two days after I had taken my treasure home my mood had changed, and another three-quarters-full bottle was added to my collection.

There may be men with so little of the idealist in their natures that they will condemn such an accumulation of unfinished bottles as an imbecile extravagance. I think they are in error. I some-times wonder whether the bottles of medicine that I finished or the bottles that I left unfinished did me the greater good. The virtue of a medicine probably lies to a considerable extent in the will to get well with which one purchases it. Besides, very often the only way to counteract the effect of the advertisement is to go out and buy the remedy that is advertised.

There are only two of the advertised remedies, I fancy, that I have ardently longed for and that

yet I had never the courage to obtain for myself.
One was a cure for blushing. Had it been called
Nonblusho and sold in packets at chemists' shops,
I think I should have tried a shilling's worth of it.
But, so far as I can remember, one had to write
for it, and I could not sit down and write on so
delicate a subject to a stranger. I could not face
the possibility that the letter might be opened by
a lady clerk who would laugh jeeringly. I might,
of course, have begun my letter: "Dear Sir, I have
a cousin who blushes a great deal," and asked for
the remedy as if for another. But I was all simplicity and slow to think of such subtle devices.
The other remedy I never dared to send for was
a machine for curing ugly or misshapen noses. I
do not know how widespread is the misery of noses,
but when I was a child I would have taken almost
anybody's nose in exchange for my own. I once
fought a boy over an insult to my nose, and it was
none the better as a result of his overwhelming
victory. I used to be told that I had had a bad
fall on it in infancy, and even the friendliest of my
friends treated it as a matter for which I needed to
be consoled rather than to be praised. Hence,
when I reached the age at which one reads the advertisements in papers, I used to be filled with
longing when I came to the advertisement about
ugly or misshapen noses. But here again the dread of
ridicule prevented me from writing; and now I shall
go to my grave without that lean and delicate bridge
to my nose that, if I had been given three wishes by a
fairy, would once have been one of my choices.

I suppose the nose machine can in strictness hardly
be called a patent medicine; but it appeals to the

same love of the ideal. The electric brush for which I paid I forget how much as a cure for baldness is in the same category; and, like a patent medicine, it lies on my shelves honored but unused. The world is so full of a number of things that most of us simply have not the time to make use of half the remedies we bring into the house. Do not despise them, however. They represent for us, even though the dust gathers on them, the ideal of getting well and the ideal of looking well, and it is an inspiration to come on them suddenly in moments of depression.

I confess that, having a vein of Scottish blood in me, I have scruples that these things should go unused, and I have often tried to persuade others to finish the bottles that I had failed to get through myself. I even made earnest supplications to a friend to try the electric brush that I had got for baldness as a cure for his rheumatism. After all, few of these things can hurt anybody. I remember my uncle had a great black instrument shaped rather like a bassoon which, instead of blowing into, as you would into a musical instrument, he inhaled from in deep breaths. It was, I believe, a cure for asthma, and he had not asthma, but he had smoker's throat, and that served. When at length he grew tired of it and it was laid aside for good in the medicine cupboard, I used privately in his absence to take it out of its long box and draw in deep breaths from it myself. It had a pleasant, sweet, cool taste, somewhat like a cachou; and it made an agreeable change from the monotony of too many sugar-coated pills.

You will understand, then, why I write enthusiastically in defense of patent remedies. I have enjoyed so many of them, and I do not remember any of them ever doing me any harm. I avoid only medicated wines, for I do not like to mix my pleasures. I have a friend who is a teetotaler and who speaks highly of medicated port. Not being a teetotaler, however, I like medicine to look and taste a little less like the sort of thing one drinks for amusement in a public house.

CONFESSIONS OF A SMOKER [1]

BY

Christopher Morley

TRUE smokers are born and not made. I remember my grandfather with his snowy beard gloriously stained by nicotine; from my first years I never saw my father out of reach of his pipe, save when asleep. Of what avail for my mother to promise unheard bonuses if I did not smoke until I was twenty? By the time I was eight years old I had constructed a pipe of an acorn and a straw, and had experimented with excelsior as fuel. From that time I passed through the well-known stages of dried bean-pod cigars, hayseed, corn silk, tea leaves, and (first ascent of the true Olympus) Recruits Little Cigars smoked in a lumber-yard during school recess. Thence it was but a step to the first bag of Bull Durham and a twenty-five-cent pipe with a curved bone stem.

I never knew the traditional pangs of Huck Finn and the other heroes of fiction. I never yet found a tobacco that cost me a moment's unease— but stay, there was a cunning mixture devised by some comrades at college that harbored in its fragrant shreds neatly chopped sections of rubber bands. That was sheer poison, I grant you.

The weed needs no new acolyte to hymn her

[1] From *Shandygaff* by Christopher Morley, published by Doubleday, Page and Company.

222

sanctities. Where Raleigh, Pepys, Tennyson, Kingsley, Calverley, Barrie, and the whimful Elia best of all—where these have spoken so greatly, the feeble voice may well shrink. But that is the joy of true worship: ranks and hierarchies are lost, all are brothers in the mystery, and amid approving puffs of rich Virginia the older saints of the mellow leaf genially greet the new freshman, be he never so humble.

What would one not have given to smoke a pipe out with the great ones of the empire! That wainscoted back parlor at the Salutation and Cat, for instance, where Lamb and Coleridge used to talk into the small hours "quaffing egg flip, devouring Welsh rabbits, and smoking pipes of Orinooko." Or the back garden in Chelsea where Carlyle and Emerson counted the afternoon well spent, though neither one had said a hundred words—had they not smoked together? Or Piscator and Viator, as they trudged together to "prevent the sunrise" on Amwell Hill—did not the reek of their tobacco trail most bluely on the sweet morning air? Or old Fitz, walking on the Deben wall at Woodbridge, on his way to go sailing with Posh down to Bawdsey Ferry—what mixture did he fill and light? Something recommended by Will Thackeray, I'll be sworn. Or, to come down to more recent days, think of Captain Joseph Conrad at his lodgings in Bessborough Gardens, lighting that apocalyptic pipe that preceded the first manuscript page of *Almayer's Folly*. Could I only have been the privileged landlady's daughter who cleared away the Captain's breakfast dishes that morning! I wonder if she remembers the incident?

It is the heart of fellowship, the core and pith and symbol of masculine friendship and good talk. Your cigar will do for drummers, your cigarettes for the dilettante smoker, but for the ripened, boneset votary nothing but a briar will suffice. Away with meerschaum, calabash, cob, and clay; they have their purpose in the inscrutable order of things, like crossing sweepers and presidents of women's clubs; but when Damon and Pythias meet to talk things over, well-caked briars are in order. Cigars are all right in fiction: for Prince Florizel and Colonel Geraldine when they visit the famous Divan in Rupert Street. It was Leigh Hunt, in the immortal Wishing Cap Papers (so little read, alas!), who uttered the finest plea for cigars that this language affords, but I will wager not a director of the United Cigar Stores ever read it.

The fine art of smoking used, in older days, to have an etiquette, a usage, and traditions of its own, which a more hurried and hygienic age has discarded. It was the height of courtesy to ask your friend to let you taste his pipe, and draw therefrom three or four mouthfuls of smoke. This afforded opportunity for a gracious exchange of compliments. "Will it please you to impart your whiff?" was the accepted phrase. And then, having savored his mixture, you would have said; "In truth, a very excellent leaf," offering your own with proper deprecations. This, and many other excellent things, we learn from Mr. Apperson's noble book *The Social History of Smoking* which should be prayer book and breviary to every smoker con amore.

But the pipe rises perhaps to its highest function as the solace and companion of lonely vigils. We all look back with tender affection on the joys of tobacco shared with a boon comrade on some walking trip, some high-hearted adventure, over the malt-stained counters of some remote alehouse. These are the memories that are bittersweet beyond the compass of halting words. Never again perhaps will we throw care over the hedge and stride with Mifflin down the Banbury Road, filling the air with laughter and the fumes of Murray's Mellow. But even deeper is the tribute we pay to the sour old elbow of briar, the dented, blackened cutty that has been with us through a thousand soundless midnights and a hundred weary dawns when cocks were crowing in the bleak air and the pen faltered in the hand. Then is the pipe an angel and minister of grace. Clocks run down and pens grow rusty, but if your pouch be full your pipe wil! never fail you.

How great is the witching power of this sovereign rite! I cannot even read in a book of some one enjoying a pipe without my fingers itching to light up and puff with him. My mouth has been sore and baked a hundred times after an evening with Elia. The rogue simply can't help talking about tobacco, and I strike a match for every essay. God bless him and his dear Orinooko! Or Parson Adams in *Joseph Andrews*—he lights a pipe on every page!

I cannot light up in a wind. It is too precious a rite to be consummated in a draught. I hide behind a tree, a wall, a hedge, or bury my head in my coat. People see me in the street, vainly seeking shelter. It is a weakness, though not a shameful one. But set me in a tavern corner, and fill the pouch with Quiet Moments (do you know that English mixture?) and I am yours to the last ash.

I wonder after all what was the sweetest pipe I ever smoked? I have a tender spot in memory for a fill of Murray's Mellow that Mifflin and I had in the old smoking room of the Three Crowns Inn at Lichfield. We weren't really thirsty, but we drank cider there in honor of Dr. Johnson, sitting in his chair and beneath his bust. Then there were those pipes we used to smoke at twilight sitting on the steps of 17 Heriot Row, the old home of R. L. S. in Edinburgh, as we waited for Leerie to come by and light the lamps. Oh, pipes of youth, that can never come again!

When George Fox was a young man, sorely troubled by visions of the devil, a preacher told him to smoke tobacco and sing hymns.

Not such bad advice.

ESSAYS PARTICULARLY ADAPTED FOR USE AS MODELS

Allen, Frederick Lewis. *Sleeping Outdoors*, in *The Century Magazine*, November, 1913.

Hall, James Norman. *Reminiscences of a Middle-Western School*, in *The Atlantic Monthly*, June, 1923; and *Sing a Song of Sixpence*, in *The Atlantic Monthly*, December, 1925.

Hazlitt, William. *On Going a Journey*, from *Table Talk*.

Lamb, Charles. *Confessions of a Drunkard*, from *The Last Essays of Elia*.

Lynd, Robert. *The Stranger's Room*, from *The Money-Box*. D. Appleton & Company.

McFee, William. *On A Balcony* and *Harbours of Memory*, from *Harbours of Memory*. Doubleday, Page & Company.

McFee, William. *The Magic Carpet Business*, from *Swallowing the Anchor*. Doubleday, Page & Company.

Stevenson, Robert Louis. *Walking Tours*, from *Essays*. Charles Scribner's Sons.

Tanner, William M. *Essays and Essay-Writing*. The Atlantic Monthly Press. *Furnace and I* and *Thoughts while Getting Settled*.

Thoreau, Henry David. *On Walking*, from *Excursions*. Scott, Foresman and Company.

Warner, Frances Lester. *Snow on the Beach*, from *Surprising the Family*. Houghton Mifflin Company.

Warner, Frances Lester. *Supervised Suicide*, from *Groups and Couples*. Houghton Mifflin Company.

Young, Filson. *Going Away and Arriving*, from *Letters from Solitude*. Chapman and Hall, Ltd., London.

B. Opinions, Notions, and Points of View

By no large stretch of the imagination the words in this title may be considered, at least for our purpose, as synonymous. A notion has doubtless less weight and a viewpoint has probably more than an opinion; but either or any will serve to name the mental twist that helps to produce this sort of informal essay. An ability to laugh at the world is behind all such essays just as it was behind the *Tatler* and the *Spectator* of Addison and Steele, who made themselves and their periodicals by this very gift. An overly serious and didactic mind can neither conceive nor execute this essay. It takes, in Miss Repplier's words, the combination of a sad heart and a gay temper. Strongly as the writer may feel upon the matter of the subject, he yet must be able to conceal his impatience and disgust under a veil of humor. Prejudice, but not too much, a sense of balance, above all a sense of incongruity—these are the necessary ingredients.

With essays of this type the Contributors' Club of the *Atlantic Monthly* and the Lion's Mouth of *Harper's Magazine* have long delighted us. From the latter source come Frederick L. Allen's *These Intelligence Tests* and Robert Palfrey Utter's *School Ahead—Go Slow*. Without doubt Mr. Allen's essay arises from the fact that he is quite skeptical as to the thorough efficacy of the modern intelligence test and not a little amused by it; and just as surely Mr. Utter's reflects his honest opinion that much time is wasted in our public schools; but rather than be didactic both have wisely chosen to accomplish their purposes by being funny. Within Henry W. Nevinson's farewell words to us there doubtless lurked satire, accusation, and impatience as well as affection and tolerance; in every sentence there is something to think about; and yet taken as a whole, the essay does not leave the impression of being intolerant, didactic, or overly serious. Stark Young's *Citizen Tom*, which, one will discover, is largely narrative, accomplishes with ease and humor three things: the arraignment of a certain type of college president, an attack on a pernicious and widespread theory of college education, and the presentation of an ideal of success. And finally among the student essays Geraldine Bailey's *On the Slavery of Confidantes* conceals by playful and much exaggerated humor what are doubtless her honest and exasperated convictions.

Essays of this type afford a chance for the expression of all manner of mental attitudes. They are more nearly "timely" than any other kind of informal essays. And their popularity was assured two centuries and more ago when Dick Steele invented them.

THESE INTELLIGENCE TESTS [1]

BY

Frederick L. Allen

LAST October I had to take a literacy test. I had recently moved to New York State, and it appeared that I could not vote in the election unless I either produced a school or college diploma or certificate, or passed a literacy test; and though I searched the house from top to bottom, not a single certificate could I find. I found documents which to my simple mind seemed to bear on the case, such as college class reports with my name in them, and letters which mentioned my being in the publishing business (a fact which ought to establish at least a fair presumption in my favor); yet when I took them to the local schoolhouse and showed them to the State of New York as embodied in the person of its authorized agent, the schoolmistress, I was told they wouldn't do. The law said certificates, and these were not certificates. So I laughed a little nervously and sat down in the schoolroom to take the test, in a tiny chair before a tiny desk designed for a child of eight, and a little deficient in knee room for a child of thirty-four.

It was a formidable paper which the schoolmistress set before me. First I had to write my name and address, which I did with great care.

[1] Reprinted by kind permission of the author and of *Harper's Magazine.*

Then came a series of detailed directions to the effect that I was to read the paragraph of text which followed and write out the answers to some questions bearing on it. The paragraph began somewhat as follows:

Theodore Roosevelt was a great American. His letters to his children have been collected in a book since his death. He was interested in animals and birds. He read many books and magazines. . . .

It ran on in this sprightly and coherent style for some distance. Then came the questions:

1. Who was a great American?
2. What has been done to his letters to his children since his death?
3. What was he interested in?
4. What did he read?

And so forth.

I started to answer the first question when suddenly (as sometimes happens) a thought struck me.

One of the candidates for Governor of New York State in the coming election was named Theodore Roosevelt—and here were humble citizens like myself, of doubtful literacy, being subtly subjected to propaganda on his behalf. Was I to submit to any such nefarious scheme? I was not. I resolved to write:

1. Alfred E. Smith; and still is.

They would throw me out of the schoolhouse for an illiterate fellow, but I would appeal the case. If necessary I would carry it to the Supreme Court, where able counsel would argue brilliantly that

Alfred E. Smith; and still is was a demonstrably literate reply. There would be a triumphant vindication, and—

But suddenly I cooled. By that time Election Day would be past, and I should have lost my vote. No, there was a better way. So very firmly I seized my pencil and wrote *Theodore Roosevelt*. I received a certificate of literacy, and a few weeks later I went to the polls—and you all know the result.

I had almost forgotten the incident when the other day I picked up a set of the intelligence tests prepared by the learned ones of Columbia University for the selection of young Columbians. As I looked at them I marveled again—as I had marveled that day in the schoolroom—at the abject docility of mind which so many examiners seem to expect of their victims. To them there is only one right answer to any question—the one they had in mind when they framed it—and all others are wrong. If they want you to write *Theodore Roosevelt*, write it you must or flunk.

With most of the Columbia tests I had no quarrel. There were printed alphabets in which you were told to cross out the letter just after A and draw a line under the second letter after K; there were nice little problems in arithmetic, and pictures of rabbits with one ear missing in which you had to point out what was the matter with the rabbit. But soon appeared a lot of questions of a different sort. Each of these questions had several answers appended to it. The miserable examinee was instructed to mark a cross before the "best answer" to each question. No chance for argument; he would be given credit if he picked the right answer and lose credit if he picked the wrong one. For example:

When you are out of funds, should you—
get to work and earn
borrow from your friends
write home to your people
steal

Now what on earth is the "best answer" to that question? I am willing to concede that the worst is *steal*. But as between the other three, it seems to me a toss-up, with the wise selection depending on the circumstances. Presumably *get to work and earn* is the answer favored on Morningside Heights: but to the average subfreshman I should certainly recommend writing home to his people, and to myself I should recommend borrowing, and then evening things up by striking the editor for more cash for my next contribution. Yet apparently there is no chance for the examinee to rise in his wrath and say, "That depends." He must pick the "right answer."

Here is another:

If you are lost in the forest in the daytime, what is the thing to do?
go straight ahead to a big tree
hurry to the nearest house you know of
sit down and cry
use the sun or compass for a guide

Now here is a very pretty problem, on which whole chapters could be written (and have been). The orthodox Boy Scout would say, *Use the sun or a compass for a guide;* but the only time I ever got lost in a forest the sun was well hidden by clouds and I had no compass—which shows that the kind of answer which will get you into Columbia won't always get you out of the woods. The fellow who would get lost in plain sunshine with a compass in his pocket would be such a nut that he ought to be admitted to a good safe campus and kept there.

There is something to be said for the answer, *Hurry to the nearest house you know of.* I happen to live in a thoroughly wooded suburb, a section so wooded that the real-estate agents sometimes pleasantly refer to it as a forest; and often visitors have told me that they got thoroughly mixed up driving around in the network of roads and succeeded in finding where I lived only by inquiring for me at the nearest house. Ought I to say to them, "Tut, tut, you should have used the sun or a compass for a guide"?

There are occasions when I should recommend going straight ahead to a big tree, climbing it, and getting a good long look at the surrounding country, being very careful—and here is a real test of intelligence—not to climb out on the end of a dead branch. But after all the most delightfully satisfactory answer is *sit down and cry.* There are few enough opportunities for a good long cry in this busy modern life of ours; so if you are all alone and there is nobody to tell you to move on, why not settle right down on a stump and enjoy yourself? Besides, after you have cried for a little while you may have a good idea about what to do next (such as not climbing out on the dead branch), or the sun may come out, or somebody may hear you and come along with a compass, or even point out the moss growing on the north side of a Doctor of Philosophy, thus enabling you to make your triumphal exit according to the best Boy Scout traditions.

In these tests there are also a number of sentences which the victim is to mark T if they could possibly be true and F if they could not; and several of these sentences seem to me equally debatable. For instance, take this one: *Coming down the hill on his bicycle the chain broke, but he rode back again to get it fixed.* I can see the examiners shaking their heads and saying, "Impossible." But who said it was a bicycle chain which broke? In my version of the incident our friend was carrying something heavy by means of a chain (very likely a dangling participle such as the examiner perpetrated in the sentence above) when the chain broke. No damage was done to his bicycle or any part thereof. Will Nicholas Murray Butler raise his right hand and swear to me that our friend could not ride back again (to the English department, let us say) to get the damage repaired?

Here is another: *Fearing that he might waken her patient by his impudent talk, the nurse gave the detested dummy what he wished.* "Impossible!" goes up the cry at Morningside Heights. But what if we were to tell them the whole sordid story? As I recall it, there were four men in the convalescent ward of a hospital, playing bridge. As the game progressed, one of them (who was not taking part in it at the moment) wandered off to the private corridor and, hateful creature that he was, demanded a kiss of a pretty nurse. Whereupon, fearing that he might awaken her patient by his impudent talk, the nurse gave the detested dummy what he wished. I am not quite sure what happened next, though it is my impression that the patient—a former Yale football star—had one eye open all the time and,

ʾdespite his enfeebled condition, got up and spoiled the dummy for any more bridge that night, subsequently marrying the nurse, much to the regret of several eligible internes. Is it impossible? It is not. Yet if you, ardent bridge player that you are, were taking the examination and marked that sentence as possible, the scoring clerks would set you down as unintelligent.

I have nothing against intelligence tests or literacy tests or any other sort of tests as such. Personally I find them as diverting and twice as ingenious as cross-word puzzles. When I see a question like *a man whose salary is $16 a week spends $10 a week, in how many weeks can he save $300?* I like to see how soon I can get the answer, which is, of course, 50 weeks or more, depending on (a) his private income, and (b) the size of the doctor's bills resulting from his attempt to live on an insufficient diet. But I do wish examiners would try not to be so arbitrary. Young John Keats was a pretty intelligent boy and as Keats, '14, might have been spoken of as one of the more successful members of the Alumni Club of London; but what chance would he have had of picking the "best answer" if he had been up against something like this (which isn't from a Columbia test but might be)?

Mark a cross before the best answer to this question: What can ail thee, knight at arms, alone and palely loitering?

I have mislaid my compass

I have indigestion and my companions have deserted me

I voted for the Republican candidate for Governor of New York

I met a lady in the meads.

SCHOOL AHEAD—GO SLOW [1]

BY
Robert Palfrey Utter

TOUSLEHEAD came breezily into the study just at the acme of one of my most delicately adjusted sentences, and announced that he had to "make a report" on Daniel Boone. If he had demanded the price of the movies, he would have been unanimously ejected. But I pride myself on the neat little historical collection in the northwest corner of the study almost as much as on the turn of my sentences. To be sure, I have never recaptured the first fine careless calculation of the one he shattered, but I should rather lose it forever than send a boy of mine to school with a bunch of withered encyclopedia stuff on a topic like that. So Touslehead and I spent a happy afternoon and evening (at least I was happy) rummaging among my almost unique pamphlets and maps. I managed to slip in a suggestion of my highly original theory about George Rogers Clark and Simon Kenton and a few other good old scouts, and sent him off next morning with a very spiffy little report such as no other boy in his class could have turned out—unless he had come to me for it. Of course, in the Carter Brown Library and there is—an almost unknown collection in Worcester—however . . . I could hardly wait—till Wednesday to hear how his report hit the class. I even meditated

[1] Reprinted by kind permission of the author and of *Harper's Magazine*.

trying to slip into the room just to see that history teacher's face.

On Wednesday afternoon I found him working over a drawing board, his arms to the elbows subdued to what he worked in, namely, colored inks. When I asked him about the report, he said they hadn't had any history that day because it was Fire Prevention Week, and they had been listening to lectures from members of the Fire Department on how much it cost the insurance companies every time there was a fire. I was a little disappointed at first, but I suggested that the delay was not wholly unfortunate since it would enable us to add evidence to show that Cresap was not responsible after all for the murder of Logan's family. Touslehead said that—aw—the report was all right; anyway he had to make a colored poster to show what happens when you light a match to see whether there is any more gasoline in the tank. I looked over his shoulder. The cartoon was rather crude, but it was vivacious and highly colored. I suggested that if he were to add an "awk!" or a "glub!" or words to that effect, tied to the victim's nose with a string, he might sell the drawing to a Sunday supplement. He explained with some heat that an explosion which was quite harmless in the supplement was deadly during Fire Prevention Week, and retorted by pointing out that my desk was a fire risk which menaced the community. I had to admit that it is piled pretty high with papers, but I reminded him that I can always draw out a slide to write on, and it always keeps itself clear because it dumps automatically when you shove it in; besides, all my ash trays are fireproof,

and I can always tell anyway when the papers
get on fire because they smell so different from
tobacco. I don't think he heard my defense; he
was too busy adding glories of orange and yellow
to his towering flames. "Gee, Dad," he remarked,
"I wisht there would be a fire like when the lumber
yard burned down—only with people jumping out
of the windows. Did you ever see one with people
jumping out of the windows?"

By the following Wednesday my eagerness had
somewhat abated; still, as soon as I decently could
after I heard Touslehead come in, I strolled casually
into his room and found him at work over his desk,
which swam before my eyes as a vague welter of
raffia, putty, toothpicks, and tinsel string. It
seemed that there had been no regular lessons;
all the pupils had been busy making "these things";
he had not finished, and had brought the work
home. His concept of the work was that he was to
reinforce a lump of putty with toothpicks and
swathe it in raffia wrapped and interwoven with
tinsel string. His explanation of the use of the
finished product was that it was "to give to an
orphan asylum." It appeared that Mrs. Orra
Kidwell wanted ten thousand of them because she
was driving a campaign to put one in the hands of
every orphan in every asylum in the state. My
memory told me nothing of Mrs. Orra Kidwell save
that she was the president of the Women's Club, but
I learned from the paper that evening that she had
been "prominently mentioned" as a candidate for the
presidency of the State Affiliation of Women's Clubs.

The next week was "Buy a Prune Week." This
year the Amalgamated Prune Producers did not

succeed in making it a national affair, but another time they expect to have every school child in the United States live mentally on prunes for a week, and physically if possible. As a state affair, the newspapers declared the week a success. In science, each child dissected a dead prune and learned the most intimate secrets of its anatomy. There was a debate in the High School auditorium as to whether the prune was the tree of knowledge or the tree from which Adam and Eve made their (alleged) fig-leaf clothes. The affirmative proved beyond a reasonable doubt that a prune diet was a short cut to wisdom, but the negative won by a striking demonstration of prune-leaf clothes on living models. In history classes, the children traced the uses of the prune in boarding houses of all ages and races from the dynasty of Thotmes III to Tipton, Indiana. In English class, each child received a prune and wrote an essay on how best to use it. With all this the children were too much occupied to learn anything, so I did not so much as ask Touslehead about Daniel Boone.

I had no better luck the next week either. It was "Own Your Own Home Week." Touslehead told me that "conspicuous realtors" were delivering lectures in all the schools. From their talks he gathered that if, when you are nine years old you pay ninety-nine cents down, and thereafter pay nine cents a day, when you are ninety you will find yourself the proud possessor of an option on a lot either in the Hopewell Addition or in the cemetery, he wasn't quite sure which. I don't know exactly what a "realtor" is, and I have no dictionary young enough to tell me, but I infer that he is a promising

sort of person whose mind is rather hazy about all terms except financial ones, for he naïvely confuses the idea of owning a home with that of buying a house.

By that time we had passed the middle of October, and for a week all lessons were suspended to prepare for the important festival of Halloween. Half the children in the city schools spent the week cutting figures of cats and witches out of black paper and pasting them on orange paper. The other half cut figures from orange paper and pasted them on black paper. The amount of paper destroyed must have been enormous. I haven't mathematics enough to calculate what it would have done if placed end to end, but it must have contributed hugely to the deforestation of the continent, and added another figure to the fortunes of paper manufacturers. Also, there is the destruction of sheets and pillowcases to make costumes for the evening exercises, the destruction of pumpkins in the attempt to make lanterns and the ultimate purchase of imitation pumpkin lanterns, the destruction of gates, fences, signs, and other movable property, and the sale of useless dewdads in black and orange from the window displays of the small retail merchants. When I think of all this, I can see clearly that the Halloween agitation in the public schools as measured in hard cash by hard citizens is worth more than history and spelling. But I do not see clearly what the connection is between black cats and All Souls, and Touslehead was so absorbed that week in the work of destruction that I hadn't the heart to ask him.

For the rest of the calendar year the children

were working too hard with preparations for Thanksgiving and Christmas to do anything with formal lessons. Besides, the paint manufacturers came along with a "Save the Surface Week" in which the pupils learned that the beauty of a building is only skin deep, and if you use up enough paint on the outside, the plumbing will take care of itself. Then the plumbers came back with a "Plumb to the Bottom Week" and the doctrine that good digestion is better than cosmetics, and the house whose plumbing is open and aboveboard need never be painted. So it was not until Christmas vacation that I had a chance to ask Touslehead about Daniel Boone. He looked at me blankly, and asked, "Who's Daniel Boone?"

There was once a time when the schoolboy of tender age was taught to proclaim at suitable intervals that his heart was God's little garden. Does the Gardener walk there still in the cool of the evening? Or is the garden now given over to propagandists and other advertisers for an experiment station? If so, I think I must take a hand myself, and teach the young idea how to shoot in self-defense.

FAREWELL TO AMERICA [1]

BY

Henry W. Nevinson

IN mist and driving snow the towers of New York fade from view. The great ship slides down the river. Already the dark, broad seas gloom before her. Good-by, most beautiful of modern cities! Good-by to glimmering spires and lighted bastions, dreamlike as the castles and cathedrals of a romantic vision, though mainly devoted to commerce and finance! Good-by to thin films of white steam that issue from central furnaces and flit in dissolving wreaths around those precipitous heights! Good-by to heaven-piled offices, so clean, so warm, where lovely stenographers, with silk stockings and powdered faces, sit leisurely at work or converse in charming ease! Good-by, New York! I am going home. I am going to an ancient city of mean and moldering streets, of ignoble coverts for mankind, extended monotonously over many miles; of grimy smoke clinging closer than a blanket; of smudgy typists who know something of powder, but little of silk and less of leisure and charming ease. Good-by, New York! I am going home.

Good-by to beautiful "apartments" and "homes"! Good-by to windows looking far over the city as

[1] Excerpt from *Farewell to America,* by H. W. Nevinson. New York: The Viking Press. Copyright, 1922, by B. W. Huebsch, Inc.

243

from a mountain peak! Good-by to central heating
and radiators, fit symbols of the hearts they warm!
Good-by to frequent and well-appointed bathrooms,
the glory of America's art! Good-by to suburban
gardens running into each other without hedge or
fence to separate friend from friend or enemy from
enemy! Good-by to shady verandas where rocking
chairs stand ranged in rows, ready for reading the
voluminous Sunday papers and the *Saturday Evening
Post!* Good-by, America! I am going home. I
am going to a land where every man's house is
his prison—a land of open fires and chilly rooms and
frozen water pipes, of washing stands and slop
pails, and one bath per household at the most; a
land of fences and hedges and walls, where people
sit aloof, and see no reason to make themselves
seasick by rocking upon the shore. Good-by,
America! I am going home.

Good-by to the copious meals—the early grapefruit, the "cereals," the eggs broken in a glass!
Good-by to oysters, large and small, to celery and
olives beside the soup, to "sea food," to sublimated
viands, to bleeding duck, to the salad course, to
the "individual pie" or the thick wedge of apple
pie, to the invariable slab of ice cream, to the coffee, also bland with cream, to iced water and home-
brewed alcohol! I am going to the land of joints
and roots and solid pudding; the land of ham-and-
eggs and violent tea; the land where oysters are
good for suicides alone, and where cream is seldom
seen; the land where mustard grows and whisky
flows. Good-by, America! I am going home.

Good-by to the long stream of motors—"limousines" or "flivvers!" Good-by to the signal

lights upon Fifth Avenue, gold, crimson, and green; the sudden halt when the red light shines, as though at a magic word an enchanted princess had fallen asleep; the hurried rush for the leisurely lunch at noon, the deliberate appearance of hustle and bustle in business, however little is accomplished, the Jews, innumerable as the Red Sea sand! Good-by to outside staircases for escape from fire! Good-by to scrappy suburbs littered with rubbish of old boards, tin pails, empty cans, and boots! Good-by to standardized villages and small towns, alike in litter, in ropes of electric wires along the streets, in clanking trolleys, in chapels, stores, railway stations, Main Streets, and isolated wooden houses flung at random over the countryside! Good-by to miles of advertisement imploring me in ten-foot letters to eat somebody's cod-fish ("No Bones!"), or smoke somebody's cigarettes ("They Satisfy!"), or sleep vith innocence in the "Faultless Night-gown!" Good-by to the long trains where one smokes ir a lavatory, and sleeps at night upon a shelf screened with heavy green curtains and heated with stifling air, while over your head or under your back a baby yells and the mother tosses moaning, until at last you reach your "stopping-off place," and a semi-negro sweeps you down with a little broom, as in a supreme rite of unction! Good-by to the house that is labeled "One Hundred Years Old," for the amazement of mortality! Good-by to thin woods, and fields inclosed with casual pales, old hoops, and lengths of wire! I am going to a land of the policeman's finger, where the horse and the bicycle still drag out a lingering life; a land of persistent and silent toil; a land of old villages and towns as little like each other as one woman is like the next; a land where trains are short, and one seldom sleeps in them, for in any direction within a day they will reach a sea; a land of vast and ancient trees, of houses time-honored three centuries ago, of cathedrals that have been growing for a thousand years, and of village churches built while people believed in God. Good-by, America! I am going home.

Good-by to the land of a new language in growth, of split infinitives and crossbred words; the land where a dinner jacket is a "Tuxedo," a spittoon a "cuspidor"; where your opinion is called your "reaction," and where "vamp," instead of meaning an improvised accompaniment to a song, means a dangerous female! Good-by to the land where grotesque exaggeration is called humor, and people gape in bewilderment at irony, as a bullock gapes at a dog straying in his field! Good-by to the land where strangers say "Glad to meet you, sir," and really seem glad; where children incessantly whine and wail their little desires, and never grow much older; where men keep their trousers up with belts that run through loops, and women have to bathe in stockings! I am going to a land of ancient speech, where we still say "record" and "concord" for "recud" and "concud"; where "unnecessarily" and "extraordinarily" must be taken at one rush, as hedge-ditch-and-rail in the hunting field; where we do not "commute" or "check" or "page," but "take a season," and "register," and "send a boy round"; where we never say we are glad to meet a stranger, and seldom are; where humor is under-statement, and irony is our habitual resource in danger or distress; where children are told they are meant to be seen and not heard; where it is bad form to express emotion, and suspenders are a strictly feminine article of attire. Good by, America! I am going home.

Good-by to the multitudinous papers, indefinite of opinion, crammed with insignificant news, and asking you to continue a first-page article on page 23, column 5! Good-by to the weary platitude accepted as wisdom's latest revelation! Good-by to the docile audiences that lap rhetoric for sustenance! Good-by to politicians contending for aims more practical than principles! Good-by to Republicans and Democrats, distinguishable only by mutual hatred! Good-by to the land where Liberals are thought dangerous, and Radicals show red! Where Mr. Gompers was called a Socialist, and Mr. Asquith would seem advanced! A land too large for concentrated indignation; a land where wealth beyond the dreams of British profiteers dwells, dresses, gorges, and luxuriates, emulated and unashamed! I am going to a land of politics violently divergent; a land where even Coalitions cannot coalesce; where meetings break up in turbulent disorder, and no platitude avails to soothe the savage breast; a land fierce for personal freedom, and indignant with rage for justice; a land where wealth is taxed out of sight, or for very shame strives to disguise its luxury; a land where an ancient order of feudal families is passing away, and Labor leaders whom Wall Street would shudder at are hailed by Lord Chancellors as the very fortifications of security. Good-by, America! I am going home.

Good-by to prose chopped up to look like verse! Good-by to the indiscriminating appetite which gulps lectures as opiates, and "printed matter" as literature! Good-by to the wizards and witches who claim to psychoanalyze my complexes, inhibitions, and silly dreams! Good-by to the exuberant religious or fantastic beliefs by which unsatisfied mankind still strives desperately to penetrate beyond the flaming bulwarks of the world! Good-by, Americans! I am going to your spiritual home.

CITIZEN TOM [1]

Stark Young

My first sight of President C— was in the telephone booth of a railway junction. "Hello,
President C— speaking," he said. And then a
moment later a tall, broad man in a blue serge
suit with heavily padded shoulders, his hair red,
his features large and decisive and full of a kind of
foolish strength, emerged and stood looking up and
down the station, large, firm, like a swelling piece
of civic virtue. I knew the outlines of the president's career. He had been first a baseball player
of renown, he had then entered the ministry, and
now after several years of service had become the
president of a New England college. In this state,
I had been told, his athletic piety and direct manhood had made him adored. There were, as might
be expected nowadays, some restless and Reddish
students who rebelled at President C—'s quality
and influence; the majority of the college body took
him for their ideal.

President C— and I became acquainted not
long after this first sight I had of him. We sat
together on a government educational commission,
a left-over from the war. He never talked easily
or was able to flow into simple human connections

From *Encaustics* by Stark Young. Reprinted by kind permission of the author.

with other men, but he frequently conducted a monologue or crashed into debate. And so, in the course of things, I had a chance to learn his theory of education.

I am not sure that I ever understood it quite, but the gist of it, as I gathered when I stripped it of its eloquence and vigor, was this: The purpose of education is making men. A man among men. It makes leaders of men, however, also. The ideal education develops both mind and body, *mens sana in corpore sano.* Men learn to mix by being at college. Nothing teaches them to mix with their fellow men so well as athletics, as clean contest. Let us never forget the noble exercise of the mind! President C— himself might never have been able to mingle with men if it had not been for baseball. It had saved him. College men learn to be men not so much through book learning as through their freshman experiences, the rough and tumble of the dormitories. College connections are valuable in after-life. The purpose of education is to make of young men citizens.

These, as the world must know by now, for he has expanded them into many addresses, were President C—'s theories of education.

I have a friend, or rather a friend of the family, who sent her son last year to President C—'s college, partly because it is well known, partly to get him into the country and out of New York. Tom, the son, by some maternal engineering, by caresses and spanks and bribes, had been got through preparatory schools, and rather miraculously past the test of college entrance · requirements. That was last year.

A week or two ago I met President C— on the street; he is naturally on another commission and had run down to New York for the meeting. We talked as we walked along Park Avenue. Finally I asked:

"What about my friend Mrs. L—'s boy, President C—? He is at your college, isn't he?"

A look of disgust came over the president's face.

"L—," he said, "oh, that chap? I think I remember him; I make an effort to keep our men individually in mind. I was gravely disappointed in the course he pursued in college. You can see he is a shy boy, with some ability, the dean tells me, if he would apply himself. But he made a total failure of it. He neglected his grades. He did not know how to mix with the men. He took no part in athletics or the life of the college. No fraternity invited him to join. He wasted the year. In the spring he decided to leave. I urged him to remain. Buckle down, I said. Play the game. If he had stayed, a fraternity would have asked him to be a member undoubtedly, he was not a bad-looking youth. But he was unapproachable apparently. He disregarded my opinion and left college."

"But suppose," I ventured, "Tom never wanted to be one of the college men? Why distort what he is to be like the others? There must be a man now and then who learns little from fraternity life, or from having freshmen rub molasses in his hair and keep him up all night, don't you think? For many men your college scheme may be quite right, but why not grant men who may be different their own kind of thing?"

"This college experience will teach them the

life of the race," the president said—though here
I can only quote his words without quite following
his meaning: "L— never gave himself the chance."

"The chance for what, President C—?" I
asked.

"A chance for learning to live among his fellow
men."

"But what's the use of learning to live with men
if you can't live with yourself?"

President C— looked at me patiently and power-
fully like a big, fine, influential spirit. I could see
him judging me as a man of little weight. I shifted
the subject slightly. I asked what Tom was doing
this year, if he had not returned to college.

"L—," the president replied, "so the dean tells
me, wrote in answer to the questionnaire that the
college sends out in August, that he had entered a
theater school."

President C— was silent and I looked at him.
Silent and swollen like that, he seemed to me like a
platitude at prayer.

But I knew that what had happened was that
Tom, timid, wrapped in his own world, dreaming,
vague, useless if you like, had got under the president's skin. It hit the president's vanity to fail
of even so negligible a worshiper.

"And how has he done?" I asked.

"Now that I can't tell you. We can probably
imagine."

"Is it a good theater school, I wonder?" I said,
tentatively.

President C— had no way of knowing that either.
But he told me the exact name of the place— Tom,
I reflected, had indeed impressed him.

"But that," I said, "is only around the corner more or less. What do you think, shall we run in and see what is going on?"

President C— looked at me a moment and decided.

"By the living God I will," he said. I knew of old that admirable oath of his, in which by putting in the living you take out the profanity. "I've never seen one of these places."

Neither had I and I said as much. And we started off to find Tom's school.

But I had seen art schools full of students. I began to think gleefully of those students coming on the run every morning and staying till the last light had faded and the janitors pulled down the blinds. And then the talk, talk, talk, looking at one another's work, criticizing, intense, happy with the head and hands working together, believing in art, in the future, delighting in the world. Many of these students were without talent, many lazy, many destined to clerkships; but for the time they moved in a happy, drifting, believing atmosphere. Then I thought of the colleges, with their muddled aims, their exhorting grades, their rules, degrees and prizes to keep the thing going. I thought of those bored groups of men around fraternity house fires, the victrola grinding, tobacco smoke rising—a scene sweetly remembered years afterward, but at the time rather flat—how little it connected with the life of the mind, with the life of human thought! Some of these college men study, some love learning, some find stimulation in a handful of professors who are hated by the faculty at large. But all are encouraged by the dean, the alumni, the fraternities and the class spirit, to hold college offices, to be leaders with buttons and pennants, to compete, to fill the time. The art school was busy, but had to get on with mere art and high hopes; it had no baseball, class honors, clubs, or letters for sweaters and caps. These sweet thoughts made me feel more gently toward President C—. I was relying on the tone of the theater school to take him down.

We entered the school to the sound of a tremendous hammering and talking. In the hallway there was a class in diction. In the auditorium itself there was a pantomime rehearsing; and on the stage some one was directing a scene from a play. Over in a far corner they were painting scenery, and two men lay sprawled on the floor around a drawing. We were presently introduced to the director. Was it always like this, we asked? Was everyone always at it? From nine in the morning until eleven at night, said the director. There were lessons in literature, in diction, fencing, dancing, stage decoration. There were rehearsals, and every night there was a performance of one-act plays, for the students must get the theater endurance. Few of them would ever be distinguished artists, but everyone worked, there was so much to be learned.

And how was Mr. Tom L— getting on? we asked.

The director beamed. Mr. L—, he said, was one of the lights of the school. He came early and stayed late. He was insatiable, he killed himself trying to learn everything. And his acting was very promising; he had in comedy a certain wistful quality that ought to go far. We might find Tom, the director said, in the basement somewhere; he was experimenting with stage lighting.

We came upon Tom on his knees with a reflecting apparatus. He was rather pale and a little thinner perhaps but his eyes were shining. He gesticulated, swept out a notebook with designs, he led us around to his machines, he chattered about his plans. "Believe me," he said, "it's a great life if you don't weaken."

Meanwhile I watched President C—. He was very reserved, very kind, in the few things he said he took a tone of national encouragement. What a big, manly spirit he represented there among the lighting machines and painted sets! And I could see that he still wanted to be the boy's ideal.

As for me I was shamelessly thrilled over seeing a man find what he wanted. I felt encouraged, set up, sentimental. On the street again a moment later I could still see that young face, a dreamer's, an artist's. He was like a blossoming tree, he was like a child listening to music.

I lost my sense of humor and began to say to President C— how splendid it was to see a chap discover like this his education and his happiness together.

The president said nothing.

I persisted. Did he not think so?

"Probably," he assented. "But still—"

"But still—?"

The president, knitting his brows together, measured his words, making me at the same moment how grateful that he should run so true to form!

"I question his judgment, nevertheless," he said. "What of his citizenship?"

A LIST OF BOOKS PARTICULARLY ADAPTED FOR USE AS MODELS

Beerbohm, Max. *An Infamous Brigade*, from *More*. Dodd, Mead and Company.

Broun, Heywood. *The Fifty-First Dragon*, from *Seeing Things at Night*. Harcourt, Brace and Company.

Cabell, James Branch. *Beyond Life* (two concluding sections). Robert M. McBride and Company.

Crothers, Samuel McChord. *The Perils of the Literate*, from *The Dame School of Experience*. Houghton Mifflin Company.

Dickinson, G. Lowes. *The Modern Pulpit*, from *Appearances*. Doubleday, Page & Company.

Galsworthy, John. *Castles in Spain*, in *The Yale Review*, October, 1921.

Hyde, Agnes Rogers. *The Modern School*, in *The Lion's Mouth*, *Harper's*, December, 1927.

Lamb, Charles. *Grace Before Meat*, from *The Essays of Elia*.

Leacock, Stephen. *Oxford as I See It*, from *My Discovery of England*. Dodd, Mead and Company.

Repplier, Agnes. *The Charm of the Familiar*, from *Essays in Miniature*. Houghton Mifflin Company.

Stevenson, Robert Louis. *An Apology for Idlers*, from *Essays*. Charles Scribner's Sons.

Tanner, William M. *Essay and Essay-Writing*. The Atlantic Monthly Press. *The Flavor of Things* and *The Passing of Friendship*.

Warner, Frances Lester. *Surprising the Family*, from *Surprising the Family*. Houghton Mifflin Company.

Woolf, Virginia. *Illness—An Unexploited Mine*, in *The Forum*, April, 1926.

C. Nature Essays

Nature inspired the writers of prose long before the essay broke its formal bonds and became the easier, more delightful type of writing that it is to-day. Bacon, it will be recalled, wrote *On Gardens*, and Sir Thomas Browne in the middle of the seventeenth century composed in his *Garden of Cyrus* a beautiful treatise on the "mystical Mathematicks" discernible in leaves, buds, and branches. In the last century, influenced no doubt by the spread of scientific knowledge, the nature essay immeasurably widened alike its range and its appeal until to-day he who would write such essays has an almost illimitable field for exploration and enjoyment.

The four essays reprinted here suggest the width and range of this subject for the essay writer. Like Richard Jefferies, you may choose to depict fully and accurately, with as many comments and digressions as you please, some one thing like the grass in July, hollyhocks by the garden fence, frost on a window-pane. Or, eschewing that method as not suited to your more philosophical temperament, you may follow the example of Hilaire Belloc and deal with the efficacy to mankind of some feature of nature. Christopher Morley in *Clouds* would awaken our sense of mystery or, perhaps better, record his own; in *Winter Mist* Robert Palfrey Utter, good-humoredly scorning the hockey players, sees himself like the moon as "the center of a circle of vague limit and vaguer content;" and among the student essays Elizabeth Botsford has portrayed the river of her childhood in varying times and seasons of the day and year and has suggested its beneficent and mysterious influence upon her life.

Or—but why cheat you of the thrill of discovering a dozen other ways of approach and execution. Only we cannot forbear the suggestion that Hardy in his novels, especially in *Far from the Madding Crowd*, *The Return of the Native*, and *Tess of the D'Urbervilles* is a treasure house of ideas and of moods which no would-be essayist of nature should allow himself to miss.

THE JULY GRASS [1]

BY

Richard Jefferies

A JULY fly went sideways over the long grass. His wings made a burr about him like a net, beating so fast they wrapped him round with a cloud. Every now and then, as he flew over the trees of grass, a taller one than common stopped him, and there he clung, and then the eye had time to see the scarlet spots—the loveliest color—on his wings. The wind swung the burnet and loosened his hold, and away he went again over the grasses, and not one jot did he care if they were *Poa* or *Festuca* or *Bromus* or *Hordeum*, or any other name. Names were nothing to him, all he had to do was to whirl his scarlet spots about in the brilliant sun, rest when he liked, and go on again. I wonder whether it is a joy to have bright scarlet spots, and to be clad in the purple and gold of life; is the color felt by the creature that wears it? The rose, restful of a dewy morn before the sunbeams have topped the garden wall, must feel a joy in its own fragrance, and know the exquisite hue of its stained petals. The rose sleeps in its beauty.

The fly whirls his scarlet-spotted wings about and splashes himself with sunlight, like the children on the sands. He thinks not of the grass and sun; he

[1] From *Field and Hedgerow*. By permission of Longmans, Green & Co.

does not heed them at all—and that is why he is
so happy—any more than the barefoot children
ask why the sea is there, or why it does not quite
dry up when it ebbs. He is unconscious; he lives
without thinking about living; and if the sunshine
were a hundred hours long, still it would not be
long enough. No, never enough of sun and slid-
ing shadows that come like a hand over the table
to lovingly reach our shoulder, never enough of the
grass that smells sweet as a flower, not if we could
live years and years equal in number to the tides
that have ebbed and flowed counting backwards
four years to every day and night, backward still
till we found out which came first, the night or the
day. The scarlet-dotted fly knows nothing of the
names of the grasses that grow here where the
sward nears the sea, and thinking of him I have
decided not to willfully seek to learn any more of
their names -either. My big grass book I have
left at home, and the dust is settling on the gold
of the binding. I have picked a handful this morning of which I know nothing. I will sit here on the
turf and the scarlet-dotted flies shall pass over me,
as if I too were but a grass. I will not think, I will
be unconscious, I will live.

Listen! that was the low sound of a summer
wavelet striking the uncovered rock over there
beneath in the green sea. All things that are beautiful are found by chance, like everything that is good.
Here by me is a praying-rug, just wide enough to
kneel on, of the richest gold inwoven with crimson.
All the Sultans of the East never had such beauty
as that to kneel on. It is, indeed, too beautiful to
kneel on, for the life in these golden flowers must

not be broken down even for that purpose. They must not be defaced, not a stem bent; it is more reverent not to kneel on them, for this carpet prays itself. I will sit by it and let it pray for me. It is so common, the bird's-foot lotus, it grows everywhere; yet if I purposely searched for days I should not have found a plot like this, so rich, so golden, so glowing with sunshine. You might pass by it in one stride, yet it is worthy to be thought of for a week and remembered for a year. Slender grasses, branched round about with slenderer boughs, each tipped with pollen and rising in tiers cone-shaped—too delicate to grow tall—cluster at the base of the mound. They dare not grow tall or the wind would snap them. A great grass, stout and thick, rises three feet by the hedge, with a head another foot nearly, very green and strong and bold, lifting itself right up to you; you must say, "What a fine grass!" Grasses whose awns succeed each other alternately; grasses whose tops seem flattened; others drooping over the shorter blades beneath; some that you can only find by parting the heavier growth around them; hundreds and hundreds, thousands and thousands. The kingly poppies on the dry summit of the mound take no heed of these, the populace, their subjects so numerous they cannot be numbered. A barren race they are, the proud poppies, lords of the July field, taking no deep root, but raising up a brilliant blazon of scarlet heraldry out of nothing. They are useless, they are bitter, they are allied to sleep and poison and everlasting night; yet they are forgiven because they are not commonplace. Nothing, no abundance of them, can ever make the poppies commonplace.

There is genius in them, the genius of color, and they are saved. Even when they take the room of the corn we must admire them. The mighty multitude of nations, the millions and millions of the grass stretching away in intertangled ranks, through pasture and mead from shore to shore, have no kinship with these, their lords. The ruler is always a foreigner. From England to China the native born is no king; the poppies are the Normans of the field. One of these on the mound is very beautiful, a width of petal, a clear silkiness of color three shades higher than the rest—it is almost dark with scarlet. I wish I could do something more than gaze at all this scarlet and gold and crimson and green, something more than see it, not exactly to drink it or inhale it, but in some way to make it part of me that I might live it.

The July grasses must be looked for in corners and out-of-the-way places, and not in the broad acres—the scythe has taken them there. By the wayside on the banks of the lane, near the gateway—look, too, in uninteresting places behind incomplete buildings on the mounds cast up from abandoned foundations where speculation has been and gone. There weeds that would not have found resting-place elsewhere grow unchecked, and uncommon species and unusually large growths appear. Like everything else that is looked for, they are found under unlikely conditions. At the back of ponds, just inside the enclosure of woods, angles of corn-fields, old quarries, that is where to find grasses, or by the sea in the brackish marsh. Some of the finest of them grow by the mere roadside; you may look for others up the lanes in the deep ruts, look

too inside the hollow trees by the stream.   In a
morning you may easily garner together a great
sheaf of this harvest.   Cut the larger stems aslant,
like the reeds imitated deep in old green glass.   You
must consider as you gather them the height and
slenderness of the stems, the droop and degree of
curve, the shape and color of the panicle, the dusting
of the pollen, the motion and sway in the wind.
The sheaf you may take home with you, but the
wind that was among it stays without.

ON A GREAT WIND [1]

BY

Hilaire Belloc

IT is an old dispute among men, or rather a dispute
as old as mankind, whether Will be a cause of
things or no; nor is there anything novel in those
moderns who affirm that Will is nothing to the
matter, save their ignorant belief that their affirma-
tion is new.

The intelligent process whereby I know that Will
not seems but is, and can alone be truly and ulti-
mately a cause, is fed with stuff and strengthens sac-
ramentally as it were, whenever I meet, and am
made the companion of, a great wind.

It is not that this lively creature of God is indeed
perfected with a soul; this it would be superstition to believe. It has no more a person than any
other of its material fellows, but in its vagary of
way, in the largeness of its apparent freedom, in
its rush of purpose, it seems to mirror the action
of mighty spirit. When a great wind comes roaring
over the eastern flats toward the North Sea, driving
over the Fens and the Wringland, it is like something of this island that must go out and wrestle
with the water, or play with it in a game or a battle;
and when, upon the western shores, the clouds come
bowling up from the horizon, messengers, outriders,

---

[1] From *First and Last.* Reprinted with the kind permission
of the author.

or comrades of a gale, it is something of the sea
determined to possess the land. The rising and
falling of such power, its hesitations, its renewed
violence, its fatigue and final repose—all these are
symbols of a mind; but more than all the rest, its
exultation! It is the shouting and the hurrahing of
the wind that suits a man.

Note you, we have not many friends. The older
we grow and the better we can sift mankind, the
fewer friends we count, although man lives by
friendship. But a great wind is every man's friend,
and its strength is the strength of good fellowship;
and even doing battle with it is something worthy
and well chosen. If there is cruelty in the sea, and
terror in high places, and malice lurking in profound darkness, there is no one of these qualities
in the wind, but only power. Here is strength too
full for such negations as cruelty, as malice, or as
fear; and that strength in a solemn manner proves
and tests health in our own souls. For with terror
(of the sort I mean—terror of the abyss or panic
at remembered pain, and in general, a losing grip
of the succors of the mind), and with malice, and
with cruelty, and with all the forms of that Evil
which lies in wait for men, there is the savor of
disease. It is an error to think of such things as
power set up in equality against justice and right
living. We were not made for them, but rather for
influences large and soundly poised; we are not
subject to them but to other powers that can always enliven and relieve. It is health in us, I say,
to be full of heartiness and of the joy of the world,
and of whether we have such health our comfort
in a great wind is a good test indeed. No man

spends his day upon the mountains when the wind is out, riding against it or pushing forward on foot through the gale, but at the end of his day feels that he has had a great host about him. It is as though he had experienced armies. The days of high winds are days of innumerable sounds, innumerable in variation of tone and of intensity, playing upon and awakening innumerable powers in man. And the days of high wind are days in which a physical compulsion has been about us and we have met pressure and blows, resisted and turned them; it enlivens us with the simulacrum of war by which nations live, and in the just pursuit of which men in companionship are at their noblest.

It is pretended sometimes (less often perhaps now than a dozen years ago) that certain ancient pursuits congenial to man will be lost to him under his new necessities; thus men sometimes talk foolishly of horses being no longer ridden, houses no longer built of wholesome wood and stone, but of metal; meat no more roasted, but only baked; and even of stomachs grown too weak for wine. There is a fashion of saying these things, and much other nastiness. Such talk is (thank God!) mere folly; for man will always at last tend to his end, which is happiness, and he will remember again to do all those things which serve that end. So it is with the uses of the wind, and especially the using of the wind with sails.

No man has known the wind by any of its names who has not sailed his own boat and felt life in the tiller. Then it is that a man has most to do with the wind, plays with it, coaxes or refuses it, is wary of it all along; yields when he must yield, but comes

up and pits himself again against its violence;
trains it, harnesses it, calls it if it fails him, de-
nounces it if it will try to be too strong, and in
every manner conceivable handles this glorious
playmate.

As for those who say that men did but use the
wind as an instrument for crossing the sea, and that
sails were mere machines to them, either they have
never sailed or they were quite unworthy of sailing.
It is not an accident that the tall ships of every age
of varying fashions so arrested human sight and
seemed so splendid. The whole of man went into
their creation, and they expressed him very well;
his cunning, and his mastery, and his adventurous
heart. For the wind is in nothing more capitally
our friend than in this, that it has been, since men
were men, their ally in the seeking of the unknown
and in their divine thirst for travel which, in its
several aspects—pilgrimage, conquest, discovery,
and, in general, enlargement—is one prime way
whereby man fills himself with being.

I love to think of those Norwegian men who set
out eagerly before the northeast wind when it
came down from their mountains in the month of
March like a god of great stature to impel them to
the West. They pushed their Long Keels out
upon the rollers, grinding the shingle of the beech
at the fjord-head. They ran down the calm narrows, they breasted and they met the open sea.
Then for days and days they drove under this
master of theirs and high friend, having the wind
for a sort of captain, and looking always out to the
sea line to find what they could find. It was the
springtime; and men feel the spring upon the sea

even more surely than they feel it upon the land. They were men whose eyes, pale with the foam, watched for a landfall, that unmistakable good sight which the wind brings us to, the cloud that does not change and that comes after the long emptiness of sea days like a vision after the sameness of our common lives. To them the land they so discovered was wholly new.

We have no cause to regret the youth of the world, if indeed the world were ever young. When we imagine in our cities that the wind no longer calls us to such things, it is only our reading that blinds us, and the picture of satiety which our reading breeds is wholly false. Any man to-day may go out and take his pleasure with the wind upon the high seas. He also will make his landfalls to-day, or in a thousand years; and the sight is always the same, and the appetite for such discoveries is wholly satisfied even though he be only sailing, as I have sailed, over seas that he has known from childhood, and come upon an island far away, mapped and well known, and visited for the hundredth time.

CLOUDS [1]

BY

Christopher Morley

W HO has ever done justice to the majesty of the
clouds?   Alice Meynell, perhaps?   George
Meredith?   Shelley, who was "gold-dusty with
tumbling amongst the stars?"   Henry Van Dyke
has sung of "The heavenly hills of Holland," but
in a somewhat treble pipe; R. L. S. said it better—
"The traveling mountains of the sky."   Ah, how
much is still to be said of those piled-up mysteries
of heaven!

We rode to-day down the Delaware Valley from
Milford to Stroudsburg.   That wonderful meadow-
land between the hills (it is just as lovely as the
English Avon, but how much more likely we are
to praise the latter!) converges in a huge V toward
the Water Gap, drawing the foam of many a mountain creek down through that matchless passway.
Over the hills which tumble steeply on either side
soared the vast Andes of the clouds, hanging pal-
pable in the sapphire of a summer sky.   What
height on height of craggy softness on those silver
steeps!   What rounded bosomy curves of golden
vapor; what sharpened pinnacles of nothingness,
spiring in ever-changing contour into the intangible
blue!   Man the finite, reveler in the explainable

[1] From *Shandygaff* by Christopher Morley, published by
Doubleday, Page and Company.

and the exact, how can his eye pierce or his speech describe the rolling robes of glory in which floating moisture clothes itself!

Mile on mile, those peaks of midsummer snow were marching the highways of the air. Fascinated, almost stupefied, we watched their miracles of form and unfathomable glory. It was as though the stockades of earth had fallen away. Palisaded, cliff on radiant cliff, the spires of the Unseeable lay bare. Ever since childhood one has dreamed of scaling the bulwarks of the clouds, of riding the ether on those strange galleons. Unconscious of their own beauty, they pass in dissolving shapes— now scudding on that waveless azure sea; now drifting with scant steerage way. If one could lie upon their opal summits, what depths and what abysses would meet the eye! What glowing chasms to catch the ardor of the sun, what chill and empty hollows of creaming mist, dropping in pale and awful spirals. Floating flat like ice floes beneath the greenish moon, or beetling up in prodigious ledges of seeming solidness on a sunny morning— are they not the most superbly heart-easing miracles of our visible world? Watch them as they shimmer down toward the Water Gap in every shade of silver and rose and opal; or delicately tinged with amber when they have caught some jeweled chain of lightning and are suffused with its lurid sparkle. Man has worshipped sticks and stones and stars; has he never bent a knee to the high gods of the clouds?

There they wander, the unfettered spirits of bliss or doom. Holding within their billowed masses the healing punishments of the rain, chaliced beakers of golden flame, lightnings instant and unbearable as the face of God—dissolving into a crystal nothing, reborn from the viewless caverns of air—here let us erect one enraptured altar to the bright mountains of the sky!

At sunset we were climbing back among the wooded hills of Pike County, fifteen hundred feet above the salt. One great castle of clouds that had long drawn our eyes was crowning some invisible airy summit far above us. As the sun dipped, it grew gray, soft, and pallid. And then one last banner of rosy light beaconed over its highest turret—a final flare of glory to signal curfew to all the other silver hills. Slowly it faded in the shadow of dusk.

We thought that was the end. But no—a little later, after we had reached the farm, we saw that the elfs of cloudland were still at play. Every few minutes the castle glowed with a sudden gush of pale blue lightning. And while we watched, with hearts almost painfully sated by beauty, through some leak the precious fire ran out; a great stalk of pure and unspeakable brightness fled passionately to earth. This happened again and again until the artery of fire was discharged. And then, slowly, slowly, the stars began to pipe up the evening breeze. Our cloud drifted gently away.

Where and in what strange new form did it greet the flush of dawn? Who knows?

WINTER MIST [1]

BY

Robert Palfrey Utter

FROM a magazine with a rather cynical cover I learned very recently that for pond skating the proper costume is brown homespun with a fur collar on the jacket, whereas for private rinks one wears a gray herringbone suit and taupe-colored alpine. Oh, barren years that I have been a skater, and no one told me of this! And here's another thing. I was patiently trying to acquire a counterturn under the idle gaze of a hockey player who had no better business till the others arrived than to watch my efforts. "What I don't see about that game," he said at last, "is who wins?" It had never occurred to me to ask. He looked bored, and I remembered that the pictures in the magazine showed the wearers of the careful costumes for rink and pond skating as having rather blank eyes that looked illimitably bored. I have hopes of the "rocker" and the "mohawk;" I might acquire a proper costume for skating on a small river if I could learn what it is; but a bored look— why, even hockey does not bore me, unless I stop to watch it. I don't wonder that those who play it look bored. Even Alexander, who played a more imaginative game than hockey, was bored—poor

[1] Reprinted by kind permission of the author and of *Harper's Magazine*.

fellow, he should have taken up fancy skating in his youth; I never heard of a human being who pretended to a complete conquest of it.

I like pond skating best by moonlight. The hollow among the hills will always have a bit of mist about it, let the sky be clear as it may. The moonlight, which seems so lucid and brilliant when you look up, is all pearl and smoke round the pond and the hills. The shore that was like iron under your heel as you came down to the ice is vague, when you look back at it from the center of the pond, as the memory of a dream. The motion is like flying in a dream; you float free and the world floats under you; your velocity is without effort and without accomplishment, for, speed as you may, you leave nothing behind and approach nothing. You look upward. The mist is overhead now; you see the moon in a "hollow halo" at the bottom of an "icy crystal cup," and you yourself are in just such another. The mist, palely opalescent, drives past her out of nothing into nowhere. Like yourself, she is the center of a circle of vague limit and vaguer content, where passes a swift, ceaseless stream of impression through a faintly luminous halo of consciousness.

If by moonlight the mist plays upon the emotions like faint, bewitching music, in sunlight it is scarcely less. More often than not when I go for my skating to our cosy little river, a winding mile from the milldam to the railroad trestle, the hills are clothed in silver mist which frames them in vignettes with blurred edges. The tone is that of Japanese paintings on white silk, their color showing soft and dull through the frost-powder with which the air is filled. At the milldam the hockey players furiously rage together, but I heed them not, and in a moment am beyond the first bend, where their clamor comes softened on the air like that of a distant convention of politic crows. The silver powder has fallen on the ice, just enough to cover earlier tracings and leave me a fresh plate to etch with grapevines and arabesques. The stream winds ahead like an unbroken road, striped across with soft-edged shadows of violet, indigo, and lavender. On one side it is bordered with leaning birch, oak, maple, hickory, and occasional groups of hemlocks under which the very air seems tinged with green. On the other, rounded masses of scrub oak and alder roll back from the edge of the ice like clouds of reddish smoke. The river narrows and turns, then spreads into a swamp, where I weave my curves round the straw-colored tussocks. Here, new as the snow is, there are earlier tracks than mine. A crow has traced his parallel hieroglyph, alternate footprints with long dashes where he trailed his middle toe as he lifted his foot and his spur as he brought it down. Under a low shrub that has hospitably scattered its seed is a dainty, close-wrought embroidery of tiny bird feet in ir-regular curves woven into a circular pattern. A silent glide toward the bank, where among bare twigs little forms flit and swing with low conversa-tional notes, brings me in company with a working crew of pine siskins, methodically rifling seed cones of birch and alder, chattering sotto voce the while. Under a leaning hemlock the writing on the snow tells of a squirrel that dropped from the lowest branch, hopped aimlessly about for a few yards,

then went up the bank. Farther on, where the
river narrows again, a flutter-headed rabbit crossing
at top speed has made a line seemingly as free from
frivolous indirection as if it had been defined by all
the ponderosities of mathematics. There is no
pursuing track. Was it his own shadow he fled, or
the shadow of a hawk?

The mist now lies along the base of the hills,
leaving the upper ridges almost imperceptibly
veiled and the rounded tops faintly softened. The
snowy slopes are etched with brush and trees so
fine and soft that they remind me of Dürer's en-
gravings, the fur of Saint Jerome's lion, the cock's
feathers in the coat of arms with the skull. From
behind the veil of the southernmost hill comes a
faint note as

> From undiscoverable lips that blow
> An immaterial horn.

It is the first far premonition of the noon train; I
pause and watch long for the next sign. At last I
hear its throbbing, which ceases as it pauses at the
flag station under the hill. There the invisible
locomotive shoots a column of silver vapor above
the surface of the mist, breaking in rounded clouds
at the top, looking like nothing so much as the
photograph of the explosion of a submarine mine,
a titanic outburst of force in static pose, a geyser
of atomized water standing like a frosted elm tree.
Then quick puffs of dusky smoke, the volley of which
does not reach my ear till the train has stuck its
black head out of fairyland and become a prosaic
reminder of dinner. High on its narrow trestle
it leaps across my little river and disappears between

the sandbanks. Far behind it the mist is again spreading into its even layers. Silence is renewed, and I can hear the musical creaking of four starlings in an apple tree as they eviscerate a few rotten apples on the upper branches. I turn and spin down the curves and reaches of the river without delaying for embroideries or arabesques. At the milldam the hockey game still rages; the players take no heed of the noon train.

> Let Zal and Rustum bluster as they will,
> Or Hatim call to supper . . .

Their minds and eyes are intent on a battered disk of hard rubber. I begin to think I have misjudged them when I consider what effort of imagination must be involved in the concentration of the faculties on such an object, transcending the call of hunger and the lure of beauty. Is it to them as is to the mystic "the great syllable Om" whereby he attains Nirvana? I cannot attain it; I can but wonder what the hockey players win one-half so precious as the stuff they miss.

A LIST OF ESSAYS PARTICULARLY ADAPTED FOR USE AS MODELS

Hudson, W. H. *The Peach Orchard* and *The Twenty-Five Ombú Trees*, from *Far Away and Long Ago*. E. P. Dutton & Co.

Hudson, W. H. *The Plains of Patagonia*, from *Idle Days in Patagonia*. E. P. Dutton & Co.

Jefferies, Richard. *Field and Hedgerow*, especially *Hours of Spring*, *Swallow-Time*, and *Birds' Nests*. Longmans, Green & Co.

Jefferies, Richard. *Round about a Great Estate*, especially *Wood-Anemones* and *The Cuckoo-Fields*. Smith, Elder & Co. London.

Smith, Logan Pearsall. *The Starry Heaven* and *The Wheat*, from *Trivia*. Doubleday, Page & Company.

Storm, Miriam. *A Woodland Valentine*, and *Minstrel Weather*. Harper and Brothers.

Tanner, William M. *Essays and Essay-Writing*. The Atlantic Monthly Press. *The Lure of the Berry, The Rock and the Pool*, and *Woodland Mysteries*.

D. Essays of Perception and Imagination

Having bitten pencils for an hour over the paragraphs proposed by the title, we have decided not to write them. Only fools, it will be recalled, rush in where angels would fear to tread. Here is a situation in which Turgeniev's words ring true. "No one man can truly help another." The essays that follow are born, not of opinions, which all may have, but of beneficent ideas, which are accorded to few, not entirely of thought, but of its more gracious mistresses and handmaidens. Most beautiful of all essays, they nurture their readers as do great poetry and great music. All four of those that follow, as well as the one quoted in the student section, are distinguished by delicate and careful workmanship. A reader who gives them their due will hardly forget the beautiful rhythms of one, the light and color of another, the effectiveness of the vowel sounds in certain paragraphs of a third. Nor can he be blind to the reality that each is somehow raised above the more common ground of experience and thought.

It is by no means expected that students will readily write essays of this type; it is fondly hoped that they may appreciate those which we have chosen to reprint.

THE HOURS OF SLEEP [1]

BY

Alice Meynell

THERE are hours claimed by Sleep, but refused to him. None the less are they his by some state within the mind, which answers rhythmically and punctually to that claim. Awake and at work, without drowsiness, without languor, and without gloom, the night mind of man is yet not his day mind; he has night powers of feeling which are at their highest in dreams, but are night's as well as sleep's. The powers of the mind in dream, which are inexplicable, are not altogether baffled because the mind is awake; it is the hour of their return as it is the hour of a tide's, and they do return.

In sleep they have their free way. Night then has nothing to hamper her influence, and she draws the emotion, the senses, and the nerves of the sleeper. She urges him upon those extremities of anger and love, contempt and terror, to which not only can no event of the real day persuade him, but for which, awake, he has perhaps not even the capacity. This increase of capacity, which is the dream's, is punctual to the night, even though sleep and the dream be kept at arm's length.

The child, not asleep, but passing through the hours of sleep and their dominions, knows that the

[1] From *The Spirit of Place*. By permission of Charles Scribner's Sons.

mood of the night will have its hour; he postpones his troubled heart, and will answer it another time, in the other state, by day. "I shall be able to bear this when I am grown up" is not oftener in a young child's mind than "I shall endure to think of it in the daytime." By this he confesses the double habit and double experience, not to be interchanged, and communicating together only by memory and hope.

Perhaps it will be found that to work all by day or all by night is to miss something of the powers of a complex mind. One might imagine the rhythmic experience of a poet, subject, like a child, to the time, and tempering the extremities of either state by messages of remembrance and expectancy.

Never to have had a brilliant dream, and never to have had any delirium, would be to live too much in the day; and hardly less would be the loss of him who had not exercised his waking thought under the influence of the hours claimed by dreams. And as to choosing between day and night, or guessing whether the state of day or dark is the truer and the more natural, he would be rash who should make too sure.

In order to live the life of night, a watcher must not wake too much. That is, he should not alter so greatly the character of night as to lose the solitude, the visible darkness, or the quietude. The hours of sleep are too much altered when they are filled by lights and crowds; and Nature is cheated so, and evaded, and her rhythm broken, as when larks caged in populous streets make ineffectual springs and sing daybreak songs when the London lamps are lighted. Nature is easily deceived; and the muse, like the lark, may be set all astray as to the hour. You may spend the peculiar hours of sleep amid so much noise and among so many people that you shall not be aware of them; you may thus merely force and prolong the day. But to do so is not to live well both lives; it is not to yield to the daily and nightly rise and fall, cradled in the swing of change.

There surely never was a poet but was now and then rocked in such a cradle of alternate hours. "It cannot be," says Herbert, "that I am he on whom Thy tempests fell all night."

It is in the hours of sleep that the mind, by some divine paradox, has the extremest sense of light. Almost the most shining lines in English poetry— lines that cast sunrise shadows—are those of Blake, written confessedly from the side of night, the side of sorrow and dreams, and those dreams the dreams of little chimney-sweepers; all is as dark as he can make it with the "bags of soot"; but the boy's dream of the green plain and the river is too bright for day. So, indeed, is another brightness of Blake's, which is also, in his poem, a child's dream, and was certainly conceived by him in the hours of sleep, in which he woke to write the *Songs of Innocence:*—

> O what land is the land of dreams?
> What are its mountains, and what are its streams?
> O father, I saw my mother there,
> Among the lilies by waters fair.
> Among the lambs clothèd in white,
> She walk'd with her Thomas in sweet delight.

To none but the hours claimed and inspired by sleep, held awake by sufferance of sleep, belongs such a vision.

Corot also took the brilliant opportunity of the hours of sleep. In some landscapes of his early manner he has the very light of dreams, and it was surely because he went abroad at the time when sleep and dreams claimed his eyes that he was able to see so spiritual an illumination. Summer is precious for a painter, chiefly because in summer so many of the hours of sleep are also hours of light. He carries the mood of man's night out into the sunshine—Corot did   so—and lives the life of night, in all its genius, in the presence of a risen sun. In the only time when the heart can dream of light, in the night of visions, with the rhythmic power of night at its dark noon in his mind, his eyes see the soaring of the actual sun.

He himself has not yet passed at that hour into the life of day. To that life belongs many another kind of work, and a sense of other kinds of beauty; but the summer daybreak was seen by Corot with the extreme perception of the life of night. Here, at last, is the explanation of all the memories of dreams recalled by these visionary paintings, done in earlier years than were those, better known, that are the Corots of all the world. Every man who knows what it is to dream of landscape meets with one of these works of Corot's first manner with a cry, not of welcome only, but of recognition. Here is morning perceived by the spirit of the hours of sleep.

THE MOWING OF A FIELD [1]

Hilaire Belloc

THERE is a valley in South England remote from ambition and from fear, where the passage of strangers is rare and unperceived, and where the scent of the grass in summer is breathed only by those who are native to that unvisited land. The roads to the Channel do not traverse it; they choose upon either side easier passes over the range. One track alone leads up through it to the hills, and this is changeable: now green where men have little occasion to go, now a good road where it nears the homesteads and the barns. The woods grow steep above the slopes; they reach sometimes the very summit of the heights, or, when they cannot attain them, fill in and clothe the coombes. And, in between, along the floor of the valley, deep pastures and their silence are bordered by lawns of chalky grass and the small yew trees of the Downs.

The clouds that visit its sky reveal themselves beyond the one great rise, and sail, white and enormous, to the other, and sink beyond that other. But the plains above which they have traveled and the Weald to which they go, the people of the valley cannot see and hardly recall. The wind, when it reaches such fields, is no longer a gale from the

[1] From *Hills and the Sea*. By permission of Charles Scribner's Sons.

salt, but fruitful and soft, an inland breeze; and those whose blood was nourished here feel in that wind the fruitfulness of our orchards and all the life that all things draw from the air.

In this place, when I was a boy, I pushed through a fringe of beeches that made a complete screen between me and the world, and I came to a glade called No Man's Land. I climbed beyond it, and I was surprised and glad, because from the ridge of that glade, I saw the sea. To this place very lately I returned.

The many things that I recovered as I came up the countryside were not less charming than when a distant memory had enshrined them, but much more. Whatever veil is thrown by a longing recollection had not intensified nor even made more mysterious the beauty of that happy ground; not in my very dreams of morning had I, in exile, seen it more beloved or more rare. Much also that I had forgotten now returned to me as I approached— a group of elms, a little turn of the parson's wall, a small paddock beyond the graveyard close, cherished by one man, with a low wall of very old stone guarding it all around. And all these things fulfilled and amplified my delight, till even the good vision of the place, which I had kept so many years, left me and was replaced by its better reality. "Here," I said to myself, "is a symbol of what some say is reserved for the soul: pleasure of a kind which cannot be imagined save in a moment when at last it is attained."

When I came to my own gate and my own field, and had before me the house I knew, I looked around a little (though it was already evening), and

I saw that the grass was standing as it should stand
when it is ready for the scythe. For in this, as in
everything that a man can do—of those things at
least which are very old—there is an exact moment
when they are done best. And it has been remarked
of whatever rules us that it works blunderingly,
seeing that the good things given to a man are not
given at the precise moment when they would have
filled him with delight. But, whether this be true
or false, we can choose the just turn of the seasons
in everything we do of our own will, and especially
in the making of hay. Many think that hay is
best made when the grass is thickest; and so they
delay until it is rank and in flower, and has already
heavily pulled the ground. And there is another
false reason for delay, which is wet weather. For
very few will understand (though it comes year
after year) that we have rain always in South
England between the sickle and the scythe, or say
just after the weeks of east wind are over. First
we have a week of sudden warmth, as though the
south had come to see us all; then we have the weeks
of east and southeast wind; and then we have
more or less of that rain of which I spoke, and
which always astonishes the world. Now it is just
before, or during, or at the very end of that rain—
but not later—that grass should be cut for hay.
True, upland grass, which is always thin, should
be cut earlier than the grass in the bottoms and
along the water meadows; but not even the latest,
even in the wettest seasons, should be left (as it is)
to flower and even to seed. For what we get when
we store our grass is not a harvest of something
ripe, but a thing just caught in its prime before

maturity: as witness that our corn and straw are best yellow, but our hay is best green. So also Death should be represented with a scythe and Time with a sickle; for Time can take only what is ripe, but Death comes always too soon. In a word, then, it is always much easier to cut grass too late than too early; and I, under that evening and come back to these pleasant fields, looked at the grass and knew that it was time. June was in full advance; it was the beginning of that season when the night has already lost her foothold of the earth and hovers over it, never quite descending, but mixing sunset with the dawn.

Next morning, before it was yet broad day, I awoke, and thought of the mowing. The birds were already chattering in the trees beside my window, all except the nightingale, which had left and flown away to the Weald, where he sings all summer by day as well as by night in the oaks and the hazel spinneys, and especially along the little river Adur, one of the rivers of the Weald. The birds and the thought of the mowing had awakened me, and I went down the stairs and along the stone floors to where I could find a scythe; and when I took it from its nail, I remembered how, fourteen years ago, I had last gone out with my scythe, just so, into the fields at morning. In between that day and this were many things, cities and armies, and a confusion of books, mountains and the desert, and horrible great breadths of sea.

When I got out into the long grass the sun was not yet risen, but there were already many colors in the eastern sky, and I made haste to sharpen my scythe, so that I might get to the cutting before the dew should dry. Some say that it is best to wait till all the dew has risen, so as to get the grass quite dry from the very first. But, though it is an advantage to get the grass quite dry, yet it is not worth while to wait till the dew has risen. For, in the first place, you lose many hours of work (and those the coolest), and next—which is more important—you lose that great ease and thickness in cutting which comes of the dew. So I at once began to sharpen my scythe.

There is an art also in the sharpening of the scythe, and it is worth describing carefully. Your blade must be dry, and that is why you will see men rubbing the scythe-blade with grass before they whet it. Then also your rubber must be quite dry, and on this account it is a good thing to lay it on your coat and keep it there during all your day's mowing. The scythe you stand upright, with the blade pointing away from you, and put your left hand firmly on the back of the blade, grasping it; then you pass the rubber first down one side of the blade-edge and then down the other, beginning near the handle and going on to the point and working quickly and hard. When you first do this you will, perhaps, cut your hand; but it is only at first that such an accident will happen to you.

To tell when the scythe is sharp enough this is the rule. First the stone clangs and grinds against the iron harshly; then it rings musically to one note; then at last, it purrs as though the iron and stone were exactly suited. When you hear this, your scythe is sharp enough; and I, when I heard it that June dawn, with everything quite silent except the birds, let down the scythe and bent myself to mow.

When one does anything anew, after so many years, one fears very much for one's trick or habit. But all things once learnt are easily recoverable, and I very soon recovered the swing and power of the mower. Mowing well and mowing badly—or rather not mowing at all—are separated by very little; as is also true of writing verse, of playing the fiddle, and of dozens of other things, but of nothing more than of believing. For the bad or young or untaught mower without tradition, the mower Promethean, the mower original and contemptuous of the past, does all these things: He leaves great crescents of grass uncut. He digs the point of the scythe hard into the ground with a jerk. He loosens the handles and even the fastening of the blade. He twists the blade with his blunders, he blunts the blade, he chips it, dulls it, or breaks it clean off at the tip. If any one is standing by he cuts him in the ankle. He sweeps up into the air wildly, with nothing to resist his stroke. He drags up earth with the grass, which is like making the meadow bleed. But the good mower who does things just as they should be done and have been for a hundred thousand years, falls into none of these fooleries. He goes forward very steadily, his scythe-blade just barely missing the ground, every grass falling; the swish and rhythm of his mowing are always the same.

So great an art can only be learned by continual practice; but this much is worth writing down, that, as in all good work, to know the thing with which you work is the core of the affair. Good

verse is best written on good paper with an easy
pen, not with a lump of coal on a whitewashed wall.
The pen thinks for you; and so does the scythe mow
for you if you treat it honorably and in a manner
that makes it recognize its service. The manner
is this. You must regard the scythe as a pendulum
that swings, not as a knife that cuts. A good
mower puts no more strength into his stroke than
into his lifting. Again, stand up to your work.
The bad mower, eager and full of pain, leans forward and tries to force the scythe through the
grass. The good mower, serene and able, stands
as nearly straight as the shape of the scythe will
let him, and follows up every stroke closely, moving
his left foot forward. Then also let every stroke
get well away. Mowing is a thing of ample gestures,
like drawing a cartoon. Then, again, get yourself
into a mechanical and repetitive mood: be thinking
of anything at all but your mowing, and be anxious
only when there seems some interruption to the
monotony of the sound. In this, mowing should
be like one's prayers—all of a sort and always the
same, and so made that you can establish a monotony and work them, as it were, with half your mind:
that happier half, the half that does not bother.

In this way, when I had recovered the art after
so many years, I went forward over the field, cutting
lane after lane through the grass, and bringing out
its most secret essences with the sweep of the scythe
until the air was full of odors. At the end of every
lane I sharpened my scythe and looked back at
the work done, and then carried my scythe down
again upon my shoulder to begin another. So, long
before the bell rang in the chapel above me—that is,

long before six o'clock, which is the time for the
Angelus—I had many swathes already lying in
order parallel like soldiery; and the high grass yet
standing, making a great contrast with the shaven
part, looked dense and high. As it says in the
Ballad of Val-ès-Dunes, where—

> The tall son of the Seven Winds
> Came riding out of Hither-hythe,

and his horse-hoofs (you will remember) trampled
into the press and made a gap in it, and his sword
(as you know)

> was like a scythe
> In Arcus when the grass is high
> And all the swathes in order lie,
> And there's the bailiff standing by
> A-gathering of the tithe.

So I mowed all that morning, till the houses
awoke in the valley, and from some of them rose a
little fragrant smoke, and men began to be seen.

I stood still and rested on my scythe to watch the
awakening of the village, when I saw coming up
to my field a man whom I had known in older
times, before I had left the Valley.

He was of that dark silent race upon which all
the learned quarrel, but which, by whatever mean-
ingless name it may be called—Iberian, or Celtic,
or what you will—is the permanent root of all
England, and makes England wealthy and pre-
serves it everywhere, except perhaps in the Fens
and in a part of Yorkshire. Everywhere else you
will find it active and strong. These people are
intensive; their thoughts and their labors turn
inward. It is on account of their presence in these

islands that our gardens are the richest in the
world. They also love low rooms and ample fires
and great warm slopes of thatch. They have, as I
believe, an older acquaintance with the English
air than any other of all the strains that make up
England. They hunted in the Weald with stones,
and camped in the pines of the green sand. They
lurked under the oaks of the upper rivers, and
saw the legionaries go up, up the straight paved
road from the sea. They helped the few pirates
to destroy the towns, and mixed with those pirates
and shared the spoils of the Roman villas, and were
glad to see the captains and the priests destroyed.
They remain; and no admixture of the Frisian pirates,
or the Breton, or the Angevin and Norman con-
querors, has very much affected their cunning eyes.

To this race, I say, belonged the man who now
approached me. And he said to me, "Mowing?"
And I answered, "Ar." Then he also said "Ar,"
as in duty bound; for so we speak to each other in
the Stenes of the Downs.

Next he told me that, as he had nothing to do, he
would lend me a hand; and I thanked him warmly,
or, as we say, "kindly." For it is a good custom
of ours always to treat bargaining as though it
were a courteous pastime; and though what he
was after was money, and what I wanted was his
labor at the least pay, yet we both played the
comedy that we were free men, the one granting a
grace and the other accepting it. For the dry
bones of commerce, avarice and method and need,
are odious to the Valley; and we cover them up
with a pretty body of fiction and observances.
Thus, when it comes to buying pigs, the buyer

does not begin to decry the pig and the vendor
to praise it, as is the custom with lesser men; but
tradition makes them do business in this fashion:—

First the buyer will go up to the seller when he
sees him in his own steading, and, looking at the
pig with admiration, the buyer will say that rain
may or may not fall, or that we shall have snow or
thunder, according to the time of the year. Then
the seller, looking critically at the pig, will agree
that the weather is as his friend maintains. There
is no haste at all; great leisure marks the dignity
of their exchange. And the next step is, that the
buyer says: "That's a fine pig you have there,
Mr.——" (giving the seller's name). "Ar, powerful fine pig." Then the seller, saying also "Mr."
(for twin brothers rocked in one cradle give each
other ceremonious observance here), the seller, I
say, admits, as though with reluctance, the strength
and beauty of the pig, and falls into deep thought.
Then the buyer says, as though moved by a great
desire, that he is ready to give so much for the pig,
naming half the proper price, or a little less. Then
the seller remains in silence for some moments; and
at last begins to shake his head slowly, till he says;
"I don't be thinking of selling the pig, anyways." He
will also add that a party only Wednesday offered
him so much for the pig—and he names about double
the proper price. Thus all ritual is duly accomplished;
and the solemn act is entered upon with reverence and
in a spirit of truth. For when the buyer uses this
phrase: "I'll tell you what I *will* do," and offers
within half a crown of the pig's value, the seller replies
that he can refuse him nothing, and names half a
crown above its value; the difference is split, the pig

is sold, and in the quiet soul of each runs the peace of something accomplished.

Thus do we buy a pig or land or labor or malt or lime, always with elaboration and set forms; and many a London man has paid double and more for his violence and his greedy haste and very un-chivalrous higgling. As happened with the land at Underwaltham, which the mortgagees had begged and implored the estate to take at twelve hundred and had privately offered to all the world at a thousand, but which a sharp direct man, of the kind that makes great fortunes, a man in a motor car, a man in a fur coat, a man of few words, bought for two thousand three hundred before my very eyes, protesting that they might take his offer or leave it; and all because he did not begin by praising the land.

Well then, this man I spoke of offered to help me and he went to get his scythe. But I went into this house and brought out a gallon jar of small ale for him and for me; for the sun was now very warm, and small ale goes well with mowing. When we had drunk some of this ale in mugs called "I see you," we took each a swathe, he a little behind me because he was the better mower; and so for many hours we swung, one before the other, mowing and mowing at the tall grass of the field. And the sun rose to noon and we were still at our mowing; and we ate food, but only for a little while, and we took again to our mowing. And at last there was nothing left but a small square of grass, standing like a square of linesmen who keep their formation, tall and unbroken, with all the dead lying around them when the battle is over and done.

Then for some little time I rested after all those

hours; and the man and I talked together, and a long way off we heard in another field the musical sharpening of a scythe.

The sunlight slanted powdered and mellow over the breadth of the valley; for day was nearing its end. I went to fetch rakes from the steading; and when I had come back the last of the grass had fallen, and all the field lay flat and smooth, with the very green short grass in lanes between the dead and yellow swathes.

These swathes we raked into cocks to keep them from the dew against our return at daybreak; and we made the cocks as tall and steep as we could, for in that shape they best keep off the dew, and it is easier also to spread them after the sun has risen. Then we raked up every straggling blade, till the whole field was a clean floor for the tedding and the carrying of the hay next morning. The grass we had mown was but a little over two acres; for that is all the pasture on my little tiny farm.

When we had done all this, there fell upon us the beneficent and deliberate evening; so that as we sat a little while together near the rakes, we saw the valley more solemn and dim around us, and all the trees and hedgerows quite still, and held by a complete silence. Then I paid my companion his wage, and bade him a good-night, till we should meet in the same place before sunrise.

He went off with a slow and steady progress, as all our peasants do, making their walking a part of the easy but continual labor of their lives. But I sat on, watching the light creep around towards the north and change, and the waning moon coming up as though by stealth behind the woods of No Man's Land.

THE PRECEPT OF PEACE [1]

Louise Imogen Guiney

A CERTAIN sort of voluntary abstraction is the oldest and choicest of social attitudes.   In France, where all æsthetic discoveries are made, it was crowned long ago: la sainte indifférence is, or may be, a cult, and le saint indifférent an articled practitioner.   For the Gallic mind, brought up at the knee of a consistent paradox, has found that not to appear concerned about a desired good is the only method to possess it; full happiness is given, in other words, to the very man who will never sue for it.   This is a secret neat as that of the Sphinx: to "go softly" among events, yet domineer them.   Without fear: not because we are brave, but because we are exempt; we bear so charmed a life that not even Baldur's mistletoe can touch us to harm us.   Without solicitude: for the essential thing is trained, falcon-like, to light from above upon our wrists, and it has become with us an automatic motion to open the hand, and drop what appertains to us no longer.   Be it renown or a new hat, the shorter stick of celery, or

> The friends to whom we had no natural right,
> The homes that were not destined to be ours,

it is all one: let it fall away! since only so, by depletions, can we buy serenity and a blithe mien.   It is

[1] From *Patrius* by Louise Imogen Guiney.

diverting to study, at the feet of Antisthenes and of
Socrates, his master, how many indispensables man
can live without; or how many he can gather together, make over into luxuries, and so abrogate
them.   Thoreau somewhere expresses himself as
full of divine pity for the "mover," who on May-
Day clouds city streets with his melancholy household caravans; fatal impedimenta for an immortal.
No: furniture is clearly a superstition.   "I have
little, I want nothing; all my treasure is in Mi-
nerva's tower."   Not that the novice may not ac-
cumulate.   Rather, let him collect beetles and
Venetian interrogation marks; if so be that he may
distinguish what is truly extrinsic to him, and
bestow these toys, eventually, on the children of
Satan who clamor at the monastery gate.   Of all
his store, unconsciously increased, he can always
part with sixteen-seventeenths, by way of concession to his individuality, and think the subtrac-
tion so much concealing marble chipped from the
heroic figure of himself.   He would be a donor from
the beginning; before he can be seen to own, he
will disencumber, and divide.   Strange and fearful
is his discovery, amid the bric-a-brac of the world,
that this knowledge, or this material benefit, is
for him alone.   He would fain beg off from the
acquisition, and shake the touch of the tangible
from his imperious wings.   It is not enough to cease
to strive for personal favor; your true indifférent is
Early Franciscan: caring not to have, he fears to
hold.   Things useful need never become to him
things desirable.   Toward all commonly-accounted
sinecures, he bears the coldest front in Nature, like
a magician walking a maze, and scornful of its

flower-bordered detentions. "I enjoy life," says Seneca, "because I am ready to leave it." Meanwhile, they who act with too jealous respect for their morrow of civilized comfort, reap only indigestion, and crow's-foot traceries for their deluded eye-corners.

Now nothing is farther from le saint indifférent than cheap indifferentism, so-called: the sickness of sophomores. His business is to hide, not to display, his lack of interest in fripperies. It is not he who looks languid, and twiddles his thumbs for sick misplacedness, like Achilles among girls. On the contrary, he is a smiling industrious elf, monstrous attentive to the canons of polite society. In relation to others, he shows what passes for animation and enthusiasm; for at all times his character is founded on control of these qualities, not on the absence of them. It flatters his sense of superiority that he may thus pull wool about the ears of joint and several. He has so strong a will that it can be crossed and counter-crossed, as by himself, so by a dozen outsiders, without a break in his apparent phlegm. He has gone through volition, and come out at the other side of it; everything with him is a specific act: he has no habits. Le saint indifférent is a dramatic wight; he loves to refuse your proffered six per cent, when, by a little haggling, he may obtain three-and-a-half. For so he gets away with his own mental processes virgin; it is inconceivable to you that, being sane, he should so comport himself. Amiable, perhaps, only by painful propulsions and sore vigilance, let him appear the mere inheritor of easy good nature. Unselfish out of sheer pride, and ever eager to

claim the slippery side of the pavement, or the
end cut of the roast (on the secret ground, be it
understood, that he is not as Capuan men, who
wince at trifles), let him have his ironic reward in
passing for one whose physical connoisseurship is
yet in the raw.   That sympathy which his rule
forbids his devoting to the usual objects, he ex-
pends, with some bravado, upon their opposites;
for he would fain seem a decent partizan of some
sort, not what he is, a bivalve intelligence, Tros
Tyriusque.   He is known here and there, for instance, as valorous in talk; yet he is by nature a
solitary, and, for the most part, somewhat less
communicative than

> The wind that sings to himself as he makes stride,
> Lonely and terrible, on the Andean height.

Imagining nothing idler than words in the face of
grave events, he condoles and congratulates with the
genteelest air in the world.   In short, while there is
anything expected of him, while there are spectators
to be fooled, the stratagems of the fellow prove inexhaustible. It is only when he is quite alone that he
drops his jaw, and stretches his legs; then heigho!
arises like a smoke, and envelopes him becomingly,
the beautiful native well-bred torpidity of the gods,
of poetic boredom, of "the Oxford manner."

"How weary, stale, flat, and unprofitable!"
sighed Hamlet of this mortal outlook. As it came
from him in the beginning, that plaint, in its sin-
cerity, can come only from the man of culture,
who feels about him vast mental spaces and depths,
and to whom the face of creation is but comparative and symbolic.   Nor will he breathe it in the

common ear, where it may woo misapprehensions, and breed ignorant rebellion. The unlettered must ever love or hate what is nearest him, and, for lack of perspective, think his own fist the size of the sun. The social prizes, which, with mellowed observers, rank as twelfth or thirteenth in order of desirability, such as wealth and a foothold in affairs, seem to him first and sole; and to them he clings like a barnacle. But to our indifférent, nothing is so vulgar as close suction. He will never tighten his fingers on loaned opportunity; he is a gentleman, the hero of the habitually relaxed grasp. A light unprejudiced hold on his profits strikes him as decent and comely, though his true artistic pleasure is still in "fallings from us, vanishings." It costs him little to loose and to forego, to unlace his tentacles, and from the many who push hard behind, to retire, as it were, on a never-guessed-at competency, "richer than untempted kings." He would not be a life prisoner, in ever so charming a bower. While the tranquil Sabine Farm is his delight, well he knows that on the dark trail ahead of him, even Sabine Farms are not sequacious. Thus he learns betimes to play the guest under his own cedars, and, with disciplinary intent, goes often from them; and, hearing his heartstrings snap the third night he is away, rejoices that he is again a freedman. Where his foot is planted (though it root not anywhere), he calls that spot home. No Unitarian in locality, it follows that he is the best of travelers, tangential merely, and pleased with each new vista of the human Past. He sometimes wishes his understanding less, that he might itch deliciously with a prejudice. With cosmic

congruities, great and general forces, he keeps, all
along, a tacit understanding, such as one has with
beloved relatives at a distance; and his finger, airily
inserted in his outer pocket, is really upon the pulse of
eternity. His vocation, however, is to bury himself in
the minor and immediate task; and from his intent
manner, he gets confounded, promptly and perma-
nently, with the victims of commercial ambition.

The true use of the much-praised Lucius Cary,
Viscount Falkland, has hardly been apprehended:
he is simply the patron saint of indifférents. From
first to last, almost alone in that discordant time,
he seems to have heard far-off resolving harmonies,
and to have been rapt away with foreknowledge.
Battle, to which all knights were bred, was penitential to him. It was but a childish means: and
to what end? He meanwhile—and no man carried
his will in better abeyance to the scheme of the
universe—wanted no diligence in camp or council.
Cares sat handsomely on him who cared not at all,
who won small comfort from the cause which his
conscience finally espoused. He labored to be a
doer, to stand well with observers; and none save
his intimate friends read his agitation and profound weariness. "I am so much taken notice of,"
he writes, "for an impatient desire for peace, that
it is necessary I should likewise make it appear how
it is not out of fear for the utmost hazard of war."
And so, driven from the ardor he had to the simula-
tion of the ardor he lacked, loyally daring, a sacrifice
to one of two transient opinions; and inly impartial
as a star, Lord Falkland fell: the young never-to-be-
forgotten martyr of Newburg field. The imminent
deed he made a work of art; and the station of the

moment the only post of honor. Life and death may
be all one to such a man; but he will at least take the
noblest pains to discriminate between Tweedledum
and Tweedledee, if he has to write a book about the
variations of their antennæ. And like the Carolian
exemplar is the disciple. The indifférent is a good
thinker, or a good fighter. He is no "immartial minion," as dear old Chapman suffers Hector to call
Tydides. Nevertheless, his sign manual is content
with humble and stagnant conditions. Talk of scaling
the Himalayas of life affects him, very palpably, as
"tall talk." He deals not with things, but with the
impressions and analogies of things. The material
counts for nothing with him: he has moulted it away.
Not so sure of the identity of the higher course of
action as he is of his consecrating dispositions, he feels
that he may make heaven again, out of sundries, as he
goes. Shall not a beggarly duty, discharged with perfect temper, land him in "the out-courts of Glory,"
quite as successfully as a grand Sunday-school excur-
sion to front the cruel Paynim foe? He thinks so.
Experts have thought so before him. Francis Drake,
with the national alarum instant in his ears, desired
first to win at bowls, on the Devon sward, "and afterwards to settle with the Don." No one will claim a
buccaneering hero for an indifférent, however. The
Jesuit novices were ball playing almost at that very
time, three hundred years ago, when some too specu-
lative companion, figuring the end of the world in a
few moments (with just leisure enough, between, to
be shriven in chapel, according to his own thrifty
mind), asked Louis of Gonzaga how he, on his part,
should employ the precious interval. "I should go
on with the game," said the most innocent and most

ascetic youth among them. But to cite the behavior
of any of the saints is to step over the playful line
allotted. Indifference of the mundane brand is
not to be confounded with their detachment, which
is emancipation wrought in the soul, and the ineffable efflorescence of the Christian spirit. Like
most supernatural virtues, it has a laic shadow; the
counsel to abstain, and to be unsolicitous, is one
not only of perfection, but also of polity. A very
little nonadhesion to common affairs, a little reserve
of unconcern, and the gay spirit of sacrifice, provide
the moral immunity which is the only real estate.
The indifférent believes in storms, since tales of
shipwreck encompass him. But once among his
own kind, he wonders that folk should be circum-
vented by merely extraneous powers! His favorite
catch, woven in among escaped dangers, rises
through the roughest weather, and daunts it:

> Now strike your sailes, ye jolly mariners,
> For we be come into a quiet rode.

No slave to any vicissitude, his imagination is, on
the contrary, the cheerful obstinate tyrant of all
that is. He lives, as Keats once said of himself,
"in a thousand worlds," withdrawing at will from
one to another, often curtailing his circumference to
enlarge his liberty. His universe is a universe of balls,
like those which the cunning Oriental carvers make
out of ivory; each entire surface perforated with the
same delicate pattern, each moving prettily and
inextricably within the other, and all but the outer
one impossible to handle. In some such innermost
asylum the right sort of dare-devil sits smiling,
while men rage or weep.

GIANNI IN CHURCH [1]

BY

Stark Young

GIANNI is the son of my laundress in Ravenna. He lives in the Via Rasponi on the ground floor of a little house, a narrow place with a tiny court into which the sunlight falls at noon and in the corner of which is a stone trough where his mother and the other women in the house do their washing. Every Friday he brings my biancheria, shining white in a basket like a platter, and stays a moment to tell me about himself, sounding his s's with that kind of whistling lisp that you hear in Romagnuolo. When he grows up, he says, after he has gone some more to school, provided, that is, his mother can keep him there, her back is not very good, he will work in the post office. If he cannot find a place there, he would like to be a clerk in a store. Gianni has a Romagna face, rather blond, with an open smile, white teeth, yellowish-brown hair and wide gray eyes. He looks friendly, honest and not self-conscious. He is strong and healthy and likes to use his mind. In general he is an ordinary Italian boy of thirteen.

Thursday after Corpus Christi in Ravenna there was a great procession that left the Duomo at half past six and marched around the town and back

[1] From Italian Notes in *Encaustics* by Stark Young. Reprinted by kind permission of the author.

again. The gold light from the west poured down the church as the procession entered and moved toward the altar in the aisle that the four young priests kept open through the press of people. Group after group, banner after banner, blue, red, yellow, white and every color, the town band leading with its horns and drums, priests, seminarians, friars, nuns, boys in black shirts, boys with blue sashes, the endless line of little communicants in their white dresses and veils and wreaths and bouquets of white flowers carrying their candles lighted, then the boys and men and youths of the choir in rose and purple, singing, then the priests of the cathedral and the bishop, in vestments of ivory-colored brocade flowered and braided with gold, walking under the gold-fringed baldachino, chanting and carrying in their midst the Host in a glittering monstrance, and finally a line of priests in black, without a banner and chanting a response to those walking with the bishop and the Host. For half an hour they came, chanting at the head of the line as it passed by the altar, and again midway the length of the church, and farther away as the end of the procession drew nearer in the streets outside. And over the heads of the crowd you could see the banners moving, pausing for a moment at the great portal and then coming through the air toward the altar, slowly, tilting slightly, like sails. The organ high up in the loft began to play, stealing out over the heads of the people like a soft trumpet and flutes. And outside in the piazza dusk had come on and the windows of the church grew dim.

The procession ended, the banners took their places at the sides of the choir and by the altar.

Benediction began. The organ played, the choir
sang. Across the carved balcony of the choir loft
stretched a hanging of crimson brocade bound
with wide gold bands. Crimson brocade with
gold hung down the pilasters of the apse and crimson
was draped around the arch. Under this arch,
high up, was swung a line of crystal chandeliers
with lighted candles in them. Lighted candles rose
seven feet high from the silver candlesticks on the
altar, with lower lights sown thickly beneath them
and tapers like stars, and from the silver altar vases
bouquets of flowers, red roses and white lilies.

Beside the altar stood the great Byzantine cross,
with its equal arms and its plaques of silver. The
music stopped and the priest at the altar began
to read the service. Clouds of incense rose, above
the candles of the altar with their twinkling lights,
past the marble and gilt and crimson, and into the
shadowed vault of the dome. The priest read, the
people made the responses. A bell rang; the Host
was elevated. The crowd dropped to their knees.
And then the music and the choir began again.

I did not see Gianni in the procession as it passed;
but later I saw him standing near the altar with the
boys in blue scarfs, looking up, his mother near.

Afterward I thought of him. Gianni was only
an ordinary boy of thirteen. If his mother lived
and could afford it, he would have a few years
more of the kind of education that schools can give.
Otherwise he might get work somewhere soon as
an apprentice or an errand boy in a shop. And
either way he would settle into the life of Ravenna
and so run his course. But it was interesting to consider what all this that we had seen at the Duomo

might mean to him. I wondered what ideas it might give him.

Even if Gianni never gets these ideas quite into words—which is a process we have come to think necessary, though it by no means is—he might possess them at least as habit or experience and as extensions in his living. He might possess them vaguely somehow as patterns for living.

It had not been an extraordinary procession. Such a one it was as had repeated itself thus simply from generation to generation and century to century. Gianni's father had seen it every year of his life, no doubt, and his father's father and his father and so on back, everyone in the family except perhaps one uncle Gianni had told me of who deserted his family and ran off and was now in hell. And it was only a friendly community affair after all, among the people, the little communicants, the Franciscans, the priests and sisters, the boys' clubs, the candles, God, the gold and silver and flowers, the evening light.

But from that procession Gianni might know what it is to take part in a society, with every one together following some idea of pleasure or beauty or devotion; he might learn what it is to be a social member, no matter how narrow and cramped your days are or how few people you can really know and talk with. And this was just as it was with the prayers he said and heard, which set forth certain typical sins of the human race and led the mind of the sinner toward them rather than toward the numberless private varieties of evil that he might stew out of himself; and just as it was with the service he heard repeated in the churches from

year to year, always the same and the same all
over the world, which led the mind not so much to
an individual as to a general and social side of
religion.

But the Duomo, as much as anyone in Ravenna
did, he owned. From it and his moments in it
there flowed into him things he might never be
able to describe or even to recognize as ideas in
his head, but which would nevertheless have been
a part of his existence. He might live in a narrow
dark little house, but here there was space, great
stretches of stone floor and wall and columns rising
up to high arches and to the wide dusk and glow
of the ceiling and dome. He might have from that
the experience of space, space in things, and space
perhaps in thoughts and in actions. There was
present here in the lines of the pilasters, in the
altar, in the doorways the quality of elegance, a
distinction of choice and development that Gianni
might never quite recognize though he might learn
to resent its absence.

In the Duomo there was to be seen the use and
integrity of materials, the hard lines of stone left
hard, the rich texture of silk, the luxury and biting
suavity of gold and gilding, the paler and more
accessible ornament of silver, and the softened
permanence of wood; in all of them the essential
nature of the material worked in was brought to
the service of the end desired.

In the shadows, the lights, the motions, the music,
used to express what was in the breast of the people
kneeling there, Gianni might get a sense of the ex-
tension beyond words and speech of a part of human
living, and so be ready always to admit in himself

and in all life the presence and possibility of an element elusive and invisible but no less real on that account. From that ancient cross gleaming with its silver plaques in the altar light, and the antique marbles here and there, he might feel the oneness of time and of men's thoughts and hopes. And though all his life he goes about clothed in poor worsted as he does now and though he is cramped into a narrow channel of modern labor and never has much chance at all to grow or spread, Gianni from the great spaces there in the Duomo, the carved and painted and gilded wood, the brocade and crystal and marble, and the superb sweep of those columns and arches, will nevertheless have had the idea of magnificence.

A LIST OF ESSAYS PARTICULARLY ADAPTED FOR USE AS MODELS

Belloc, Hilaire. *On an Unknown Country*, from *On Nothing*. Metheun & Co., Ltd., London.

Hudson, W. H. *"Gone Back*," from *Idle Days in Patagonia*. E. P. Dutton & Co.

Hunt, Leigh. *Colour*, in *Romantic Prose of the Early Nineteenth Century*. The Modern Student's Library. Charles Scribner's Sons.

Meynell, Alice. *Rejection, The Colour of Life*, and *The Rhythm of Life*, from *The Rhythm of Life*. Charles Scribner's Sons.

Tanner, William M. *Essays and Essay-Writing*. The Atlantic Monthly Press. *Returning*.

Warner, Frances Lester. *"Thundering Water*," from *Surprising the Family*. Houghton Mifflin Company.

White, Stewart Edward. *On Lying Awake at Night*, from *The Forest*. Doubleday, Page & Company.

Woolf, Virginia. *Street Haunting*, in *The Yale Review*, October, 1927.

A COLLECTION OF STUDENT ESSAYS

Explanatory Note: The following essays, which further exemplify the types explained and illustrated in the preceding pages, are written by students of the University of Minnesota and of Smith College.

ANGEL

BY

Marjorie Lawson
—Smith College

OUR family has never risen to the dignity of keeping
a real maid, one, I have always imagined, who would
wear a black uniform and starched frills for her cap and
apron. But we have always had Angel.

I could have been only about three when Angel came
for the first time, yet I distinctly remember her arrival.
She was a plump, rosy young woman with light-brown
hair and a queer Slavic voice. She wore a blue gingham
dress and large, creaky black shoes that buttoned on in-
definitely up under her dress. I stood peering around the
corner into the hall at her as she tried to make Mother
understand her fragmentary English. I still remember
that I wore white ribbed stockings, wrinkled at the knees,
and dangled about my ankles a wooden horse on wheels
tied to a string. When Mother noticed me, she called me
forth from my retreat, and, horse and all, introduced me to
the new "woman." Her name, we afterwards discovered,
was Mrs. Andel, but she pronounced it so curiously that I
called her "Angel," which she remained ever after.

She was at once put to work about the house. I liked
her very much, and she could not rid herself of my attentions. She made matters worse by being most indulgent.
She set me on the box of our carpet sweeper, which had
a marvelous squeak, quavering the same tune over and
over. She would have been forced to ride me all day had
not Mother come to the rescue.

After that first time she came almost daily for more
than ten years. I was always interested to see how she

would look when she arrived in the morning. Mother gave her our old clothes, and she usually came garbed in state. Amused as I was, I never dared laugh because she was proud of this strange collection of garments and took off with reverent care her hat, so stylish on Mother, so ridiculous on her who had never worn hats before.

On days when Mother was at home I was never allowed to bother Angel, but when Mother was out, I used to leave everything to watch her Sometimes she had to wash. I can still see her as she used to stand over the boiler, her smiling face obscured by steam, a long stick in her hand, stirring and stirring. When she hung the clothes up to dry, I was custodian of the clothespins. I remember my pleasure at plunging my hand into the bag, and my disappointment at always drawing forth one instead of a handful of the elusive things. I could not be cast down, however, for even without maternal consent I was helping. My importance undoubtedly delayed Angel a great deal because I insisted upon following her everywhere and upon handing her every clothespin myself. When she ironed I used to stand, absorbed, at the end of her board. I can yet feel the warmth of the room and smell the freshly starched and ironed clothes, can see her plump, shiny red hands as she thumped the iron on the board, can hear her thin voice vaguely humming a tuneless Hungarian folk song.

Sometimes she washed windows. She sat on the sill so that only her feet were inside, and then, as she polished away the white cloud that had dried on the glass, I got an increasingly comprehensive picture of her framed in the window. On these occasions she wore a cloth tied around her head in gypsy fashion, and she seemed a strange and unfamiliar figure of some other world until the rattle of the window as she rubbed vigorously and her feet, swinging impersonally from the sill, reminded me that she was only Angel.

Always, when she had some leisure, she would produce

her embroidery, most remarkable work. Much of it was really beautiful, but the part that was for her kitchen, as she said, most interested me. There were yards and yards of a shelf cover with a border done in red cross-stitch of every kitchen utensil ever used; there was a table cover depicting in pink and blue the love affair of two fat kewpies on a background of umbrella trees; there was a motto in black and yellow threatening eternal punishment to her who did not keep her kitchen clean; there was a bureau scarf with orange-breasted bluebirds flying recklessly about among purple daisies and red roses.

She liked to talk as she worked; in fact, we could not prevent her. When she first came, her knowledge of English included only about a dozen words. I shall never forget the first discussion she had with Mother about the war, which had just broken out in Europe. She needed a word for war and for a moment was speechless. Then, pointing her finger like a pistol at Mother, she cried, "Pooh, pooh!" as she pulled the trigger. Despite Mother's ill-concealed amusement, she continued to discuss the "pooh-pooh in Europe," firing her pistol in a realistic fashion each time.

Her brother had been one of the gardeners of Franz Joseph, Emperor of Austria and Hungary, the "Kink," as she called him. She loved to tell us of his great gardens. She loved, too, to tell us of her girlhood in the old country. Her descriptions of Prague, its bridges and its university, of the winter carnivals at Vienna to which she had gone, of the fresh beauty of the rural district in which she had lived—these impressed me greatly. In spite of her rotundity she could dance with a certain dash and grace the old folk dances.

She was easily delighted by attention. Once Father took her for a ride in our car, and I can yet see her beaming face as she majestically occupied the back seat and hear her chuckles as she was bounced over a bump. She was a sympathetic person to tell one's jokes to. Mother was

altogether unappreciative of mine, and, since they had
to be told, I used to relate them impressively and at
length to Angel. She always laughed whether I had
come to the funny part or not.

She was just as easily sorrowful. When I came home
crying over a scratched knee, she used to wash it for me,
tears in her own eyes. When I was somewhat older, my
playmate, a little boy, named Jack, and I meanly took
advantage of her weakness by telling her, just to make
her weep, all the sad news we heard in our explorations
about the neighborhood. She never suspected us of this
baseness and was very kind. Her skill at making muffins
was unsurpassed. I vividly remember the hot, crisp ones
she made us that day Jack and I fell violently ill from
eating so many. She always had severe qualms of conscience about the nourishment of our family, and thus
we ate too well for some years. At one time I had a forlorn goldfish which she used to feed secretly and against
Mother's advice. Then, overcome with remorse, she con-
fessed her crime to Mother who usually scolded her somewhat, for excessive kindness was her gravest sin. When
the poor fish at last feebly passed away from overindulgence, she wept heartily, no doubt partly because of her
own guilt.

I can to this day recall many impressions of Angel:
her quick, creaking steps and then her rosy, chuckling
face in the doorway; her red, thick-fingered hands smooth-
ing starched, white linen; her high voice like a tinny violin
quavering faintly above the swish of a scrubbing brush;
her fine brown hair straggling from its tight knot at the
top of her head and being pushed back by a hastily-wiped
arm; her squat figure trotting breathlessly away down
the street after a distant trolley car. I can think of no one
in appearance less like the popular conception of an angel;
yet as far as any human being approaches the angels—in
kindness, in sympathy, in loyalty, in simplicity—Angel
deserved her name.

PONTA DELGATA

BY

Henry Johnson
—University of Minnesota

Paradoxical as it may seem, though Ponta Delgata lives in memory as an earthly paradise, I have no desire to revisit it. I am quite sure that, if the opportunity ever presents itself, I shall say No, for unless I could recreate within myself the identical mental and physical states, the results would probably be disappointing. It would mean the shattering of a beautiful illusion. I paid a rather high price to have that scene printed in indelible colors upon my memory, and, whether it be illusion or reality, I refuse to allow it to be destroyed.

I said Ponta Delgata lives in my memory, and *lives* is exactly the word I wish to use. Through an experience which has become hazy and indistinct, this scene shines with undimmed brightness. The prophet on lonely Patmos saw no more clearly the jasper walls and gem-studded gates of the Promised City than I see in my memory that little white- and red-tiled town, huddled between the high mountains and the blue waters of the Atlantic. After seven years, I can still see the clouds gathering and breaking up again around the high mountain peaks, hear the bells from the tower of the old Jesuit church, and feel the caressing softness of the south wind on my bare arms.

For those who must know, Ponta Delgata is to be found on the island of St. Michael's in the Azores group, not far from Flores in the Azores, where Sir Richard Grenville lay. To-day it is a place almost forgotten; but, when the doughty captains of good Queen Bess plundered Spanish galleons laden with gold and silver from the land of the Incas, the Azores were the rendezvous of many a tall-masted fleet.

But it was not of stately, gold-laden Spanish ships or of the *Revenge* and Sir Richard Grenville that I thought when the U. S. S. *Quincy* dropped anchor outside the little harbor of Ponta Delgata. I was thinking of Ulysses and his sea-weary men when they reached the land of the Lotus-eaters. For the crew of the *Quincy*,

> Most weary seemed the sea, weary the oar,
> Weary the wandering fields of barren foam.

And it was not an imaginary weariness. Seven days before, in the cold gray light of a winter morning, we had slipped out of the mouth of the Loire for what we thought would be a short and easy run. But the Bay of Biscay is never quiet and the Atlantic very seldom peaceful in the winter time; consequently, we were four days overdue at our destination.

To the ordinary traveler who crosses the Atlantic on board a floating palace, sea weariness can mean nothing. He may become a trifle bored from overeating and from lack of exercise, but that is all. It is quite a different experience when one must really fight the overpowering and merciless sea for every inch of headway that is made. After two days of this, even the most hardened sea dog goes about the ship with a set face. A sullen silence takes possession of everyone from the captain down to the coal-passers. Like snails they withdraw into their shells. There is no unnecessary talking, for talking takes energy, and of that there is none to spare. Only the weak break and whimper under the strain. Not until it is over does one realize that one has been drawing heavily on the last reserve of physical and mental energy.

In such a state I found myself on the morning of our arrival at Ponta Delgata. As I dragged myself up the narrow engine-room ladder at eight bells, I thought only of my bunk where I could lie down and sleep until the eight-to-twelve went on at night again. I had stood the four-to-eight that morning for a sick shipmate, and I felt as if I wanted to sleep the rest of my life. I did not care where we were; I was interested in sleep and nothing else. But I had no more than stepped out of the hatchway before it dawned upon my dazed understanding that the world had been recreated over night.

I forgot about the overpowering desire to sleep. I went up on the forecastle deck and looked toward land. Before me mountains rose right out of the sea and a little town, which glistened red and white in the morning sun, clung to the rocky shore. Clouds hid the tops of the mountains; but on the slopes about the town I could see the pale green of pineapple fields. The soft breeze was just strong enough to make the blue water dance and break occasionally into little bursts of gleaming white. Here was a paradise if any ever existed.

I pulled off my blouse, made a pillow of it, and lay on the deck. In that hour I wanted for nothing. I felt as if I should be satisfied to lie there and look at that fairyland for all eternity. If Ulysses and his men had been there, I would have joined in their song,

> Our island home is far beyond the wave;
> We will no longer roam!

I slept the sleep of exhaustion; and when I awoke, I felt the heave and fall of the ship and the throb of the engines. I sat up and looked around. Darkness had fallen. I heard no sound but the swish of water and the dull thumping of the propeller. Ahead nothing but stars and sea. Was it only a dream? I looked back over the stern of the heaving ship; and I saw the intermittent flashes of a light, and beyond that, against a dark blot, a cluster of small lights twinkled like stars. No, it was not a dream. Ponta Delgata was slipping rapidly astern.

LEWIS CARROLL, DREAMER

BY

Eleanor Lincoln

—University of Minnesota

IT all began in the big morris chair by the window. Mother settled down one night with Kay on one arm and me on the other as she did every evening, but she had a new book—a tan book with a round-faced rabbit in waistcoat and breeches on the outside, who was taking a pair of gloves from a very tall, very thin, little girl with very straight, bobbed hair, and a worried expression on her face. It did not do any good to ask Mother about pictures. She always said, "Wait and see." So we stretched our legs out straight along the wide, flat, wooden arms of the old chair and waited.

I knew before Mother had been reading very long, that I should like Alice, for the arm of the chair did not feel hard. Sometimes when Mother read, if she came to long descriptions or uninteresting places, that arm became most terribly uncomfortable. I went to bed every night for the next week worrying about Alice, or the poor dormouse stuffed into the teapot, or the remarkable Father William with a wriggling eel balanced on his nose. They had such unusual and harrowing experiences that I was in constant anxiety over one or another. What if the Mad Hatter should suffer permanent injury from the bite which he absent-mindedly took out of the teacup? What became of the pig baby after it ran away into the woods? A forest is a very poor place for an unattended baby. What if the caterpillar, sage though he was, should fall from the toadstool? All these problems were bad enough, not to mention Alice's dreadful experiences with little doors and lost keys and seas of tears.

318

It was years before Alice's adventures became funny to me,—not until the little tan book was nearly worn out, and I knew what mock-turtle soup really was. After that my jaw did not hurt, and the tears did not come to my eyes when Alice ate the wrong cake and bumped her chin on her toes.

It is strange that no one else ever wrote down a dream. Everyone loves to tell them at breakfast time, before they fade away into the land of forgotten dreams, and everyone has some which are as queer and as fascinating as Alice's. A clergyman told me, only yesterday, that his night's rest had been simply ruined because he had been obsessed all night with the idea that he was rolling a hoop down Nicollet Avenue, and a very honest and dignified college professor told me that he had tried to steal apples from a neighbor's tree for two successive nights, but that they had turned to eggs as fast as he picked them.

Lewis Carroll must have been a wonderful dreamer. I can just imagine him coming downstairs after breakfast to a little girl with long, straight-bobbed hair, and long, thin legs, who is fairly trembling with eagerness until he takes her up on his knee and tells her what Alice did last night. He must have been quite worried sometimes because Alice got into such heart-rending predicaments that sometimes it took a great deal of dreaming and worrying to get her out.

One would never connect little Alice and her experiences with a Syllabus of Plane Geometry, nor Lewis Carroll with the quiet, unromantic C. L. Dodgson. It would be like mixing "shoes and ships and sealing wax and cabbages and kings," but what a comfort he must have been to struggling young mathematicians at Christ's. No one who had helped Alice through so many trials could have lost patience with a poor youth who could not realize that if certain letters lie on certain other letters, be they as remote as A and Z, "the homologous sides are equal." In fact, it is not surprising to me that a man who spent his days with prisms and parallelograms should find his nights made terrible by seas of tears, frog footmen, and grinning Cheshire cats.

I have always thought of Lewis Carroll as a boy. I don't know why, because he would make a delightful grandfather, but in my mind he will always be a tall, slim boy stretched out on the grass of a little hillock. Sometimes he looks up at the sky and the clouds and builds castles and ships. Sometimes his eyes close, and he dozes there in the sun. When this happens, I see two white rabbit's ears peeping up over a grass tuft and hear a faint but harsh "Off with his head!" What fun he must have had just lying there on the grass watching the Walrus and the Carpenter stroll up and down the sand, speculating on how long it would take to sweep it all away.

> "If seven maids with seven mops
>   Swept it for half a year,
> Do you suppose," the Walrus said,
>   "That they could get it clear?"
> "I doubt it," said the Carpenter,
>   And shed a bitter tear.

Lewis Carroll need never be lonesome, for when air-castles failed, the Caterpillar or the March Hare or Tweedledee and Tweedledum would appear from "nowhere in particular" to visit with him. And if those failed, there were all the new creatures whom he knew, but whom Alice never met even in her extensive travels through the Land of the Looking Glass. He knew nobility in abundance who afforded excellent company even when they were short-tempered and explosive like the Red Queen, or ruthless and choleric like the screaming Duchess.

Lewis Carroll must have grown old. Even boys who exist only in Wonderland have to grow old. But when he could not lie on grassy mounds because the ground was too hard, and the damp earth made his legs ache with rheumatism, I can see a queer company,—Alice, nibbling cake, an agitated white rabbit in black frock coat nervously muttering, "The Duchess, the Duchess"; three young oysters, the knave of hearts, and all the rest gathered about an old man who dozes before the fire.

HUSBANDS, BLACK AND WHITE

BY

Ruth Carlson
—University of Minnesota

LITTLE girls who have long hair parted in the middle, just a little curly at the ends, and who look about them eagerly in round-eyed wonderment when they go to the Zoo are quite apt to look like Alice in Wonderland. So it is not surprising that once when I was standing on the very tip of my toes before the lion's cage looking in amazement into the cavernous depths of that beast's mouth, a lady beside me said, "Look, Milly, quick! Doesn't this little girl here with the blue ribbons 'round her hair look just exactly like Alice in Wonderland?" And, of course, that settled it then and there; I knew that I must be beautiful, bewitchingly beautiful—for Alice in Wonderland was the very loveliest little girl in the whole world—and the lady of the Zoo had said I looked like her. I sang for joy all the way home.

That night in bed I thought it all over. Perhaps thinking about Alice so constantly, and adoring her, and forever trying to fall down holes as she had done had something to do with it. Or perhaps it was eating one of every kind of pills in the medicine cabinet in a vain attempt to change my size. Anyway, we looked alike. Suddenly I was conscious of a great sense of power. I decided to marry somebody very soon. Beautiful people always did. I thought and thought, and then I remembered Prince Charming, Cinderella's Prince Charming. We were married the next day at high noon down under the apple tree, and the Prince was very nervous for fear Cinderella would discover us, and after it was all over he called me his "Fair Betrothed." The story books say that Cinderella and her Prince lived happily ever after, but the story books don't know. They don't know how the Prince finally agreed to leave his wife after I had smiled winsomely at him all one morning, and whispered to him—softly so that Cinderella on the next page couldn't hear, "You must marry me, oh Prince, because I am beautiful. I look like Alice in Wonderland, you know, and she is far lovelier than Cinderella."

But after a while, I grew tired of the Prince, and one Monday morning after breakfast, I married King Arthur. I came to know his knights very well, but several of the ladies of the Court tried to put poison in my milk, as some one did in a book called *Peacock Rose* which our maid left on the pantry shelf; so I eloped with young Lochinvar, who rode out of the West to carry me off with him. That was on a moonlit night, and I distinctly remember the nightingale's singing to us as we rode through the dark.

Then I married Robinson Crusoe. It was great fun living on the desert island—only my mother made me come home for lunch.

I was wedded to the Pied Piper, too, and he played the wedding march on his slim reed pipe. We lived inside the mountain, with all the little children whom my husband had piped away from Hamelin Town. I took care of them all very nicely, wiping their noses for them when they needed it, and kissing their bumps when they fell down.

I married Toby Tyler two weeks later, but one afternoon he fell off my lap into the lake, and sank without a word to his watery grave. I wore a black hair ribbon for days in memory of him.

Robin Hood was next, I think. We spent our honeymoon in the forest of Arden, where everything was lovely and cool and green, and I wore a leaf-green frock and a feather in my hat. But every afternoon at three o'clock I had to go home to practice my music lesson.

I met Uncle Tom in school, and I don't mind telling you that I married him, too, because I felt so sorry for him. He cried, and I did, too, when I left him at the end of a month, but I had promised to marry Santa Claus. The wedding took place under the Christmas Tree. It was snowing out-of-doors, and away off in the distance some children were singing, "Hark, the herald angels sing"—and a candle dripped down onto Santa's beard.

They were delightfully exciting, all these secret marriages of mine, and I felt sure that if people knew about them there would be a poem about me in the paper, something like this:

> There is a fair lady
> Who ties up her hair in blue;
> She has so many husbands
> She doesn't know what to do.

And when my mother and Aunt Amy shook their heads and clicked through their teeth because a lady in the paper had three husbands, I almost fell out of my little red chair laughing at what they would do if they knew that I had had twenty-three of them!

One day I found a husband for Aunt Amy, and when I told her about it, she blushed clear down her neck and sort of giggled. But I went on telling her about him, how tall and handsome he was with piercing eyes and a great many brains, and how he had said he would like to marry her. Aunt Amy blew her nose nervously and said,

"Oh, I 'spect it's that new minister. He just pesters the life out of me."

I shook my head.

"No?" Aunt Amy leaned forward in her chair and stuck her hairpins into her hair more firmly. "It isn't Mr. Holiday, is it—and his wife dead only three years!"

"No, Aunt Amy," I said, going closer to her, "it isn't Mr. Holiday. It is (and I lowered my voice impressively), it is—Sherlock Holmes."

Aunt Amy's mouth shut into a tight line, and she told me to go straight downstairs. It is surprising, indeed, how ungrateful one's aunts can be. I went toward the door with a lump in my throat, for I had thought she would be so pleased.

"Aunt Amy," I said wistfully, "if you don't like Sherlock Holmes, perhaps Rip Van Winkle would do. He likes to sleep just like you do, and he's every bit as old as you are—" But Aunt Amy's door banged in my face.

This little affair, however, did not dampen my own zeal for husbands. I married Nils, who had the wonderful adventures, and Hans Brinker, and the Katzenjammers, and Wee Willie Winkie during the next week. On the eve of my marriage to the Raggedy Man, my big sister Virginia called me into her room. She took me onto her lap and held me tight for a minute.

"Will you miss me, little sister," she whispered close to my ear, "after to-morrow when I go away with Steve?"

"Sure, I will, Virginia," I said, closing one eye and watching the lights dance in and out of the ring on her finger. Then, suddenly tearful, "Please don't marry Steve, Virginia."

Virginia laughed softly and kissed the top of my head.

"But I must marry Steve, darling. You see, I love him."

I sat up and looked at her for a minute, and then I told what I had been thinking for almost two years.

"I want you to marry a prince, though," I told her, "and Steve isn't a prince at all. He hasn't any flashing armor, or any plume in his hat or even a milk-white steed. Why don't you marry Prince Charming? Cinderella won't care. Or there's King Arthur, and Sir Launcelot, and Sir Galahad, and King Midas. Please, please don't marry Steve. He doesn't even call you his 'Fair Betrothed,' does he, Virginia?"

Virginia only laughed again and trotted me off to bed, telling me about the long white veil she would wear to-morrow, which, she said, looked like a misty, white trail of happiness. That night I cried myself to sleep thinking about Steve, and about Toby Tyler in the bottom of the lake.

Two days after Virginia went away with Steve, Rumpel-stiltzkin sought my hand in marriage, but I refused him, and locked him up in the bookcase while I went calling with my mother. He is such an ill-tempered little dwarf.

My last husband was Gulliver, the traveling man. He is always on the road, so he doesn't bother me much, but I'm tired of him. I wish I could find a new one—not one like Steve, one in a book, I mean—but there aren't any that I should really want now. Perhaps, after all, Rumpelstiltzkin will have to do.

WINTER IN HOLLAND

BY

Louise Boerlage

—University of Minnesota

THE first of November was a welcome day in my Dutch childhood. Then the smith would return the stoves after having taken care of them for six months. That day the smith's helpers in blue blouses would rush through the streets hauling rattling and clanging stoves and stove-pipes in handcars over the cobble-stones. The whole house would smell of damp smoke and heated grease; but who would mind that? Soon in every one of the living rooms a roaring peat-fire would burn in a square iron stove, surmounted by a dragon or spreading eagle for a handle. By the stove stood the shining copper peatbox with brass knobs, and the brass prongs with which some one now and then would pick up a brick of peat to throw into the stove.

With the arrival of the stoves came the peatman. Every morning he would go through the streets yelling "Harde en losse"; that is, hard bricks of peat and bricks loosely hanging together, not quite so old in formation. The hard peat looked dark brown or black with a slight molddust on the surface, whereas the loose quality was reddish brown and showed the interweaving roots, branches and even leaves, which made up the brick. We children did not know the peatman's name, but we used to call him "turfman," which means peatman, and we always addressed him so for friendly conversation. He was not a city man and spoke in a strange dialect of the north, which fascinated us. He was, indeed, an interesting man. He wore a brown blouse of

327

heavy wool with sleeves cut just above the elbow, show-ing his blue cotton shirt sleeves, dark baggy skipper's trousers, black wooden shoes instead of white, from which the hay filling protruded, and a dark silk cap. He wore, also, small golden rings in his ears.

He lived with his family on one of the many peat barges which came to lie in the city canals every winter. In November the barges would still be heaped high with peat, neatly stacked on the low decks. A small ladder would lead to the top layer, from which every morning the dogcart was loaded. Then the peatman would go from street to street, running behind the cart, which the furiously barking, impatient dogs kept hurtling along the cobbled pavement. A word was sufficient to halt the dogs, but no amount of persuasion could ever induce them to keep up a rationally even pace. Sometimes the man would jump on the cart and hang on in an uncom-fortable position, but at every turn he had to jump off again to guide the dogs. After reaching the proper dis-trict, the exhausted beasts would sink down at a word and lie panting before the cart while the "turfman's" voice would sing out loudly, "Harde en losse."

Our "turfman's" barge was called "Antonia," and we often passed it on our walks with Mother. The prow, in the shape of a mermaid, was built high above the water. The name "Antonia" was painted in black letters on a golden sash, which gracefully waved from the mermaid's waist. Against the pile of peat leaned a tiny green cabin with a door opening into the small front part of the deck, and on either side a little square window with white cur-tains held back by red ribbons. This served as entrance to the hold, which it supplied with air and light.

In the hold the peatman lived with his family. There they cooked, ate and slept. A little cylindrical stove was all that they needed for their simple cooking. On warm days the stove was carried upon the deck in the shelter of the mermaid's flowing golden hair. There the "turfvrouw," as we called the wife, would tend to her household duties.

She was a large woman and wore ample woolen skirts which made her appear still larger. Her dark bodice was buttoned to the chin and covered over the shoulders by a red kerchief with large white dots. She wore a similar kerchief on her head. Her little girl, Keetje, was dressed exactly like the mother, the long ample skirts standing out from her little body and giving an impression of elaborateness in her movements.

Keetje used to help the "turfvrouw" wash clothes in pails of water dipped from the canal on long poles, and soon the ship would look gay with a clothesline of red petticoats, checkered towels and blue blouses swinging in the wind on top of the dark peat pile.

With the month of November the long winter evenings would begin. After supper the heavy red plush curtains in our sitting room would be drawn together, and the whole family gathered around the large oblong table, which was covered with a Persian cloth. Mother had the place of honor in a large chair behind the tea tray on the table. By her side stood her work basket, from which she would pick pieces of mending. She was entirely the center of the family group as she sat there with a ready smile on her happy, round face. Father would bring his books and papers from his study, over which he would bend, not too absorbedly to share in the conversation, for this was the time for the family and not for study. We children, too, would be there with home work or picture books. Annetje would learn her spelling lesson, her brown curls falling over the book, and Zusje and Henk would be telling each other stories from the colored pictures before them.

Tea-time to a Dutch family in those days, as now, was the culmination of home enjoyment. The whole atmosphere was sociable; the wheeze of the gas lamp, the scratching of Father's pen on the paper, the crushing of Mother's

sewing, and, above all, the comfortable warmth in the
room.   At a quarter of eight, Sien would bring the tea
water.   Silently she would enter the room in her long
black gown and beautifully-starched white apron and
collars, her face as unruffled as her brown hair which she
wore parted and pulled back in immaculate neatness.
Sien always knew what time it was, no matter when asked
or where.   With the brass kettle of boiling water she
would bring the "tea stove."   This was a little stand of
carved wood about two feet high, holding a brass re-
ceptacle with a glowing brick of peat.   It was placed near
Mother's chair and the kettle set over the hot peat.   Soon
the simmering of the boiling kettle and the faint, sweetish
scent of glowing peat would complete the familiar home
atmosphere.

Eight o'clock was bedtime for us children.   Occasionally, when a favorite caller was expected, we might stay
to shake hands, and then, after a cooky and a glass of
milk, we would go upstairs, accompanied by Jet, who was
to see all little tasks performed.   We loved Jet dearly.
She wore a dark serge dress, the tight bodice of which
was fastened with a seemingly interminable row of shiny
buttons from the chin to below the waist.   Her little
bright eyes looked like a pair of the same buttons.   After
Jet had gone down, Mother would slip away from the tea
table for a moment to see us in bed.

Tea time in Holland is still the time for informal and
semi-formal calls.   Very strong tea Mother would pour,
and as the feast of St. Nicolaas was nearing, brittle spice
cookies would be offered called "Klaasmannetjes."

In America Christmas is a combination of the religious
and the jolly.   In Holland the two are separated; the
quiet element of good will is kept for Christmas proper,
and all the noise and hilarity and the exchange of gifts
come three weeks earlier, on the fifth of December, St.
Nicolaas Eve.   St. Nicolaas, or Sint Niklaas, has often
been wrongly identified with Santa Claus, but his is a

very different personality. He is not the funny little man from the north in his reindeer sleigh; he is a very dignified bishop who comes in a boat from Spain, accompanied by Piet, his Moorish servant, and by a beautiful white horse upon which he rides over the roofs to listen through the chimneys and to learn whether the children are good and deserve lovely toys.

Great preparations are always made for his arrival. Father and Mother used to shop and plan just as American fathers and mothers do before Christmas. However, the celebration of the day was different from that of Christmas. The night before every member of the family would place a shoe under the mantelpiece with a handful of straw and some sugar for the white horse, and we children would sing some little Sint Niklaas songs into the chimney. The next morning the hay and the sugar would be replaced by some little surprise. That was a sure sign that Sint Niklaas had passed and that he would return again after supper. To shorten the long wait during the day Mother planned to let us visit the children of the poor under the supervision of Johan, who used to come every afternoon to polish the shoes, sharpen knives, and tend to the front door in a pink-and-white striped coat. Johan showed great enthusiasm for these excursions and was very clever in sneaking the packages into the homes without being observed. Then we would all run chuckling with pleasure in not being discovered. For Sint Niklaas presents are supposed to come as a surprise, and the giver must always try to remain a mystery.

After an early supper Sint Niklaas would be in the drawing room ready to receive us. He looked very stately, indeed, in his long white robe with trailing red mantle, in his brocaded slippers and miter and with his golden staff. Behind him stood Piet, holding in one black hand a switch-broom to be given as an only present to children who had been bad; in the other a large bag, in which extremely bad children were to be taken away to Spain.   None of our friends was ever taken away in the bag.

All were to shake hands with Sint Niklaas and with Piet, beginning with Henk, the littlest one, who would be the first to recite a poem painfully learned for the occasion.   Whether Father and Mother, too, had to fulfill this requirement we children had no time to observe, for before us lay the wonderful table laden with presents, at which every one was assigned a place marked with large initials made of chocolate.   Father would take Henk and all would join hands, Sien, Jet and Johan included, and all would walk around the table three times.   Then we turned to say "Thank you, Sint Niklaas," and lo—the saint had vanished! But from the chimney came a shower of oranges, apples and "pepernoten," small ginger cookies the size of beans. Rolling over the floor we would grab and scramble amid shouts of laughter.   Piet must have done that, for he was not a bad fellow after all.   With a "Thank you, Sint Niklaas" called up the chimney, we would go back to the table.

St. Nicolaas gifts are always strictly anonymous.   Father and Mother would distribute the presents, but we children were to help Sien, Jet and Johan to theirs.   For each of the women there would always be, besides a main gift, a large gingerbread man, traditionally called the "lover," with pink sugar buttons and sugar pills for eyes.   Johan would receive a similar "ladylove" with his present.

Presents for grown-ups were supposed to be accompanied by little original poems, taunts about minor faults. Even Father and Mother could not escape them.   The poems very often furnished clues as to the giver.

After we children had enjoyed our presents for a while, it would be time to go to bed.   Weary with excitement, we would go upstairs, our favorite toys in our arms.   Then Father and Mother and possibly the friends who had acted the parts of the sainted bishop and Piet would quietly enjoy the rest of the evening with the traditional cup of hot spiced wine and almond pastry.

Christmas was a time for quiet enjoyment and for letter writing. In Holland it was officially celebrated two days in succession, on the twenty-fifth and the twenty-sixth of December. There would be church services and carol concerts on both days, so that everyone might have a share in the celebration. For us children Mother would provide some special fun such as clothes for theatrical performances or matting for Indian camps. This would be sure to keep us busy all day and leave Father and Mother free to write letters.

No shower of letters and cards arrived at Christmas for that was the day to think of friends and the time to write the letters, no matter when they arrived. Father always had a list of names before him, which he checked systematically as he wrote, but Mother, more impulsive, would write feverishly, her face flushed with excitement, her thoughts far ahead of her words. Now and then she would exclaim, "En nicht Betsy, niet te vergeten! en oh de oude mevrouw de Kraai en, en—" [1] There was hardly time for meals for fear that some one should be left out.

On the second Christmas day, as Sien was out, there would be only cold yellow saffron rice for supper. We liked it immensely; it suggested "a special day." It was a day of good will and everything connected with it shared in the atmosphere.

Soon after Christmas, New Year's Eve would follow. This was a time of serious contemplation and promises when Father and Mother would talk to us about bad habits which were to be overcome, but especially about our progress during the year, encouraging us in efforts which we had almost but not quite accomplished. How clearly I remember how Mother used to describe to us her ideal child; how reasonably attainable this ideal seemed to us and how sure we were that we would not disappoint her.

[1] "And cousin Betsy! Don't let us forget her, and oh! old Mrs. de Kraai, and, and—"

Suddenly from the big town tower would come the twelve slow, so heavy strokes, and at the signal all the churches far and near would ring out their joyous, hopeful peals. It was the most impressive night of the year.

January and February were cold months in Holland. As a rule there would be little snow but plenty of ice for skating. The narrow canals were soon covered with ice, and a good frost a few days in succession would transform them into thoroughfares. The canals are interconnected, and people would come from everywhere. Many a peasant in his wide trousers and silk cap, or farmer's daughter with her short black cape over her shoulders, under which her skirts stood out like a fan, would take the afternoon to skate to town. Some would push before them green box-sleighs containing everything imaginable from cabbages to babies. Farmers would go to market on their skates carrying big reed baskets pending from wooden yokes across their shoulders. Fishermen would come from Katwyk in high silk caps, bushy side-whiskers and earrings of gold, and fishermen's wives with red-lined black cloth capes and blue cotton aprons, carrying baskets of fish on their heads in perfect balance. The ice would be dotted with swiftly moving people describing long, graceful curves, and scores of little boys with flying red and blue scarfs, wildly swinging their arms in superfluous efforts at speed. Parties of men and women in elegant sporting clothes would be touring the country, for practically every town and village in Holland can be reached by water. Four or six would skate together holding onto a long pole and gliding forth with long, even strokes, making excellent progress. The low-bladed, long Dutch skates are well adapted for long trips.

In the evening the contours of the canals and the bridges were outlined with thousands of tiny oil-filled glasses in which lighted wicks burned with winking flames. It was a wonderful sight, these rows of little lights against the dark sky and the white ice under foot. Then there would

be ice feasts and contests and races, when all participants
would appear in jaeger underwear and skate in stocking
feet, as wooden shoes and baggy trousers would be a
hindrance to speed. To the winner usually a pair of
skates was given, or sometimes a decorated ham.

Abram, the son of Naatje, the fire-and-water woman,
once won such a ham. All cheered and danced around him
in a circle, while he held his trophy high above his head.
Abram was an excellent skater, and we were very proud
to know him, for he belonged to the rescue squad.

Those days Naatje herself would leave her shop a while
in the care of a neighbor and set up a "koekesopie," where
she sold coffee and biscuits. The "koekesopie" was a
hut built of matting and set upon a heap of straw on the
ice. There many a traveler would stumble in across the
tangling straw to sink exhausted and the little old woman
would pour her hot coffee for him. Often Andries would
join the group with his accordion and play and sing
familiar airs for us.

Every once in a while the "koekesopie" had to be
moved to a fresh spot on the ice and then all the boys
would push and tug and scrape up the hay till finally
they had the little woman comfortably installed again
in her cozy corner behind the "tea stove."

Naatje had a tiny shop in the back street where she
sold bricks of smouldering peat in "tests," which were
red earthenware receptacles, made for the purpose, and
pailfuls of hot water, for a penny each. Especially on
Saturday evening when in the back street all the children
had to have baths, she kept a good business. She also sold
twine, scrubbing brushes, sand to scour brick sidewalks,
green liquid soap, marbles, kites and cheap candy. A
tingling bell on a loose wire announced all customers as
the door opened, and went on tingling long after she had
appeared from the inner room behind the crooked glass
door. She had sore feet and moved very slowly and with
effort, but she always waited on her customers good-

naturedly for the penny sales. She was a kindly little person with a wrinkled face under her carefully fluted white cap.

How I love to recall those winter days of long ago in Holland! The blue-bloused helpers with their noisy, clanging stoves and pipes; the cries of the friendly peatmen; the evenings at home around the tea table; the gay skaters on the wide, silvery canals: old Naatje in her "koekesopie" who in answer to her tingling bell sold hot baths on Saturday nights to dirty and reluctant children!

THE KITCHEN STOVE

BY

Helen Foot

—University of Minnesota

"WHAT's the use?" quoth the young poet. "I write a little ditty to spring, and I find a thousand poets, dead and gone, have sung the praises of sweet spring and the pretty birds, and a hundred thousand poets have chanted of their loves and of the home and hearth. What is there left for me but to restate the old?" And of these it is true, as the Preacher said, that, "There is no new thing under the sun."

But were I a poet, what pæans would I raise to the kitchen stove! Not your modern thing of blue and white enamel, dependable as the sunrise, with all the accomplishments of the virtuous woman whose price is far above rubies. Not the personification you can leave to cook the dinner, and sweep the floor, and answer the doorbell while you go serenely to church. No; but the old-fashioned, temperamental, cast-iron stove, which one day bakes an angel food to charm a gourmet, and on the next burns the johnnycake. The cool, painted beauty may compel our admiration by her perfection; but who, being imperfect, would live with intolerable perfection? Squatting in the corner, the ugly, black giantess, "not too bright or good for human nature's daily food," wins our love in spite of, even because of, her eccentricities.

The difference lies in their diet. The gas or electric stove stands aloof on its slender, elegant legs, cold and austere, like some Utopian's dream of future humanity— a frail, chinless being subsisting on rarefied liquids and odors. But the old wood stove is a jovial, chuckling

337

Falstaff, fat and well-fed, fond of the good things of
this world.

I speak of the wood stove. Coal is, to my mind, little
better than gas. For the stove fed on coal is like Falstaff
fed with cottage cheese and rye krisp and baked potatoes;
the old thief would not have been our witty, roistering
Falstaff without his sack and sugar. Your coal stove may
hiss and sputter and occasionally rattle in its throat; but
it cannot chuckle quietly along, nor laugh uproariously, as
the wood stove does over a hardwood knot or a pitch-pine
stick.

Consider further the deficiencies of the coal hod. For,
since the coal hod is to the coal stove as the wood box
is to the wood stove, it is evident that the coal hod must
take the place of, and fulfill the functions of, the wood
box. Picture yourself, with dangling feet, seated comfortably on the edge of the coal hod. Picture yourself
munching pleasantly on bits of coal. You have never
munched wood? You have never tasted with Epicurean nicety the sweet, resinous flavor of well-seasoned
fir, or the ranker pungence of cottonwood? A delight
awaits you.

I am aware, of course, that dentists condemn our modern diet for its too easy mastication. A light midday
lunch of coal would, I doubt not, strengthen not only the
teeth, but the moral fiber as well, and produce efficient,
iron-willed men. In fact, as a delicious breakfast, tempting to the jaded appetite of the commercial-looking youth,
I recommend a good coal diet of egg, buckwheat, and
nut, topped off perhaps with a West Virginia splint. But
for you who are not commercial minded, who would be
a philosopher rather than a Midas, I recommend a soft
pine splint. Composing yourself on the wood box, ru-
minate on a piece of wood, and draw inspiration from the
homely warm-hearted goddess beside you.

Such at least is the kitchen stove on the farm, particularly in winter. Then we become pagan fire worshipers.

The stove, swart, Ethiope divinity, is the warm, pulsating heart of the farm; life and vigor flow from her, and to her all life returns.   No African savage, cowering in the gloomy depths of tropical forests, worships his deity more sincerely than we our iron image.   When a sluggish sun rises reluctantly, and through the short day hides sullenly behind heavy clouds, then, under the direction of the high priestess, we feed the sacrificial fires and hover in shivering adoration round the altar, imploring the grace and mercy of our goddess.

You accuse me of gross exaggeration?   You brand yourself; you are not one of the elect; you are city bred.   I know whereof I speak.   We had a furnace in our house, I admit, but he was worse than temperamental.   Extending his arteries to the farthest cells of the house, he pretended to be greater and more powerful than the squat patron of the kitchen, but he was a huge, impotent hypocrite.   Since nothing short of hot weather could induce him to warm more than one half of the house at a time, we cut off the circulation of most of his arteries and confined his influence to the dining room and the downstairs bedroom, where he half-heartedly tempered the wintry winds. Theoretically our upstairs bedrooms were heated with the gracious warmth which worked its way through the ceilings from the kitchen, or which through quickly opened and closed doors escaped up the stairway and along the halls. But though our supreme deity was powerful, she was no miracle worker; actually we slept in a cold storage plant.

Looking back, I might rhapsodize on the joys of that life.   To wake refreshed; to spring lightly from the bed into the keen, crisp, invigorating air; to take our morning exercise before the open window, gladdened by the first gray streaks in the east which gave promise that perhaps the night was not really permanent; and then to dress, caroling blithely in our several keys:

Bliss was it in that dawn to be alive,
But to be young was very heaven!

I might so rhapsodize, but I won't; I was brought up on the story of little George and the cherry tree.

On mornings when the mercury shrank down out of sight in its tube, much persuasive calling and a final authoritative command to get up were necessary to startle us from the cradling warmth of our beds. Once up we dressed expeditiously, with no waste of time or movement. In that keen, crisp, invigorating air we learned how many of life's little tasks are fretting trivialities, hampering superfluities. And not one of us had sufficient of the martyr's spirit to exercise or take a sponge bath. With uncombed hair, unbuttoned clothes, and trailing shoe laces, we dashed from the bleak arctic regions, down the long, dark stairs to the temperate zone of the kitchen, to shiver pleasurably in the little circle of tropic heat which enveloped the stove. Thus our day began rightly, with praises of our goddess.

Indeed, there was no lack of praise of her glory. Rather we were in danger of becoming like the early Christian hermits and ascetics who gave their whole lives to the magnification of the Lord, forgetful of worldly duties. We would have imitated them, had not a stern Fate, to whose decrees even the gods must bend, forced us five days a week to tear ourselves away from the holy altars. Fortified by a benediction of hot bricks, we fared out from the temple, battling against biting winds and stinging snows to lesser temples of learning, where uncertain warmth from an unseen source was substituted for our household deity. How eagerly at night, the winds moderated by our expectations, we returned, confident that the high priestess still tended the eternal fires and, against our arrival, had prepared offerings—but not burnt offerings; for she was a good cook, and never scorched the beans.

Happy those days when Fate did not drive us out! Then we learned to know our goddess; how truly godlike she could be in wrath and sheer perversity, and how if we forsook her stern commandments she could punish us. Woe unto us if we, her acolytes, let her sacred fires burn out, or if we neglected her decree: "Thou shalt clean out my ashes every Saturday." But perfect love is possible only where there is service, and so we loved our majestic queen far more in service than if she had asked of us naught but glorification of her name.

Such days ended ideally. We cleaned and scrubbed the temple and polished the nickeled scroll work which adorned our goddess. In the happy consciousness of duties well performed, we gathered close around her, singing perhaps. And then the high priestess would chant appropriate words from her great wealth:

> But when Boreas is loosed,
> And the snow is hurled under Arcturus,
> Then these nations, in sooth,
> Shudder and shiver with cold.

We cowered and shivered in spite of the warmth, as the eerie wail began:

> O the long and dreary Winter!
> O the cold and cruel Winter!

But we relaxed at the more cheerful tones:

> Then nightly sings the staring owl
> Tu-whit!
> To-who! A merry note!
> While greasy Joan doth keel the pot.

As the wind shrieked and howled outside, mingling its blustering with the musical chant of the priestess, we shuddered and worshiped.

Then some one would turn the light out, and we would sit quietly in the warm, friendly dark, pierced by narrow red shafts glimmering from cracks and screw holes. And the beneficent goddess chuckled softly, expounding the great commandment in her law: "Laugh much, and take life as it comes."

ON THE SLAVERY OF CONFIDANTES

Geraldine Bailey

—Smith College

EVERYONE to his own taste, as the old woman said when she kissed the cow—but the story is one-sided. No one knows whether the cow enjoyed the taste of the old woman. Maybe she was long and lank and brown like the Ancient Mariner and the cow's gentle Jersey blood revolted from her skinny hand. But this is off the point, for no confider holds his victim with skinny hands. Rather does he hook in his victim with a gentle flow of conversation about the weather and an offer for a walk. Then when far away from help the confider lays his burden of sin or sorrow, as the case may be, on the confidante's soul. The confider enjoys it, as the old woman did. The confidante gives mentally a low bellow of pain like the cow.

For no one can really enjoy another's life. We come suddenly on this earth, eat, drink, live for fifty, sixty, seventy years and disappear as suddenly. In such a short space we have no time for another's life. To keep in the running we must have our own loves, hates and jealousies. The poor cow probably longed for her own romance. She bit the May violets reflectively and built golden stables in the air from her bovine brain. Tenderly, she mused on the juicy hay in the silver-fretted manger among her loving friends. And all this fell because of an old woman's affection and desire for sympathy.

The story is unfortunately true. Many people seem determined to find a confidante and admirer. They want a friend, motherly or fatherly, as their sex may be, whose shoulder they can spot with tears and whose handker-

chiefs they can borrow and never return. Some unfor-
tunates always seem chosen to be the confidantes. Max
Beerbohm once said that the world was divided into
hosts and guests, and that the supreme example of what
a host and hostess should not be was Macbeth and Lady
Macbeth. Another division of the world would be into
confidantes and confiders, and the best example of the
confider would be the Ancient Mariner who talked to the
Wedding Guest until "he went like one that hath been
stunned" and

> A sadder and a wiser man
> He rose the morrow morn.

No wonder, for the poor man by then was suffering from
all the neurotic disorders which our modern alienists can
invent. Yet, if on that morrow morn the Wedding Guest
could have seen his future, he would never have risen but
would probably have ended his troubles then and there.
For he was a man doomed to other confidences more
tedious than the Ancient Mariner's and not so pleasantly put in rime. Ladies would hunt him down in dark
corners to talk personally of their daughters' prospects and
ask his advice. He would have to spend his life dodging
traveling salesmen, friends from his old home town, and
social misfits. He would have to despair with Mormons
over the horrors of polygamy or sympathize with monks
over the cheerlessness of celibacy or exult with Califor-
nians over the glory of California. The Wedding Guest
missed a wedding, but his troubles had only begun. In
the future he would probably miss his own while a tramp
told him it was drink that did it.

For the Wedding Guest was a marked man. He had
the kindly face which makes timid hearts blossom out like
flowers and him curse bitterly in his heart. So often we
see a beautiful woman the friend and close companion of
a dowdier, plainer one. Jealous tongues say that she
chooses the friend as a foil to her beauty, but the truth of

the matter lies in another direction. She confides and the other, flattered albeit bored, listens.

So Nature makes confidantes, and society creates classes of them, too. Hairdressers, priests and dogs are probably the greatest sufferers. But doctors and lawyers rank high also. In their offices how many stories are told of unhappy lives, of tragic beginnings and more tragic endings, of children born into the world to no purpose and considered as good riddance if they died, of marriages broken because the husband found the wife unfaithful or objected to the way she wore her hats. At the hairdresser's more intimate little stories are told of what was heard through keyholes or what was the mistress to do when the cook kissed the milkman every night on the back-porch and the children asked who made God. To the rattle of marcelling irons come sorrows of the kitchen, pantry and linen-closet.

The saddest, most depressing confidences are reserved for animals. Their dumb eyes speak with encouragement and love, in novels at least, when their masters tell them their misfortunes. Many a horse's face has been worn bare by a Merton of the Movies who leans and weeps against the head of his good old pard, his only friend. Lapdogs reign supreme as the confidantes of city apartments while the good old pards are equally honored on lonely plains in the West.

Meanwhile our hairdressers, lawyers and animals are down-trodden classes. For their protection, confidences should be strictly forbidden. No secrets could be exchanged in corners, no shoulders could be spotted, no handkerchiefs borrowed to be never returned. A law should be passed for the protection of our citizens against all ancient mariners, and no old women should be allowed to kiss cows.

THE RIVER

BY

Elizabeth Botsford

—Smith College

Heaven lies about us in our infancy.

ALL winter the river sprawled in its ungainly shape, icebound and motionless. The channel alone was open, resisting stubbornly the paralyzing cold of intense winter nights. It was a jagged crevice filled with black whirling emptiness, absorbing the heavy snows with a prolonged menacing hiss. The hills were white and poised, with the brittle outline of naked trees patterned thickly upon them.

While the river held its frozen enmity, all sympathetic life waited. The levee was a graveyard of over-turned skiffs, locked boathouses and unused docks. Fishermen spent the slow days in cluttered stores along Second Street, rolling forth through sagging layers of pipe smoke their long pointless stories like sonorous clouds which hung heavily about the stove, lifted, thinned out into silence and were lost into the tall shelves of canned goods and army blankets. Or they slept like tired bears in the musty back rooms of harness shops and boarding houses, emerging just before dusk to stumble, bleary-eyed, down to the river front, and to speculate dully upon the weather. Some sat through the chill afternoons in a flimsy hut over a hole in the ice, huddling around the bright glow of a lantern to spear fish when they wavered to the surface for air. Others, bolder, in the loneliness of the islands and bottom lands left between their traps a faint chain-work of foot prints, which the snow covered and recovered

345

silently with infinite patience. The wind roared down the broad valley toward some tremendous climax—and hushed, in prolonged monotonous intervals. One sound was always there, unchanging, unceasing, the oppressed voice of the river under the ice.

But some March day, a quick wind must come to lash a gauntlet down across the river's face; to wake it, stirring and snarling; to set the ice trembling at the answering challenge of the current. Now the clouds hounded a newly gilded sun over the gray sky. The wind flaunted long streamers of sunlight at the sullen river, poked at it with soft western fingers, jabbed it with needle points of warmth from southern hills. Tired of the mockery, the river rose in mad stampede.

From far to the north the ice came like a herd of rage-driven cattle, with white tossing heads and glittering horns. It milled at the bends, crowded over the dams, rushed over the docks and the levee; shattered a skiff, rammed a house boat and heaved on. From back streams and side streams the ice gathering madness, tumbling its heavy death southward, snorting, pawing and jostling. Then, gently, the sun calmed the anger; and the swift water moved more slowly, spread out widely over the banks and the lowlands, as cattle weary of running fall to grazing.

It was the first thrilling portent of spring. Then I used to lie awake nights listening for the wild geese to come hurrying on their clamorous way to northern lakes and marshes. Out of the blowing darkness their hoarse rhythmic cries rose suddenly, filled with a strange triumph that set me trembling and straining—alien voices. Flock after flock went over in a single night without hesitancy, as though, visible only to them, a beacon flared in the north promising what their eagerness needed.

When the ice went out, a change came over the levee as if the sweeping motion had stripped off the apathy of winter. The men reappeared from their hibernation, and came early each morning down to their docks. They painted, sawed and hammered over their battered skiffs; they mended their nets and sent their duck dogs in swimming. The river front echoed to the sputter and gasp of engines clearing their throats of the last year's use and the winter's abandon. Oarlocks screeched and a boat slid down from the dry docks with a shrill rasp that startled the swallows from housebuilding in the piles of the high wagon bridge. One day a house boat was towed away by a roaring launch, and sailed northward against the current with portly self-esteem. The next, the first steamboat of the season rounded the bend below the town with three proud whistles. The tall smoke funnels reared like immense antlers over the point, and the men ran whooping down to the wharf to meet it. "It's the *Ellen R*," they cried, "No—the *Fury*." "It's the *Dandelion*. There's old Jim waving from the pilot house." "Well, boys, the winter's over."

Now the snow shrank back into the valleys and vanished. Green crept into the hills, the willows feathered themselves with jade and ruffled their plumage. The river was benevolent and generous. It welcomed the fishermen's light boats and the boys' naked timid bodies. It was amorous of the sun, and grew more beautiful daily like a woman in love. A southwest wind and wild geese cries had wrought again the old metamorphosis.

Ten miles or so up the river, past the old Stone House, around the shoulder of Black Bird Island, lay the house boat. It crowded in close under three tall maples that stood up above all else to mark for straining eyes this sanctuary. A long, straight dam reached out a friendly hand, and the current, swirling in behind it, drew one in to the shore to a deep, quiet pool. There was the house boat with the shadow of leaves on its roof and the lapping of water at its hull, absorbing so much of the smell and sounds of the river that it became less a house and a home and more a mere shelter from the sun and sudden storms. It seemed conscious of its incongruity, and worked back into the rocks and trees. Out on the shore, the clearing was a pool of precious sunlight and bee-worn daisies guarded on two sides by willow thickets. Behind it the dark woods stretched back several miles over the bottoms to the hills which rose up steeply. Round warm hills crowned with rich fields of grain and farms of industrious men. At noon they were almost within touch, each boulder and twisted pine in boldly chiseled relief. When dusk came, they withdrew slowly, swathing themselves in a remote blue veil. At night they were only shapes of intense blackness. The hills across the river opened wide-armed valleys that held, even at midday, deep soft shadows. Peace was an invisible mist over it all.

This was a world for a child, full of mysteries, adventures and exquisite delights. There were woods full of rotting logs, brambles and flickering lights to scramble through. Narrow sloughs to be penetrated, shoving one's boat along through pickerel weed and the heavy sweet odor of water lilies until one came to an emerald wilderness of fallen moss-drenched trees and tall rushes that was impassable. There were long golden bars with the stories of snipe written delicately upon the wet edges, and the bolder tale of a turtle's clumsy progress. One could find turtle's eggs buried in the hot, dry sand by poking over it with a sharp stick, nests of them; or perhaps only the shrivelled shells in the midst of the scurrying tracks of a weasel. Rabbits hid their bobbing white tails in a willow copse, snakes lay in neat revolting coils on sunny rocks. A crayfish built a strange little pile of mud balls beside his hole. In the clear shallow waters a clam left a blunt aimless trail that one could follow to find him at the end with his shapeless white body protruding from the shell, pushing himself along. A snail moving over a dry board left a train of thin silver. Countless things for a child to see and learn. A lost heritage to be reclaimed. I had it all as a birthright.

My teacher, to acquaint me with all these secrets, was

an old riverman. How old Mr. Mertes was I never really knew. He was past the age when years continued to leave a mark upon him, as unalterable as the hills. He was thin and bent from a long life pulling at the oars, as brown as a dried apple. His eyes were two brilliant blue spiders set in a network of wrinkles. They had a perpetually weary look as though he had faced too many seasons of wind and sun and rain. He never was without a stained and battered hat pulled down over his close-shaven gray hair, with fish hooks stuck in the band much as an old lady thrusts pins in the bosom of her dress. He was shabby and worn, yet a remarkable man. A skiff became an intelligent, sensitive creature under his hands, he could feather an oar as lightly as a bird trails a wing across the water, he could make a whistle out of a willow stick. He was a past master in Izaak Walton's quiet art of fishing. He knew all the deep, motionless black pools where the crappee lay, the yellow reefs for pike, the swift water around rocks or under grassy over-hanging banks that bass loved. Crayfish, bullheads, worms and minnows, he used them all for bait in their most effective season. As long as there were any fish to be caught, he would catch them. His patience was inexhaustible, his name a byword up and down the river. Woods and river were his summer home; his knowledge of them was half instinctive, half accumulated by years of intimate association. He was a man who had seen time pass bodily before his eyes. When the city, now flourishing and self-important, was only a cluster of shacks surrounded by a frail stockade, he had seen the Indians swim their spotted ponies from shore to shore just above the house boat. He remembered the old-time trappers and hunters, the woodsmen who had come down with the logs in the spring singing and shouting; he had seen the first steamboat climb slowly up against the current, heard the drawn-out, melodious voice of the roustabouts on the prow calling back the soundings to the pilot. He had shot deer on

Prairie Island, now a haunt only for rabbit and duck; he recalled days when he had caught over a hundred fish in an afternoon, and black bass leaped into the boat. His head must have been full of stories, but for the most part he was surprisingly reticent. Only occasionally when we sat in the dark together, his mind delved down into the deep pocket of his memory to bring forth a shining tale and hold it briefly before me. More often he sat unmoving for hours at a time, with his gnarled hands folded in his lap, staring at something I could not see, his spirit gone from his tired body back to younger, stronger days.

They were thrilling to me, the stories he and my father exchanged in the night, men's stories of hunting, of boats and fishing, all in times that were like history to me, so far behind as measured in the short years of my life. Throughout the summer other men drifted in to stay a day or a week, and then drift on. Crazy Nate Ward with his endless talk of southern levees and cottonfields, the fabulous wealth of his brother's plantation; Harry Vale, never quite sober and always sullen, the Beau Brummel of river towns, continually boasting of his drunken escapades; and poor Tom Miller who had lost all his teeth, and lived on coffee, milk-soaked bread and his rich memories. Too weak to work any more he went up and down the river in his ancient skiff stopping at camp after camp where his friends would give him food, a place to rest his fragile bones and a kindly audience for his rambling talk, patient because they knew, as he did, that death was very close behind the wake of his boat. Whole afternoons they spent out under the trees, spinning their yarns slowly out into the sunlight like golden tops.

But out of all these years images remain, more poignantly clear because the moments can never be physically recalled. I can remember mornings, waking gradually with the growing intensity of the sun in my face, and the swelling songs of birds and crickets in my ears; of becoming conscious of lifting mists, the bright calm of the river and the sharpening outlines of trees and vivid hills. The heat became an invisible golden haze that was suspended in sagging hammocks from bush to bush, and from tree to tree. The coolness slunk away to interweave in slender threads with the twisted roots, to spread like dew over leaves in a dark hollow, to cling shadowlike under the north side of logs.

I remember fishing in breathless afternoons, when the skiff swung in close to the bank beneath an old elm hung perilously over the water and a grapevine that trailed down like a translucent curtain around the prow with its fringes stirring in the current. Mr. Mertes drowsed over his long bamboo pole, curiously relaxed; his eyes fixed upon his motionless bobber in a sleeping blue stare.

"Mebbe," he would say more to himself than to me, "mebbe ther' a pike layin' in here, or a couple of crappee. We might even find a bass. You can't tell—." And his voice dozed off.

The wind went to rest in the cool hills, the sunlight blazing on the placid river was too bright and lonely. The heat made a third person in the boat, a heavy undeniable presence like one who says nothing but never lets you forget he is there. For us there was the thick pattern of leaves against the sky and the opposite pattern of sunlight shifting on our arms. The quiet was rather an absence of noise and the presence of sounds blending and diffusing melodiously. We could hear two muskrats not far away in the willows intent upon tender green sprouts; a chipmunk gabbling crossly at some disturbance. Redstarts tinkered up and down the branches above us, and from lush meadows inland came the soft clang of a cowbell and a dog's earnest barking. They fused with the shrill racket of the crickets and the galump-galump of the frogs. The heat blurred the sharp angles. A water snake writhed on to a piece of brush and curled up comfortably. The sun dried the shining moisture from his skin and left him a dusty gray. Not a fish worked or even touched our bait.

If I tried to speak, I had forgotten what I had said before I finished speaking. It didn't matter. Nothing mattered. We just sat watching our bobbers nodding on the lazy current. A turtle fell off his log with a great plop. It startled a pewee into song. And a butterfly that had rested for hours on my knee moved his golden brown wings dreamily and flew away. Or perhaps a bobber gurgled down out of sight suddenly and we awoke long enough to land a flapping silver crappee, or a painted sunfish, to change the water on the minnows, to bait up again. But then before the ripples had ceased to widen we were overcome by this insinuous languor. We said nothing. We dozed and waited.

Sometimes storms thundered down upon us. One moment all would be placid and heavy. The next, a black cloud leaped over the hills with sweeping out-riders. The willow leaves turned up their silver palms in surrender, the grasses bent down before a rising wind. The blue castle of the sky was besieged by black and livid-green armies; it was taken completely. Heavy explosions shook the quiet trees, the river writhed and tossed in agony at the violation of its priceless peace. The world grew dark and was split by jagged shafts of lightning from some immense long-bow. The rain marched down the valley like steady gray infantry, enveloping one calm hill after another in its ranks. The first large wet drops increased swiftly in speed and violence until they came stinging down, dry and sharp like hail. The tumult and chaos was short-lived. As quickly as the attack had come it vanished, the last rear guards trailed into the east. The rain moved on rapidly and the returning sun found a purged world with every wild rose exquisitely jeweled.

At sunset, the darkness crept down the river, out of the woods and the deep recesses of the hills. The day's heat eased away and a wet coolness flooded into its place. Now the brilliance and certainty of the day were gone. Shadows smothered the river, trees and dams were scarcely discernible, strange bulks. The stars were tired and faint, but there was the soft radiant promise of a moon behind the willows. The house boat drew the night about it closely, pressing against the bank. The droning silence of the afternoon was gone, there was a hush upon which the silent noises of the night were imprinted as the footprints of snipe are traced upon thick, smooth mud, the low whirl of the water around a point, the infinitesimal hum of mosquitoes, the deep vibrant chorus of frogs that was so unbreaking that it became part of the quiet, and now and then the broad flat sound of a fish leaping out of the water and falling back upon the unbroken surface. You could not see the motion of the river but you could feel its power. It swept the darkness with it like a mist. Likewise the air had the imperceptible flowing quality of the current. And you could not see the dipping and rising motion of the swallows and bats, but you could sense their swift passage. If you stood outside, the tips of their wings might brush your face. They were shadows that lived. All night smells rose up, long, twisting, wet smells of roots and snake holes and decaying grass, the sweet dewy smell of freshened leaves and daisies, the heavy fragrancy of damp and new-cut hay, the strong reek of water-soaked wood and spiders.

This I remember of seining minnows in the moonlight, how the sand bar lay like a rounded sheet of silver with silver ripples breaking at its edge, how the dark sheen of the river wound by like an immense glistening python, how the hills were like warm black heads sleeping against one another with the night pulled up close under their chins. Over the meadows and woods of the river bottom was a cloak of shimmering light, and the fireflies in the deep grass swung tiny winking lanterns. All familiar sights and sounds have an eeriness in the night, and this was not the world I had known under the noon sun. There was mystery in this nocturnal adventure. Strange voices in the murmuring and gurgling of the waters about our skiff, wet fingers reaching over the oarlocks, songs muffled beneath the keel, a groan as our boat grated on the sand. When we stepped out, the water reached up its warm caressing hands to our knees before our groping feet touched bottom. Now came the tense moment as we unrolled our net and waded out into the shallows. We could hear the faint fluttering music of thousands of minnows moving swiftly in some weird dance to the rhythm of their tiny darting tails. They were about our feet, hundreds of them. It was like walking barefooted through wet grass, it sent a shiver up one's spine, a tickling sensation. Silently we made a wide arc with our seine and drew it to shore. A panic among the minnows, a mad rush. They battered against our ankles like harmless little bullets. Enchantment—to stand alone in the moonlight and feel the water alive about one's feet. Then we pulled the net up on the sand and the haul spilled out on the bar like a line of leaping silver flames.

Time passed with the slow sapphire procession of the river. Each day merged into the next, and each in itself was complete, satisfying and untroubled. The whole was a perfect harmony.

Now it has all changed. It is a change in me. There is a veil, fragile and impassable between me and my former existence. I am no longer an intimate part of nature, but moving outside, out of tune, foreign to all that I knew so well. Something has happened to me—call it education, sophistication or what you will. The spell is broken, I have lost my place and must forever feel this intangible barrier between me and the precious world of my childhood.

ON PROGRESS—FORWARD AND BACKWARD

BY

Elizabeth Hall

—Smith College

To one who seldom dreams, dreams when they do occur, take on a vital meaning. So vivid are they, so real, that they acquire a living significance, and become part of one's philosophy of life.

I was terrified, inexplicably so, like a savage who sees in nature some overwhelming phenomenon which he can not explain. I rushed to the stairs only to find them crowded with girls, like myself frantic, terror stricken, grasping for some reality in the sudden immensity which was everywhere. A ghastly blue light was over everything, and one was conscious of illimitable absence, a totality of blankness. I do not know how long it was before I realized that this was the end of the world, the millennium, that immortality or death lay beyond the translucent blue atmosphere. Some one gasped "The world has stopped revolving," and I realized with a sudden and awful consciousness that there was no motion anywhere, no wind, no breathing, no gravitation. I could feel the absence of a force which I had never before perceived as existent. Some one was praying, but like everything else the prayer was quite empty. It too had no motion, no life. I felt myself being forced slowly and relentlessly to the earth by some cold, unseen power from above. I could not go forward—there was no more future, no way of escape. I tried to scream—and suddenly a great tremor ran through the tense emptiness, a leaf rustled outside, and I knew that once again the earth was revolving and that man might live.

355

I believe in dreams, but I believe that they arise from some previous suggestion in conscious thought; and so, because I am mystically minded, I believe that this was more than a dream, that it was a direct revelation to me of an underlying principle of life. It took me back to Ephesus in the sixth century before Christ, when Heraclitus expounded his doctrines of ceaseless flux, and it made me wonder whether the early Greek philosophers were not right in assigning one underlying force or substance to the whole order of the world. Or perhaps Bergson comes nearer with his theory of temporalism wherein the essence of life and mind is movement and development in time.

But aside from armchair philosophizing, there is for me a fascinating theory of life in this thought of motion. Motion and progress and life are one, and do not and can not exist independently. When actual physical motion ceases, all life will cease; and though the earth may still hang in space, the principle that causes growth will be absent, and further life will be impossible. The vague distances will press slowly and surely in upon us, and at last the earth will be forced into incalculable units of nothing flying about in emptiness.

But since we do not expect this cessation of motion to occur in the near future, what about motion as a philosophy of living action? Any "big-business" man will tell us that progress is the essential fact of life. Only so long as we go on from one level to another do we really live, and if we stop, the result is stagnation and at last self-annihilation. The "big-business" man, however, does not realize that there is progress in retrogression, that motion does not necessarily have to be forward to mean advance and life. Though there would seem to be a contradiction in terms, there is such a thing as progress backwards. It may not be recognized in the economic world, but in the scholarly world it must be, and in the world of homely, every-day people, it surely is.

Progress backward is based on the cry of old age, "Those were the good old days," combined with the belief of youth that "we can recreate them, if not in material reality at least in the reality of inspiration." We turn back to the long ago and through the length of days we see the past glorified. We also have perspective to see the advantages and disadvantages of the time in their real relation, and if we have minds that believe in progress through retrogression, we see how we have sacrificed essential beauty and truth to unessential comfort and modernity.

So the scholar lays aside the confusion of the present, closes his ears to the "wild and whirling words" of those who wrangle heatedly over nonessentials, and turns back to the life that has gone before. Here where the conflicts have been quiet for centuries, he finds the realities that underlie all turmoil, and he sees the continuity and motion of purpose which runs through all things. In a sense reversion and retrogression, but is not the revealing of truth, whether new or rediscovered, always progress?

When the scientist can no longer go ahead to fresh discoveries and new truths, and when the scholar has forgotten how to turn back to rediscover the truths of a bygone age, then indeed will the end of the world come. Motion and progress will stop, and so must life, because there will be no breath of truth stirring, no reality in past or future, no motion anywhere.